A HISTORY OF WRITING

GLOBALITIES
Series editor: Jeremy Black

GLOBALITIES is a series which reinterprets world history in a
concise yet thoughtful way, looking at major issues over large
time-spans and political spaces; such issues can be political,
ecological, scientific, technological or intellectual. Rather than
adopting a narrow chronological or geographical approach,
books in the series are conceptual in focus yet present an array of
historical data to justify their arguments. They often involve a
multi-disciplinary approach, juxtaposing different subject-areas
such as economics and religion or literature and politics.

In the same series

Why Wars Happen
Jeremy Black

A History of Language
Steven Roger Fischer

The Nemesis of Power
A History of International Relations Theories
Harald Kleinschmidt

Geopolitics and Globalization in the Twentieth Century
Brian W. Blouet

Monarchies 1000 – 2000
W. M. Spellman

A History of
Writing

STEVEN ROGER FISCHER

REAKTION BOOKS

Dedicated to Sir Robert Evans

Published by Reaktion Books Ltd
79 Farringdon Road, London EC1M 3JU, UK

www.reaktionbooks.co.uk

First published 2001
Copyright © Steven Roger Fischer 2001

Printed and bound in Great Britain by
St Edmundsbury Press, Bury St Edmunds, Suffolk

British Library Cataloguing in Publication Data
Fischer, Steven Roger
   A history of writing. – (Globalities)
   1. Writing – History
   I. Title
   411'.09

ISBN 1 86189 101 6

Contents

Preface

This introduction to a history of writing is meant to serve as useful preliminary reading for university students and others who wish to have a general and up-to-date overview of writing's remarkable story. Central to the book's theme are the origins, forms, functions and chronological changes of the world's major writing systems and their scripts.

Writing's social dynamics are addressed at each stage. Since *Homo erectus*, hominids appear to have distinguished themselves from other creatures by forming societies based on speech. What now distinguishes modern *Homo sapiens sapiens* is a global society based most importantly on writing. Once the specialized domain of only a few thousands, today writing is a skill practised by about 85 per cent of the world's population – some five billion people. All modern society rests on writing's plinth.

Most writing systems and scripts that have existed are now extinct. Only minute vestiges of one of the most ancient – Egyptian hieroglyphs – live on, unrecognized, in the Latin alphabet in which English, among hundreds of other languages, is conveyed today. (Our *m*, for example, ultimately derives from the Egyptians' consonantal *n*-sign, depicting waves.) In consequence of a series of fortuitous developments, the Latin alphabet has become the world's most important writing system. Though language's vehicle, it will possibly outlive most of Earth's natural languages. How humankind writes today, and its larger significance for the emergent global society, can be better appreciated through an understanding of where writing came from, which is the theme of this book.

Writing fascinates everyone. For nearly six thousand years, each age has embraced this wonder, surely society's most versatile and entertaining tool. Today, ancient writing in particular intrigues, as it permits the past to speak to us in tongues long extinct. Here, writing becomes the ultimate time machine. Notwithstanding, all writing remains an artifice, an imperfect device seemingly fashioned, if only at first blush, to reproduce human speech. There have been endless ways to accomplish this. History has now reduced and refined these to a small number of 'best' solutions. Readers will appreciate, though, that the historical process of reduction and refinement is still continuing, as society discovers new needs and new answers. It is for this reason that, much more slowly than the languages they transmit, writing systems and scripts are forever in flux.

But writing is much more than Voltaire's 'painting of the voice'. It has become human knowledge's ultimate tool (science), society's cultural medium (literature), the means of democratic expression and popular information (the press) and an art form in itself (calligraphy), to mention only some manifestations. Today, writing systems based entirely on electronic communication are rapidly encroaching on what has, until now, been the domain of speech-based writing. Computers can now 'write' both messages and entire programs between themselves. At the same time, they are elaborating new systems of their own that transcend everything we have understood to be described by the word *writing*. Even the substances on which writing takes place are metamorphosing: e-ink (electronic ink) on plastic screens, thin as paper, might one day replace the ubiquitous substance which itself earlier replaced parchment. Writing changes as humanity changes. It is a gauge of the human condition.

Several insights will, I hope, become evident in the course of this brief overview. No-one 'invented' writing. Perhaps no-one independently ever 're-invented' writing, either, be it in China or Mesoamerica. All writing systems appear to be descendants of earlier prototypes or systems, whose idea of graphically depicting human speech, scheme for accomplishing this, and/or graphic signs used in this process were borrowed and adapted or converted to fit some other people's language and social needs.

Jeremy Black of Exeter University and Michael Leaman of Reaktion Books, within a week of one another, independently proposed that I should write this book, and later furnished valuable suggestions. I am very grateful to both.

A philological and linguistic career spanning more than 30 years – eighteen of which have been dedicated to ancient writing and decipherment (in particular, the scripts of Crete and Easter Island) – has often brought me together with outstanding personalities in the field of epigraphy, the study of ancient inscriptions. The roll call of 'unforgettables' is too long to intone here, but I wish to mention a few who have indelibly marked the parchment of my life, each in her or his special way: †Thomas Barthel, Emmett L. Bennett, Jr, William Bright, Nikolai Butinov, †John Chadwick, Brian Colless, Yves Duhoux, Paul Faure, Irina Fedorova, †Yuri Knorozov, †Ben Leaf, Jacques Raison, †Fritz Schachermeyr, †Linda Schele, David Stuart and George Stuart.

A personal thanks to Sir David Attenborough for his perfect encouragement.

And, above all, to Taki.

Steven Roger Fischer
Waiheke Island, New Zealand
October 2000

ONE

From Notches to Tablets

A history of writing should be predicated on an understanding of what constitutes 'writing'. The proposition is not so simple. Most readers familiar with only one consonant-and-vowel alphabetic writing system – conveying spacially separated ink-printed letters in divided words from left to right in descending horizontal lines – will perhaps be only faintly aware that the world of writing embraces so much more.

Communication of human thought, in general, can be achieved in many different ways, speech being only one of them. And writing, among other uses, is only one form of conveying human speech. Nevertheless, modern society, it appears, has exalted this distinctive form of communication. Perhaps this is partly because, as a representation of external realities, communication through graphic art seems more objective, more substantial, than linguistic communication.[1] Even abstract notions can be transcribed graphically through this 'solidifying symbolic system'. The roots of this system are to be found in human beings' fundamental need to store information in order to communicate, whether to themselves or to others, at a distance in time or space.

Since one knows writing only for what it is now, it is difficult – perhaps even pointless – to provide a definition of it that presumes to include all past, present and future meanings. Whether it is of utilitarian advantage to see in 'full' writing a 'system of graphic symbols that can be used to convey any and all thought'[2] is a moot point. Just as valid would be the equally unspecific definition of writing as 'the graphic counterpart of speech, the fixing of spoken language in a permanent or semi-permanent form'.[3] Yet this, too, seems to miss so much of what writing is about. One might accept that it is indeed the sequencing of standardized symbols (characters, signs or sign components) in order to graphically reproduce human speech, thought and other things in part or whole. This might, in fact, be the most general definition of writing possible at present. How well each system then accomplished this in the past was determined by the relative need of each society as it grew more complex. But this definition, too, remains just this: a limiting definition of something rather special that appears to resist limitation.

It may be best to avoid the 'pitfall' of a formal definition altogether, as writing has been, is and will be so many different things to so many different peoples in so many different ages. Instead, for the immediate purpose of this history of writing, one should perhaps address the more relevant question of 'complete writing', here defined as the fulfilment of three criteria:[4]

- ◆ Complete writing must have as its purpose communication;

- ◆ Complete writing must consist of artificial graphic marks on a durable or electronic surface;

- ◆ Complete writing must use marks that relate conventionally to articulate speech (the systematic arrangement of significant vocal sounds) or electronic programing in such a way that communication is achieved.

Every graphic expression that constitutes early writing – early writing fulfils at least one, but never all, of these three criteria – can be regarded as 'writing' in its largest sense, though it remains 'incomplete writing'. Some sort of communication is taking place, albeit of a limited, localized and/or ambiguous nature.

Writing did not emerge from nowhere. Divine provenance has been many peoples' preferred cliché. In fact, this fiction survived in Europe well into the 1800s, and is still embraced by certain communities in the US and in Islamic countries. Others have asserted that complete writing – writing fulfilling the three criteria – was 'invented' around the middle of the fourth millennium BC by a Sumerian in Uruk consciously searching for a better method to deal with complex accounting. Others see complete writing as the result of group effort or accidental discovery. Still others believe complete writing to have had multiple origins, for various reasons. Then there are those who assert that complete writing is the product of a long evolution of early writing over a wide region of trade.

There is certainly no 'evolution' in the history of writing, not in the sense the word generally conveys. Writing systems do not change of their own accord in a natural process; they are deliberately elaborated or changed by human agents – drawing from a wide variety of existing resources – in order to achieve any number of specific goals.[5] Perhaps the most common goal is the best graphic reproduction of the writer's speech. Constant small changes to a writing system's script over many centuries, even millennia, will result in enormous differences in that script's later appearance and use.

Before complete writing – that is, before the fulfilment of the three criteria – many processes akin to writing obtained. However, to call these processes 'proto-writing'[6] would perhaps be to award them a status and/or role they do not deserve and never fulfilled. On the other hand, pictography ('picture-writing') and logography ('word-writing', whereby the depicted object is to be spoken aloud) might justifiably be called 'pre-writing'. Elaborating on nineteenth-century German speculations, American linguist Leonhard Bloomfield distinguished in the 1930s between 'picture writing' and 'real writing', with the latter also fulfilling certain essential criteria (signs had to represent linguistic elements of some kind, and be limited in number).[7] A distinction has also been drawn between primitive 'semasiography' (whereby graphic marks convey meaning without recourse to language) and 'full writing', with only the latter to be regarded as writing in the 'true' sense.[8]

Whatever one's formal position regarding early writing attempts, graphic expression appears to be a very 'recent' phenomenon among hominids: the earliest 'engravings' appear to date from about 100,000 years ago (some say much earlier). However, our ancestors' regular series of incised dots, lines or hatch marks (allegedly tallies or lunar calendars) in no way suggest a link to articulate speech – though these 'proto-scribes' certainly spoke as fluently as we do today.

Before complete writing, humankind made use of a wealth of graphic symbols and mnemonics (memory tools) of various kinds in order to store information. Rock art has always possessed a repertoire of universal symbols: anthropomorphs (human-like figures), flora, fauna, the Sun, stars, comets and many more, including untold geometric designs. For the most part, these were graphic reproductions of the commonest phenomena of the physical world. At the same time, mnemonics were used in linguistic contexts, too, with knot records, pictographs, notched bones or staffs, message sticks or boards, string games for chanting, coloured pebbles and so forth linking physical objects with speech. Over many thousands of years, graphic art and such mnemonics grew ever closer in specific social contexts.

Eventually, they merged, to become *graphic mnemonics*.

KNOT RECORDS

One of the ancient world's commonest mnemonics was the knot record, which dates back at least to the Early Neolithic (the last period of the Stone Age).[9] Such records could be simple knots in a single strand or complicated series of colour-coded knots on strings attached to higher-order strings. Knot records reached their peak of development, it appears, with the Inca's *quipu*s (illus. 1). These comprised an elaborate means of counting: different knots in various positions depicted numerical quantities, the knots' colours representing, it has been alleged, individual commodities.

The Inca of ancient Peru used mnemonics almost exclusively to achieve what writing achieved in the same or similar contexts in other societies. The Inca had several different types of knots to record their empire's daily and long-term mercantile transactions and payment of tribute. Each knot held a specific decimal value (no knot in a certain place meant 'zero'). For example, one overhand knot above two overhand knots above a group of seven knots recorded the number '127'. Thus, there were specific cord places for the concepts 'hundreds', 'tens' and 'ones'. Bunches of strings of knots could be tied off with summation

1 The *quipu* of an Inca imperial accountant. From Félipe Guaman Poma de Ayala, *Nueva crónica y buen gobierno, c.* 1613.

cords. A special class of *quipu*-reading clerks oversaw and managed this highly complicated and efficient system. Even after the Spanish conquest of the 1500s, the *quipu* was retained for daily record-keeping.

Though not as elaborate as those of the Inca, similar prehistoric *quipu* can be found from Alaska to Chile; indeed, they are the Pacific Rim's indigenous record-keeping system. The South-East Marquesan *tuhuna 'o'ono* bards, for example, used bundles of woven coconut fibre from which hung small strings of knots called *ta'o mata* that could also be used to enumerate generations. On ancient Ra'ivavae in the Austral Islands, south of Tahiti, genealogical records were kept by means of knotted hibiscus-bark cords. Similar phenomena can be found throughout the world. In his Scythian campaign, the Persian king Darius left Greek allies guarding a rear bridge with instructions to untie one knot in a 60-knot thong each day: if they finished untying all 60 before his return, they were to sail home to Greece. Knot records are a much more versatile mnemonic than simple tally sticks or notched staffs. Permitting greater categorical variety and complexity, they can easily be 'erased' or 'rewritten' by mere retying.

Some scholars claim that these knotted strings or cords were the only primitive form of 'writing' developed in the Andes.[10] But phonetic writing did apparently exist there (see Chapter 6). And knotted strings do not comprise writing. They are memory prompts. Though the knots' purpose is communication, they are not artificial graphic marks conveyed on a durable surface, and their use has no conventional relation to articulate speech.

NOTCHES

Slashes in the bark of a tree – like rocks placed on a grave, branches rearranged over a path or an ochre handprint on a rock face – represent 'idea transmission'. That is, they communicate something to others beyond immediate hearing. Here, marking and mnemonics were often combined to produce marking *as* mnemonics. The idea is extremely old, possibly older than the earliest known cave art.

Perhaps even *Homo erectus* used notches as mnemonics. Artefacts unearthed at Bilzingsleben in Germany that date to at least 412,000 years ago – several bones revealing cut lines at regular intervals – have been interpreted by their discoverer as intentional 'engraving' (that is, graphic symbols of some kind). It is evident that the notches are markings; what they mean, if anything, is unclear.

Subtle but consistent differences in stone and bone markings by *Homo sapiens sapiens* craftsmen beginning around 100,000 years ago indicate purposeful engraving. Discovered in South Africa's famous Blombos Cave, two pieces of elaborately cross-hatched ochre represent early evidence of symbolic thinking to their discoverer. Other early artefacts, such as the Ishango Bone from Zaire (illus. 2; see also illus. 176), indicate similar markings made over a span of time; when counted, the marks on some of these artefacts appear to correspond with lunar cycles. However, other explanations are also possible. What is important here is that, tens of thousands of years ago, graphic marks,

2 Three views of the Ishango Bone from Zaire, radiocarbon-dated to *c.* 9000 BC. Perhaps a numerical or even calendrical (lunar) notation, the Ishango Bone has been called the 'earliest writing implement'.

however primitive, were probably recording some sort of human perception, for whatever reason. This was information storage.

Among more recent preliterate peoples, notches served the same purpose as knot records. For example, the *rākau whaka-papa*, or 'genealogical boards', of pre-European Māori of New Zealand bore notches, each one representing the name of an ancestor. These were simple memory aids whose marks do not relate conventionally to articulate speech.

PICTOGRAPHY

Knot records and notches can recall categories, record numbers and prompt memory. However, neither can convey particulars such as qualities and characteristics. Only pictures can do this. The need to convey a larger variety of information prompted, in addition to the above, recording with one or more pictorial symbols – that is, pictography. Pictography is the fortuitous marriage of marks and mnemonics.

3 Some cave art is understood to be pictorial communication of a kind. Engraved 'P' symbols appear on top of a horse at Les Trois Frères in southern France, their significance unknown. At adjoining Tuc d'Audoubert, more than 80 such symbols, engraved using various tools, surround a second horse.

4 A Cheyenne pictographic 'letter' from Turtle-Following-His-Wife to his son Little-Man: 'I send you $53 and ask you to come home.'

Pictorial messages were already being conveyed tens of thousands of years ago, too. In many ways, cave art can be understood to be pictorial communication (illus. 3).[11] The pictography of Native Americans has attracted much attention in recent years. Here, pictograms are usually simple marks either engraved or painted on walls and rocks – rock art or pet-roglyphs. But a few messages also involve quite elaborate pic-tography, listing warriors' names by painting distinctive features: Red Crow, Charging Hawk and so forth. In nine-teenth-century America, some tribes, such as the Cheyenne, even sent pictographic 'letters' to one another (illus. 4).

Pictography can convey a very complicated message without direct recourse to articulate speech. However, unlike knot records and notches, pictography does convey phonetic values by depicting specific objects and thus prompting their spoken identification. An Abnaki hunter in Maine, for example, could leave outside his wigwam a *wikhegan* – a birchbark scroll – depicting a man in a canoe and a deer, a man on foot pointing at a squiggle, and a snow-shoed man pulling a sled. Its message would be: 'I'm crossing the lake to hunt deer, turning off before the next lake, and won't be back until spring.'[12] This was com-munication through graphic art conveying a limited message within a limited domain.

The Ashanti people of Africa decorate their houses, utensils and other things with pictures recalling proverbs – a crocodile with a mudfish in its jaws can mean, among other things, 'If the mudfish gets anything, it will ultimately go to the crocodile.'[13] The purpose of such a picture is also communication; it is graphic art on a durable surface, and it is related to articulate speech. However, this 'sentence writing'[14] only prompts the mind of those who have already learnt the proverbs. Its 'signs' are not conventional but iconic, relating only to each proverb. Too much remains encoded in the Ashanti system, in other words, to represent an efficacious medium of general communi-cation.

Though some Chinese characters (also used in Japanese writ-ing) are pictographic in origin – like 'woman', 'child' and 'paddy-field' – one has to be told each meaning before recognizing the referents. For this reason, Chinese writing is not a pictography but a mixed logography (to be precise, a morpho-syllabography; see Chapter 5). That is, its characters hold sound and sense both, and must be individually learnt, not merely 'recognized'.

Pictography also happens to be the 'default script' of modern technology, as in electronic circuit diagrams. In this context, cultural ambiguities are intentionally avoided by standardizing symbols to maximize international comprehension. Within its limited domain, among specialists trained in the art, pictography can be extremely useful, in certain circumstances surpassing the efficacy of complete writing.

However, all pictography is 'incomplete writing'. This is because it does not use marks that relate conventionally to articulate speech. Pictography generally avoids speech.

TALLIES

Early humans, marking mnemonically, evidently realized that a similar process could be used to record counts. For example, if one could notch lunar phases one by one as they were watched – if this is what those earliest artefacts really depict – then one could also represent abstracts, such as numbers. Perhaps it was in this way that the first tallies were created.

The earliest known notched artefacts themselves might be such tallies: marks on bone to represent different people, a passage of time (rather than witnessed events), a hunting success. (Gunfighters once notched their Colt 45's with 'kills'; fighter pilots 'notched' using special emblems on the sides of their aeroplanes.) Tally sticks belong to the oldest forms of record-keeping. Native Australians even used these to send messages to one another over distances, with the number of notches on the stick signifying the amount of whatever the pre-arranged message was about.

Apparently, each ancient people possessed a regional variant of tally sticks. Standard values of notches would be known by all in the society. Throughout the European Middle Ages, customs officials' fixtures were the tally stick and notching knife. The British Exchequer, for example, used tally sticks to record receipts from around AD 1100 to 1826. (Many sticks also bore explanatory notes in Latin, and later in English.) This system followed a general principle: the larger the sum of payment, the more wood would be notched from the tally stick. £1,000 was a straight notch, indented, four inches wide; a halfpenny was a simple punched hole.

Tallies have long existed alongside complete writing. They are easily used by illiterate people, and they are often quicker, less cumbersome and less expensive than writing. Though their purpose is communication, and though they use artificial 'signs' on durable material, these are merely standardized notches and holes signifying units, not articulate speech.

FURTHER MNEMONICS AND SIGNAL MESSAGES

Many further tools have aided memory and/or conveyed human thought and speech over distance, all of which inflated the repertoire of resources that would eventually yield complete writing. Probably dating from Palæolithic times (the early Stone Age), string figures (used by one person) or 'cat's cradles' (used by two persons) – designs woven on the hands with a loop of string – have been known in nearly all preliterate societies.[15] Encoding genealogies, histories, songs, chants and more, this 'writing in air' has communication as its purpose, with conventional figures relating immediately to articulate speech, but lacks graphic marks on a durable surface. Signalling – whether by hand and face (sign language), sound, flags, smoke, fired powders, reflections on metals, electronics or other means – is similar, in that while many signal messages are now alphabet-based, they too lack conventional graphic marks on durable material.

Indexical symbols relating to something – five objects for five sheep, for example – have been used by many peoples for many thousands of years. To name one custom, the Yoruba of Africa have always used pebbles as indexical symbols; these could even assume homophonic value (an important component of some phonetic writing), whereby one word sounds identical to another with a different meaning. To arrange a tryst, for example, a Yoruba man would leave six pebbles for a woman to find –Yoruba *efa*, or 'six', also means 'attracted'. If the woman was willing, she left eight pebbles as an answer: Yoruba *eyo*, or 'eight', also means 'agreed'.

Some regard the coloured pebbles of southern France's Azilian culture of *c.* 8000 BC to be the world's 'first pictographic writing' (illus. 5). However, these crosses, stripes and other designs painted on pebbles do not portray easily recognizable natural phenomena.[16] More significantly, like the Yoruba peb-

5 A few of the coloured designs on Azilian pebbles from Mas d'Azil, Ariège, southern France, *c.* 8000 BC.

bles the Azilian do not appear to have used marks that related conventionally to articulate speech. It is entirely possible that their pebbles figure among the world's earliest examples of indexical symbols. However, they are not even 'incomplete writing'.

The nineteenth-century 'memory boards' of the Luba people of Africa supposedly contained Luba history. 'Read' by experts, the boards' patterns, colours, materials, configurations and general shape aided the 'reader's' memory. Each Luba board is different in these characteristics, and even a single board can evoke different recitations by different experts – even by the same expert on different occasions. Though the Luba 'memory boards' comprise graphic art on a durable surface whose purpose is communication, they are not complete writing either: they, too, lack conventional marks relating immediately to articulate speech.

GRAPHIC SYMBOLS

Complete writing's crucible was accountancy.[17] Only social necessity could produce such an eminent tool as complete writing. In the ancient Middle East, around six thousand years ago, Sumer's expanding society somehow had to administer and manage its raw materials, manufactured goods, workers, duties, planted fields, tributes, royal and temple inventories, incomes and expenditures. Time-honoured mnemonics no longer sufficed; something radically new was needed.

Marking possession, an important part of book-keeping, probably provided some of the world's earliest graphic symbols.[18] Possession markers occur with seals in apparently the same social contexts as complete writing occurs later. The Vinča culture

(5300–4300 BC) of the central Balkans produced pottery and other clay objects bearing incised symbols of some sort.[19] There appear to be 210 symbols in all, 30 of these being main symbols, the remainder variations and compounds. The Vinča settlement at Tordos in Romania has revealed a great number of these: from simple + or - to more complicated combs and a swastika (illus. 6). At Tartaria, twenty km east of Tordos, three clay 'tablets' initially claimed to be of the same Vinča culture were unearthed in 1961 (illus. 7); however, they might also be a local version of the much later Minoan hieroglyphic script (see Chapter 3).[20] Comparable symbols have been found at some 37 other sites dating from the same period.

Most, but certainly not all, of these artefacts appear to evidence a 'graphic symbol inventory' of some sort that was available to artisans in the central Balkans perhaps as early as 6,500 years ago.[21] (A 'symbol' is a graphic mark that stands for something else, while a 'sign' is a conventional component of a writ-

6 Some of the incised symbols that appear on pottery from the Vinča settlement at Tordos, 5300–4300 BC.

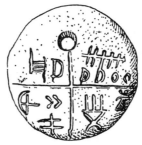

7 The three baked clay 'tablets' unearthed at Tartaria. Initially claimed to be from the Vinča culture, they might have been manufactured much later, according to some scholars.

8 Bulgarian copper-age graphic symbols from before 4000 BC: (left) 'plaque' from Gradeshnitsa, h: 12 cm; (right) clay 'seal' from Karanovo, diam: 6 cm.

ing system.) The discovery of two 'similar' clay artefacts in Bulgaria, radiocarbon-dated to before 4000 BC and bearing marks that could perhaps be graphic symbols, has been cited as additional evidence for this Balkan inventory (illus. 8). The current opinion is that these earliest Balkan symbols appear to comprise a decorative or emblematic inventory with no immediate relation to articulate speech.[22] That is, they are neither *logographs* (whole-word signs depicting one object to be spoken aloud) nor *phonographs* (signs holding a purely phonetic or sound value).

Others have claimed that the earliest 'writing' is found in China, also dating to around 4000 BC. On pottery fragments from the Yangshao culture that were excavated at Banpo near Xian City in 1954–7 are incised marks that Chinese scholars have interpreted as numbers. However, not all specialists agree.

TOKENS

The 'Gelb Dictum' (so-called after its author, American epigrapher Ignace Gelb) – 'At the basis of all writing stands the picture'[23] – appears to be rudely contradicted by the theory of the token as the ultimate origin of complete writing. This recent theory professes that early tokens were counters in a rudimentary book-keeping system; that their form indicated the product counted; that one token equalled one counted unit; and that these tokens led directly to complete writing. This theory has won many adherents in recent years. Generally accepted by the 1980s, it encountered critique in the 1990s; now, a compromise stance is emerging.

Complete writing was doubtless born out of the need to record the things of everyday life. Goods were perhaps tallied for many thousands of years in the Middle East using small clay tokens (illus. 9) – 'counters', like chits, though their exact purpose is still debated. Why clay? It is an abundant material in the Middle East, easy to work with, easy to erase and just as easy to preserve: simply let it dry in the sun or bake it. Most importantly, clay can easily be impressed with graphic marks representing stored information. Large numbers of these clay artefacts – bearing parallel, perpendicular and curved lines and dating from 8000–1500 BC – have appeared at archæological sites from eastern Iran to southern Turkey and Israel. (Significantly, Egypt has revealed none so far.) Most come from ancient Sumer, today's Iraq. Some were fashioned to resemble cones, spheres or other shapes.

The fourth millennium BC brought an innovation in the use of these small clay counters (if this was what the tokens were). Little clay 'envelopes' called *bullæ* sometimes enclosed them. The *bullæ* were then marked and impressed on their outside, so one did not have to break them open to learn how many tokens of which commodity were inside. Already in the 1930s, this process was recognized as perhaps the 'beginning' of complete writing.[24]

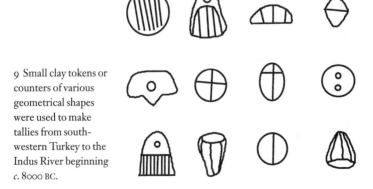

9 Small clay tokens or counters of various geometrical shapes were used to make tallies from south-western Turkey to the Indus River beginning *c.* 8000 BC.

According to recent theory, the *bullæ* markings soon became standardized and systematized.[25] This development produced a new semiotic relation in record-keeping: indirectness. (Semiotics involves the relation of symbols and signs to meaning.) That is, the external marks and impressions on the *bullæ* envelopes were symbols of symbols: each token inside a *bulla* represented one sheep, for example, and the external impression on the *bulla* stood for the type of tokens ('sheep tokens') inside. The external two-dimensional graphic symbols suddenly began substituting for the internal three-dimensional token symbols. Simultaneously with their system of secondary symbol impressions, the Sumerians were also elaborating a numerical system using 'count stones' of different shapes denoting numerical categories. (These were true 'ideograms' – signs that stand for ideas, not things; numbers are ideas.) Count stones, like the tokens, were impressed on the outside of *bullæ* envelopes. One could now 'read' on the outside of a *bulla* how many tokens were contained inside. *Bullæ* were thus 'inscribed' with both the type and the quantity of their contents. Once these secondary outside symbols came to be interpreted and used as primary 'signs', complete writing as we know it was born. According to the token theory, that is.

The leading proponent of this theory, archæologist Denise Schmandt-Besserat, believes that tokens' different forms represent different commodities: metal goods, species of animals, various textiles and so forth. She compares the tokens' forms with the earliest stylized cuneiform glyphs of the Sumerians, which have no apparent pictographic provenance, and finds strong similarities. As a result, she has claimed that the non-pictographic cuneiforms actually derive from *bullæ* impressions (illus. 10). Schmandt-Besserat sees two basic kinds of tokens: simple, like later cuneiform's numerical signs, and complex, like cuneiform's logographic signs.

Critics have voiced misgivings about this theory.[26] One of its main weaknesses, they say, is that it does not account for many of the approximately fifteen hundred Sumerian signs. (If tokens enabled the Sumerian system, they should have inspired most of the signs.) Further, cuneiform's origin seems to have been localized in Sumer, yet tokens are found over a much

clay token	pictogram incised in clay	cuneiform sign
⊕ >	⊕ >	田
(8000 – 3000 BC)	*(Archaic Uruk, c. 3000 BC)*	*(Lagesh, c. 2400 BC)*

10 How the Mesopotamian cuneiform for 'sheep' might have derived from an earlier token and/or *bulla* impression.

wider area. Schmandt-Besserat's database appears not to support her own findings, another critic alleges: 'sheep' tokens, expected to be the most common, occur only fifteen times in seven thousand years, whereas 'nail' and 'work, build' are the two most common; one must also question the alleged uniformity of token meanings over such a range of time and space. The general impression is that 'various people at various times exploited the few geometric shapes that are relatively easy to make in clay and used them as counters for whatever other purposes they, as individuals, chose.'[27] Perhaps most importantly, the *bullæ* accounting system appears to be more complicated and sophisticated than the simple clay tablet it is alleged to have inspired.

Much still speaks for the token theory. Quantitatively, fewer tokens can be dated to the period following 3000 BC once complete writing became more common, implying that tokens were being superseded by something better. A compromise appraisal currently views the tokens of the ancient Middle East as a supplementary explanation of the origins of some early Sumerian signs. Indeed, the token system appears to have contributed to the emergence of complete writing. But tokens did not enable this on their own.

PHONETIZATION AND THE FIRST TABLETS

One might be tempted to agree with linguist Florian Coulmas: 'The decisive step in the development of writing is *phonetization*: that is, the transition from pictorial icon to phonetic symbol.'[28]

11 Inscribed clay tablet from Jemdet Nasr, near Kish, southern Iraq, Late Proto-literate (Uruk IV) period, *c.* 3300 BC. At this early stage, many signs still depicted everyday objects.

Yet the 'reader' of a sheep pictogram or token, for example, would have sounded out 'sheep' as soon as s/he recognized the animal or the token's form. In the pictorial icon (image or likeness) phonetization – turning an image into speech sound(s) – already lay. The same is true with count stones and their impressions. Though phonetization is generally regarded to be a critical criterion in defining 'writing proper',[29] it is implicit in each graphic system. One sees a picture of something ('sheep') or a symbolic count I I I ('three') and one's mind automatically puts a name to it, however rudimentary the graphic likeness or prelearnt unit. Phonetization is not automatically complete writing.

Dating to *c.* 3300 BC from Uruk on the lower Euphrates between Babylon and the Persian Gulf, the earliest of all clay tablets is only one step up from the *bullæ* system, still comprising a system of numerals and (perhaps standardized, stylized) pictograms identifying commodities (illus. 11). In one system of accounting (there were several), numerals were made by pressing the round end of a reed stylus vertically into the clay (full hole = 10), at an angle left to right (hole with cavity = 5), or a number of other possibilities to signify multiples of these. The smallest accounting unit was made by impressing the edge of

| ½ | I | 10 | 60 | 600 | 3,600 |

12 In Sumerian accounting, these standardized marks on soft clay were used to count humans, livestock, vessels, stone and wooden implements, fish, and dairy and textile products.

the stylus downwards, leaving a mark like the heel of a shoe (illus. 12). An obvious improvement on the *bullæ* impressions, the two systems – *bullæ* and tablets – co-existed for many centuries. The message of both was always: 'so and so many of such and such a commodity'. More was not demanded of this system.

Though this is still not complete writing, as it fails to use marks that relate conventionally to articulate speech, it is nevertheless the successful conveyance of complex ideas through graphic art (illus. 13). It displays more sophisticated accounting techniques to accommodate a more elaborate economy. And in the phonetization or 'sounding out' of these earliest pictograms – 'foot', 'hand', 'head' – one is also acknowledging the special relation between an object, its graphic representation and its phonetic value or cue. Over time, pictograms became standardized and abstract, but retained their phonetic value. There came a point when the object itself was often no longer recognizable in the pictogram, though the pictogram's relation to the object and its phonetic value were: the pictogram became a symbol. Sumer's earliest clay tablets already exhibit many such symbols. Scribes could easily 'read' these within the system's limited domain. However, the symbols were still unable to convey 'any and all thought' because they were bound to a system-external referent (illus. 14).

These early clay tablets show at least fifteen hundred different pictograms and symbols, each standing for one concrete object. Because abstract ideas or names were difficult to convey

13 Though perfectly comprehensible to its erstwhile scribe, this pictographic clay tablet from Kish (*c.* 3300 BC) reveals little that is legible today. The 'foot' in the lower left rectangle perhaps means 'go' or 'come'; the profile heads might be 'man' or 'slave'.

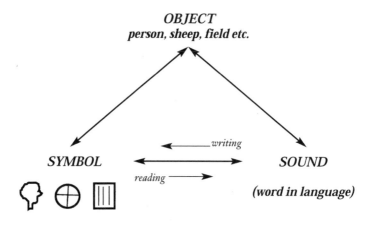

OBJECT
person, sheep, field etc.

SYMBOL ←——— *writing*

reading ——→

SOUND

(word in language)

14 Symbols in Sumerian were bound to a system-external referent.

in this way, new methods were soon devised to express them. A pictogram could now describe different things: a 'foot' was both *foot* and *walking*, a 'mouth' was both *mouth* and *speech*. Further, two pictograms could be joined: 'eye' plus 'water' meant *weeping*. One pictogram compounded with another could also denote a special category: 'plough' plus 'wood' meant *a plough*, but 'plough' plus 'man' meant *ploughman*. For those in the society using these methods, rudimentary 'reading' was possible. For those not in that society, a 'slit triangle' (*vagina/girl*) joined with 'three hills' (*foreign*) would hardly have been immediately identifiable as *foreign girl* or *female slave*. This was still not complete writing. It remained mnemonics, though very elaborate and systematized mnemonics adequate to meet the immediate demands of its users.

However, a new system – or a radical extension of this mnemonic one's adequacy – was needed if people wished to convey more or reduce ambiguity. The answer lay in *systemic phoneticism* – that is, in systematically co-ordinating sounds and symbols (including pictograms) to create 'signs' of a writing system. Graphic symbols became signs of a writing system only when the phonetic value of a symbol began superseding its semantic value within a system of limited, similar values. This cut the link to the system-external referent and prioritized the system's potential to express nearly everything in articulate speech. No longer perceiving in the graphic symbol (or pictogram) merely an external object or abstract ('sky'), one started reading a sound (Sumerian *an*) for its own independent value.

The systemic phonetic solution was possibly prompted by the nature of Sumer's language. Sumerian was mostly monosyllabic (one syllable for each word root), with a large number of homophones (like English 'to', 'too' and 'two'). Perhaps more importantly, Sumerian was agglutinative, attaching to core words prefixes and suffixes that could not stand alone, so sound words had to show these necessary attachments, too, in order to make sense of a spoken statement. When sound assumed priority in the system, incomplete writing became complete writing. This process appears to have occurred around 3700 BC. The transition expanded writing's capabilities exponentially – and inspired immediate adaptations from the Nile to the Indus Valley.

A symbol's sound had assumed systemic status to become a sign. Though perhaps prompted by the special nature of the Sumerian language, the solution had been enabled by the *rebus principle*. Perfectly suited to monosyllabic languages like Sumerian, this principle allows a picture of something to express a syllable in spoken language, taking advantage of homophonics. In this way, a picture of the monosyllabic word *eye* would also stand for the word *I*. 'Saw', the tool, would also be the past verb *saw*. 'Bill', the beak, would be the proper name *Bill*. Using pictures alone, one could 'write', then, the sentence: *I saw Bill* (illus. 15). Many scholars see the rebus principle as the 'key' to the transition from pictography to complete writing.[30]

This was not an 'evolutionary' process. It was a sudden, localized event that occurred as a direct result of a perceived social need: better communication in recording accounts. The social requirements had been accumulating for a long time. The

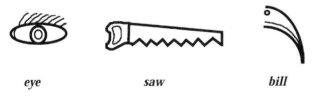

eye   *saw*   **bill**

15 Using the rebus principle to 'write' *I saw Bill*.

graphic apparatus had been provided. A problem had presented itself, and a solution was needed. The solution lay in a new form of writing that now fulfilled the three criteria. That is, it:

- had as its purpose communication;
- consisted of artificial graphic marks on a durable surface;
- used marks that related conventionally to articulate speech in such a way that communication was achieved.

Complete writing was the result (illus. 16).

Sumerian systemic phoneticism remained at first merely a minor tool for specifying isolated particles of information, such as transcribing foreign words or phonetically sounding out hard-to-identify signs that held several possible meanings. (For example, sometimes the phonetic marker *mesh* was suffixed to a sign in order to show that the plural was meant; before, one would have drawn multiple symbols to show plurality.) From the early fourth to the early third millennium BC, most Mesopotamian writing remained essentially pictographic, with only limited phoneticism. However, by 2600 BC the number of elements in the Sumerian writing system had been reduced, through increased use of phonetic writing, from fifteen hundred pictograms and symbols to about eight hundred pictograms, symbols and signs. Logography (whole-word writing, including homophonic) and phonography (exclusively phonetic writing) did not fully develop in Mesopotamia until about 2400 BC.

Yet Sumer's idea of systemic phoneticism, already at its inception, evidently spread far beyond the Tigris and Euphrates, both east to the Indus and west to the Nile, where the idea took root among other rising civilizations. Different languages and different social needs now demanded new solutions of their own.[31]

Most scholars still prefer to believe that writing originated independently in many regions of the world as an expression of a society's having attained an 'advanced' level of civilization.

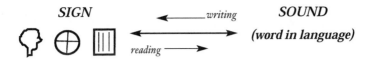

16 Systemic phoneticism: Complete writing became possible once sign and sound were no longer bound to a system-external object (compare illus. 14) – one started reading a sign for its sound value alone within a standardized system of limited signs.

However, writing is not an automatic reward of social sophistication. Writing must be *elaborated*, and this entails a protracted process determined by evolving social needs. Though there are other possible interpretations, the cumulative weight of evidence urges the consideration that the idea of complete writing may have emerged only once in humankind's history. Drawing from a standardized repertoire of pictograms and symbols – the distillation of a long development from notches to tablets – the Sumerians of Mesopotamia elaborated what has since become humankind's most versatile tool. All other writing systems and scripts are, then, perhaps derivatives of this one original idea – systemic phoneticism – that emerged between 6,000 and 5,700 years ago in Mesopotamia.

TWO

Talking Art

Once symbol became sign around 3700 BC, graphic art began to 'talk'. Pictorial writing was phonetic writing. It was precisely this conscious exploitation of the phonographic in the pictographic that turned incomplete writing into complete writing.[1] A picture of an ox had originally meant only 'ox', prompting one to say the word aloud. With the new rebus principle, one began pronouncing sounds that no longer conveyed only the graphic image. The rebus principle was Sumer's unique contribution to humankind.

It is accepted by most linguists that all complete writing (except computer programs) expresses the utterances of a particular language. However, it is not a matter of course that complete writing will say 'everything' in that language. Some writing systems are reserved for ritual use – Easter Island's *rongorongo*, early Chinese divinations, early Hebrew scripture. Many forms of writing started their life as a bound vehicle, then broke free to express other things as well. All such early, limited stages encompass complete writing even though this complete writing might have been unable to convey 'everything' in its respective language. Easter Island's writing never grew beyond this threshold; Chinese writing went on to become the ancient world's most voluminous system.

From Mesopotamia, as we have seen, the rebus principle diffused to the Nile, the Iranian Plateau and the Indus Valley (and perhaps also to the Balkans). Local needs then adapted or converted this new writing using logography, phonography and determinatives ('sign identifiers') in combination with each other – creating *mixed systems*, still the most prevalent form of writing.

In Egypt, several hundred logographic 'hieroglyphs' formed

the bulk of the local system, written in ink on papyrus. (Crucial to the history of writing, Egypt also innovated a handful of logo-consonantal signs: pictures standing only for the sound of their beginning consonant.) This new Egyptian writing soon appeared in a flowing cursive version. In contrast, in Mesopotamia a logosyllabic system prevailed that used wedges of sign components impressed into soft clay in order to form *in-di-vi-du-al* words according to a relatively small inventory of standard configurations.

Egypt's hieroglyphs and Mesopotamia's cuneiforms drew from the same well – logography or word-writing – according to the needs of their underlying languages. As it happened, the two languages differed fundamentally, and so two wholly different writing systems emerged. Yet both served thriving societies eminently for over 3,400 years. Similar clay-impressed writing in the Indus Valley, still undeciphered, thrived for half this time span, then succumbed. All the writing systems of ancient Afro-Asia appear to relate to one another in some way, either by immediate borrowing and adaptation (conversion) or by indirect influence (illus. 17).[2]

The era of papyrus and clay – writing's longest (paper has been the world's preferred writing material for only the past five hundred years) – witnessed the rapid rise of urban federations that would also survive, in various forms, for three and a half millennia. Writing is not a criterion for civilization. Recent archæological findings suggest that urban activity obtained in

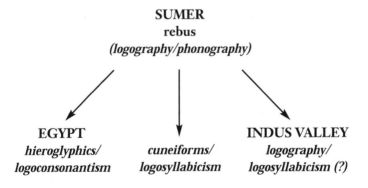

17 How the earliest Afro-Asiatic writing systems were related.

north-eastern Syria as early as 4000 BC. That is, the development of kingdoms or early states may have occurred before the emergence of complete writing. However, Egypt's Upper and Lower Kingdoms united a few centuries after the hieroglyphs' elaboration there. Similarly, Mesopotamian city-states grew into powerful empires once complete writing had emerged in that region. No direct causal relationship held, of course, but few would dispute writing's role in stimulating the economic expansion that empowered such events.

In time, the individual signs of these early writing systems assumed lives of their own, wholly divorcing themselves from the eternal world of objective phenomena. They became stylized and widened their systemic functions. The lengthening texts that used these signs diversified, no longer simply tallying and sealing, but soon invoking, propagandizing, dedicating and otherwise prolonging the spoken word in a multitude of ways. Even more societies borrowed and adapted the wonder of this new form of writing, each in unique fashion.

Within a thousand years, phonetic writing had made itself the most fundamental tool of ascending civilizations.[3]

EGYPTIAN WRITING

Ancient Egyptians called writing *mdw-nṯr* – 'god's words' – because they believed it to be the gift of Thoth, the ibis-headed scribe of the gods, healer, lord of all wisdom and patron of scholars. It was the Greek Clement of Alexandria, writing some eighteen hundred years ago, who first called the Egyptians' writing *hierogluphiká* – 'sacred carvings'. Few writing systems in the world have been as beautiful or as captivating. None has had such far-reaching effects on humankind.

Excavations have only recently revealed that fully developed hieroglyphs read in rebus fashion were in use at Abydos – Upper Egypt's 'power centre' five hundred km south of Cairo – as early as 3400 BC. Already by this early Gerzean or Narqada II period, before the unification of Upper and Lower Egypt, Sumer's idea of rebus writing, possibly only part of a larger cultural transmission,[4] had evidently inspired those rulers of Upper Egypt who sought a more efficient administration. Writing in the form of logograms and phonograms was apparently already appreciated as an advantageous vehicle for information storage and control. It is possible that Egypt's hieroglyphic writing emerged as part of the same social momentum that eventually produced the unification of Upper and Lower Egypt several centuries later, around 3100 BC.[5]

Egypt had borrowed from Sumer not simply the 'idea of writing', but logography, phonography and linearity with sequencing. The Egyptian sign inventory was codified very early on, with set phonetic values and sign usages.[6] Then, recognizing specific requirements of the Egyptian language, scribes innovated new writing tools. One of these was acrophony, the use of a hieroglyph to represent only a word's beginning consonant: the leg sign represented *b*, for example. (In contrast, Sumerian scribes used signs representing whole syllables, not individual consonants.) The Egyptians also elaborated signs standing for two consonants and for three consonants; signs representing phonetic complements (additional, reinforcing signs to ensure that the reader knows what is intended); signs that were individual logograms ('word-signs') and determinatives ('identifiers'); the use of much redundancy (repeating things to lessen ambiguity); and other usages (illus. 18). One sign could be both a logogram and a phonogram. Frequently, only context determined which reading obtained.

One of the most interesting features of the hieroglyphs was the frequent use of sign complementing or redundancy. Many hieroglyphs were complemented by supporting signs that constituted not a separate sign class but a different sign function. If we were to do this in English, for example, we would follow a sign of a human eye with the letter *i* to identify its correct pronunciation. In Egyptian hieroglyphs, the scribe commonly repeated the final consonant of a main sign in this way as a phonetic complement. Sometimes, he did this twice, or even three times, merely to ensure the reader's comprehension (illus. 19).

Another fascinating feature of Egyptian hieroglyphs is the use of determinatives or sign identifiers (one also finds this in other, much later, writing systems). Determinatives are very different from phonetic complements in that they identify sound,

1. Uni-consonantal:

2. Bi-consonantal:

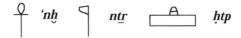

3. Tri-consonantal:

4. Phonetic complements:

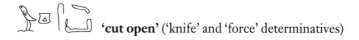

5. Determinatives (*identifying logograms*):

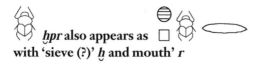

18 Some types of hieroglyphs (logograms, phonograms and determinatives).

nfr also appears as
with 'horned viper' *f* and 'mouth' *r*

ḫpr also appears as
with 'sieve (?)' *ḫ* and mouth' *r*

19 Redundancy in Egyptian hieroglyphs.

not sense. They are logograms, or word signs, stuck onto the end of phonograms – sound signs – particularly in cases when the word's sound holds ambiguity (as with English homonyms *Bill* and *bill*), in order to identify the precise meaning of the desired word. As determinatives must be as clear as possible, many are actually pictographic rather than logographic (illus. 20). And to ensure correct identification of the desired word, scribes often employed two or more determinatives per word (see illus. 18.5).

The frequent use of some 26 uni-consonantal signs – each conveying only one consonant – was doubtless the most remarkable innovation of ancient Egyptian scribes (illus. 21). This was the world's first alphabet, though it did not include vowels nor did its use customarily set these consonantal signs apart from the other phonetic signs of Egyptian hieroglyphs. The consonantal signs were almost always used together with the full inventory of logograms, phonograms and determinatives. It appears that Egyptian scribes comprehended the consonantal alphabetic principle – that is, writing only with consonants – shortly before 2000 BC. The idea then spread quickly among Semitic vassals (see Chapter 3). The Egyptians themselves used it only in rare circumstances, as for graffiti. The rigid conservatism of hieroglyphic and hieratic writing apparently exerted an inertia that could brook no radical changes. In this way, alphabetism, perhaps Egypt's greatest achievement, fell by the wayside in the land of its origin.

In these ways, Egyptian hieroglyphic writing furnished word 'skeletons' to which the reader needed only to add the appropriate vowels, again obvious to native speakers only from context.[7] (As ancient Egyptians did not mark vowels in most instances,

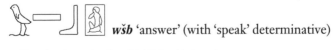

20 Egyptian determinatives (highlighted in boxes).

Sign	Transcription/Meaning	Sound
𓄿	ꜣ / vulture	glottal stop
𓇋	i / flowering reed	I
𓇋𓇋	y / two flowering reeds	Y
\\	y / oblique strokes	Y
𓂝	ꜥ / forearm and hand	Semitic *ꜥayin*
𓅱	w / quail chick	W
𓏲	w / cursive for	W
𓃀	b / foot	B
𓊪	p / mat	P
𓆑	f / horned viper	F
𓅓	m / mat	M
∿∿∿∿	n / water	N
𓂋	r / mouth	R
𓉐	ḥ / reed shelter	H
𓎛	ḥ / twisted flax	H (slightly gutteral)
𓐍	ḫ / sieve (?)	KH (as in Scottish *loch*)
𓄡	ẖ / animal's belly	KH (soft)
𓋴	s / door bolt	S
𓋳	ś / folded cloth	S
𓈙	š / pool	SH
𓈎	ḳ / hill	Q
𓎡	k / basket with handle	K
𓎼	g / jar stand (?)	G
𓏏	t / loaf	T
𓍿	ṯ / tethering rope	CH (as in *chin*)
𓂧	d / hand	D
𓆓	ḏ / snake	J

2 I Uni-consonantal signs: the Old Egyptian 'consonantal alphabet'.

Wsr-mȝ'.t-R'-stp-n-R'
(User-maatre-setepenre)

Moved forward to show respect, the sun is the logogram for the god Re.

Kneeling figure is the logogram for Maat, goddess of justice.

The jackal head is the tri-consonantal sign *wsr*, also reproducing the words *be strong*.

God Re is again moved forward in the second part of the image.

Adze on a block of wood is the tri-consonantal sign *stp*, also reproducing the word *chosen*.

Water is the uni-consonantal sign *n*.

22 Reading Egyptian hieroglyphs: 'the Maat of Re is strong, one chosen for Re', one possible translation of the *prænomen*, or throne name, of Ramesses II on an inlaid tile, *c*. 1250 BC.

the vocalic values of ancient Egyptian words are generally unknown. Some values have, however, been retrieved through educated guesswork in light of contemporaneous cuneiform and other scripts conveying ancient Egyptian proper names.) One reads hieroglyphs either from right to left or from left to right; some texts follow from top to bottom (illus. 22). Signs always 'face' the start position of each line: if one should read from right to left, then the bird's beak, for example, is facing right. Right-to-left reading was the 'default' reading direction, if there was no clear reason to choose otherwise – ease of reading, royal respect (demanding transposition of certain royal signs), artistic symmetry and so forth. Once formalized in such ways, a process that apparently occurred between *c*. 3500 and 2500 BC, hieroglyphs remained little changed for thousands of years (illus. 23). Most writing in northern Africa and the Middle East has maintained a right-to-left reading direction ever since.

The individual hieroglyphs were taken or elaborated from the inventory of traditional Egyptian art.[8] (This tendency to borrow only the idea and/or restricted functions of writing, while expressing one's own language through indigenous signs,

23 The early rebus stage of Egyptian writing: the Plaque of Akha, *c.* 2900 BC, identified with Men(es), traditional founder of the First Dynasty.

has been repeated throughout history; see the examples of Ægean syllabic writing in Chapter 3, and of Easter Island signs in Chapter 7.) The textual stages of Egyptian writing are: Old Egyptian, the language of the Old Kingdom (*c.* 2650–2135 BC), when the first continuous texts appear; Middle Egyptian, the 'classical' stage of Egyptian (*c.* 2135–1785 BC); Late Egyptian, in particular the secular documents of the Ramesside Period (*c.* 1300–1080 BC); Demotic (*c.* 700 BC–fifth century AD), the script used for the vernacular language also called Demotic; and the separate, mostly Greek-derived Coptic script (as of the fourth century AD) that conveyed the Coptic language, the only known stage of Egyptian with two dialects, Sa'idic and Bohairic (illus. 24).[9]

Egyptian hieroglyphs constitute perhaps the world's most beautiful writing system, at least as perceived today. Most writing systems or scripts are functional, not beautiful. It is true that the calligraphy of Arabic and East Asian (Chinese and Japanese) writing displays a gracefulness of form seldom attained by other scripts. However, Egyptian hieroglyphs are both decoration and script at the same time, and are never intrusive (illus. 25). Some believe only the Maya script of Mesoamerica approaches the grandeur of ancient Egyptian writing.

Over some four thousand years, Egyptian writing developed four 'distinct but interrelated' scripts, which were frequently written in complementary usage: hieroglyphic, hieratic, demotic and Coptic.[10] The hieroglyphic script was principally of monumental or ceremonial usage. The two cursive scripts (a

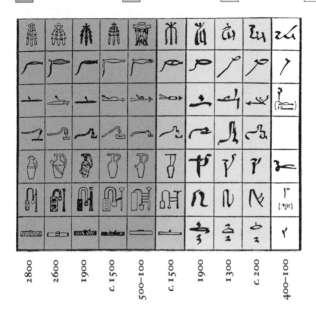

HIEROGLYPHIC					BOOK SCRIPT		HIERATIC		DEMOTIC
2800	2600	1900	c. 1500	500–100	c. 1500	1900	1300	c. 200	400–100

24 Selected signs of the three Egyptian scripts and their development.

25 The beauty of Egyptian hieroglyphs: detail of the 'reconstructed' portico of Isis' Temple at Philæ.

26 Three stages of Egypt's hieratic script: (left) Sixth Dynasty (2315–2190 BC); (centre) Middle Kingdom (2040–1710 BC); (right) Seventeenth Dynasty (1580–1555 BC).

cursive script flows freely with joined characters), hieratic and the much later demotic, were almost always written in ink on papyrus. Hieroglyphic, hieratic and demotic differ only in external appearance; in function, form and usage they are one writing system. Hieroglyphic writing originally consisted of around 2,500 signs, though only some five hundred of these were in regular use. This was the preferred script for special texts and inscriptions on metal, stone, wood and other hard surfaces, especially for ritual or propagandistic purposes, though hieroglyphs were also written in ink on papyrus, leather and ostraca (inscribed fragments of pottery).

Most writing in ancient Egypt, however, was not in hieroglyphs, which were very time-consuming to draw or engrave. Cursive hieroglyphic writing, only much later called 'hieratic', developed almost immediately as a practical tool for writing commonplace documents – letters, accounts, dockets – and, as early as the second millennium BC, also literary texts (illus. 26). Hieratic was ancient Egypt's everyday script, used for business, administration, correspondence and general literary production. A linear simplification of hieroglyphic writing, it was written exclusively from right to left on papyrus, parchment, wood, ostraca and other surfaces. Hieratic first served the Nile's accountants; then, as it was written more extensively on papyrus, it became more stylized, developing a calligraphic flourish for literary and religious compositions. More ligatures (strokes connecting two signs) were innovated to simplify book-keeping and other business requirements. Many styles and regional variants arose.

By the 25th Dynasty (middle of the first millennium BC), the chancery hands of the south, writing the 'abnormal hieratic', were no longer legible to readers of the northern hands, the new demotic script. This was because in the north, by about 700 BC, hieratic had come to be written as a form of shorthand the Egyptians called *sš-š'.t*, or 'letter writing', which the Greek historian Herodotus called *demotikós*, or 'popular'– the script 'of the people'. This demotic writing derived from the Nile Delta's business hand and, from the seventh century BC until the fifth century AD, fulfilled all of hieratic's earlier uses. (The old hieratic writing became the reserve of priests, which is why Clement of Alexandria called it *hieratikós*, or 'of the priestly class'.) Demotic is hieroglyphic in origin but highly abbreviated, with ligatured word groupings losing all graphic similarity to the original hieroglyphs. Like hieratic, demotic reads from right to left. But unlike hieratic, and beginning with the Greek Ptolemys, demotic was engraved in stone, too – such as on the famous Rosetta Stone (illus. 27).

An important social reflex of writing's elaboration along the Nile was the development of an extremely influential scribal class, something new in human history. Scribes were more highly regarded in Egypt than in Mesopotamia, where they were mere clerks; Egyptian scribes could attain great wealth, prestige and position. The most highly regarded were priestly scribes, a station reserved for a select few. As Egyptian bureaucrat Dua-Khety sailed south along the Nile around four thousand years ago, he told his son, whom he was escorting to a school for scribes: 'It is to writings that you must set your mind ... I do not see an office comparable with [the scribe's] ... I shall make you love books more than [you love] your mother, and I shall place their excellence before you.'

27 The Rosetta Stone (196 BC) memorializes Ptolemy V in three different
scripts: (top) Egyptian hieroglyphs; (centre) Egyptian demotic; (bottom) Greek.

Each scribe owned his own writing kit: a slate palette with
two shallow cups for holding red and black ink cakes, and, on a
connecting thong, a thin wooden brush case and small water jug
(see illus. 20). An ancient Egyptian scribe wrote much in the
same way as we do watercolours today. Red was used for emphasis and to divide a text under headings. A student scribe had to
learn around seven hundred signs over the course of several
years of intense effort. (This is not too dissimilar from Chinese

and Japanese education today.) Students commonly wrote on writing boards covered with gesso, a mixture of plaster and glue; the surface allowed easy erasing. The most ubiquitous writing material was papyrus – a kind of paper fashioned by pounding strips of the plant *Cyperus papyrus* into sheets.

Egypt's writing had a great material advantage over Mesopotamia's bulky, awkward clay tablets.[11] Papyrus was thin, light, flexible and easily stored. Writing on it with ink was quick; it dried easily and required less surface area per word than cuneiform wedge syllables (at least for the consonantal writing of Egyptian). The earliest-discovered papyrus comes from a First Dynasty tomb at Saqqara from *c.* 3000 BC. However, it is possible that papyrus was already used with the very first writing along the Nile, using ink with a chiselled reed pen. Papyrus writing continued in Egypt until the first few centuries AD – that is, some 3,700 years later.

Eventually, the demotic script was replaced by the invaders' Greek alphabetic script for everyday administrative purposes, as well as for writing the Egyptian language. Later, Coptic made use of mostly Greek letters to convey Egyptian words, now including vowels (see Chapter 4). Egyptian writing influenced the Meroïtic script of Meroë in the Sudan, dating from *c.* 250 BC, and also supplied the forms for the earliest identified consonantal alphabet (*c.* 2200 BC) that generated the various Semitic proto-alphabets of the Sinai and Levant. The latter became, in time, the Latin alphabet we use today.

The world's debt to the Nile is immense. It is no coincidence that our method of writing at the beginning of the third millennium AD is not too different from that of Egyptian scribes of the third millennium BC.[12] Though the idea of complete writing may have arisen in Sumer, the way we write and even some of our signs, which we call 'letters', are the ultimate descendants of ancient Egyptian founders (illus. 28).

CUNEIFORM WRITING

A history of cuneiform – the word derives from Latin *cuneus* ('wedge') and *forma* ('shape') – traces the history of logographism, or 'word-writing', to phoneticism, or 'sound-writing',

Egyptian	Proto-Sinaitic	Phoenician	Early Greek	Greek	Latin
🐂				A	A
				B	B
				Γ	G
				E	E
				K	K
				M	M
				N	N
		⊙	⊙	O	O
				P	R
	+	X	T	T	T
		W			S

28 Ancient Egyptian hieroglyphs live on, in transmuted fashion, in our own alphabet.

with sound superseding iconicity entirely. (This did not happen with Egyptian hieroglyphs.) The most important type of writing of the ancient Near East, cuneiform actually constitutes one script used by different writing systems. (In contrast, Egyptian is one writing system used by three related scripts.) The world's first complete writing, as we have seen, arose in Sumer as a response to economic needs. This response became an effective tool wielded by a bureaucratic hierarchy administering goods, services and social privilege.[13] As a result of the dynamism of Mesopotamian merchants, and of the imperialistic regimes the tool served and empowered, cuneiform writing prevailed in the region for many thousands of years.[14]

Proto-cuneiform writing, that of the tablets of Uruk and Jemdet Nasr, hardly differed from pictographic book-keeping

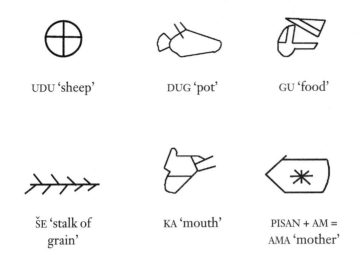

UDU 'sheep'   DUG 'pot'   GU 'food'

ŠE 'stalk of   KA 'mouth'   PISAN + AM =
grain'   AMA 'mother'

29 Proto-cuneiform signs from Uruk, late fourth millennium BC.

(illus. 29). It was drawn on clay with a pointed stylus; the impressing of wedge shapes, at various angles, came centuries later. The earliest writing is 'understood' to a certain degree, but cannot be fully 'read' in the modern sense. Whereas Egypt had codified its hieroglyphic and hieratic signs early on, and so had fossilized its system, Sumer maintained a loose inventory of about eighteen hundred pictograms and symbols for many centuries. This allowed simplification and conventionalization to occur. By 2700–2350 BC, with the tablets of Shuruppak, the inventory had been reduced to some eight hundred, with increased linearity (writing in lines of text). By about 2500 BC, nearly all graphic elements in the Sumerian writing system had become sound units. And by 2000 BC, only about 570 logograms were in everyday use.[15]

A clear script progression is evident with cuneiform writing (illus. 30). Early pictograms were replaced with wedges made by a reed stylus on soft clay, copying the original pictograms' shape. These wedges were then stylized, eventually losing identifiability. Possibly by the middle of the third millennium (*c.* 2500 BC) but certainly by the beginning of the second (*c.* 1900 BC), scribes suddenly began writing most pictograms as if they were toppled over to their left, at a 90-degree re-alignment.

| Significance | | Pictograph | Rotated | Archaic | Babylonian | Assyrian |
SUMERIAN	ENGLISH	(c. 3000 BC)	form	(c. 2500 BC)	(c. 1800 BC)	(c. 600 BC)
kur	'mountain'					
sal	'vagina/girl'					
geme	'slave girl'					
ninda	'food'					
an	'heaven'					
du	'to go, stand'					
sag	'head'					
gud	'ox'					

30 The origin and development of selected cuneiform signs from *c.* 3000 to 600 BC.

Script direction also changed: texts were no longer written from right to left vertically, but from left to right horizontally in columned lines, just as in today's newspapers (illus. 31). (Stone monuments, however, including Hammurabi's law code of the early eighteenth century BC, maintained the original orientation until *c.* 1500 BC.) Reasons for the change – whether scribal convenience or one ruler's vagary – are still unclear.[16]

Scribes trained young boys (or, rarely, girls) at special schools, as in Egypt, thus introducing the world's first formal educational systems. Pupils began by copying a teacher's sample text – a proverb, a literary fragment, gods' names and so forth – on the reverse of the teacher's soft clay tablet (illus. 32). In time, an entire social class of scribes arose, most of them employed in agriculture. Some became personal secretaries and the world's first lawyers; many exerted great social influence. However, Mesopotamia's scribes were never so revered as those along the Nile.

Most cuneiform writing occurred in clay with a reed stylus, but cuneiforms were also carved in stone and inscribed on wax, ivory, metal (including gold) and even glass. Very seldom, however, was cuneiform written in ink on papyrus, thus contrasting it greatly with Egyptian writing. Contrary to general opinion, this probably had less to do with raw materials – ancient

31 Sumerian barley account from Girsu, southern Iraq, dated 2048 BC.

32 A Babylonian pupil practised writing the word *one* over and over at Nippur *c.* 1700 BC.

Mesopotamia grew abundant papyrus – than with local need and fossilized tradition.

A stylus on clay was a fantastic tool, in many ways much more creative than today's two-dimensional pen, pencil or computer screen. The stylus, with triangular tip, could be oriented in three dimensions, and both stylus and tablet, if small, were turned in the hands simultaneously. However, to avoid confusion, a strict inventory of sign angles obtained. As a result of the physical limitations of the hand-held stylus, only rarely do cuneiform wedges slant left, straight up or up to the right. The standard shape of each sign was fixed early, and only a very limited variation was allowed.[17] Normal signs are composed of groupings – or 'cases' – of simple lines with triangular terminals (the 'wedges'), effected by holding the stylus at an angle. Once the tablet was written, it was dried in the sun, or baked if it was important enough to preserve. Ironically, destructive conflagrations have preserved some of ancient Mesopotamia's greatest libraries – because they were made of clay. In contrast, all of ancient Egypt's papyrus libraries have burnt or crumbled to dust, though many individual codices survive.

The cuneiform script was complete, capable of conveying 'any and all thought', by around 2500 BC. Essential in this process was the establishment, by convention, of a syllabary: an inventory of specific signs used purely for their syllabic sound values – *ti*, *mu*, *sa* and so forth. This began by object transfer. The Sumerian sign *mu* ('plant') was used also as the *mu* for 'year' and that for 'name'. This was then extended to function words: *mu* for 'my' and *mu* for 'third-person masculine prefix'. In time, any *mu* in the Sumerian language could be represented by the 'plant' sign, as only its sound was important in the system.[18] This is how Mesopotamia's cuneiform script, resting on the three-legged stool of pictograms/symbols, phonograms and determinatives, almost exclusively conveys a 'logosyllabic' writing system.[19] Independent whole words are represented by logograms, either single signs or sign clusters. And dependent parts of words are represented by rebus-derived syllabograms, commonly of the structure V (vowel), CV (consonant-vowel) or VC (vowel-consonant). As with Egyptian, determinatives were used to identify the significance of a word sign. Each cuneiform sign is a construct, then, of simple to complex. Though simple signs often form part of complex signs, their sound value is lost in the process: the produced graphic holds its own unique value.

The Sumerians had elaborated a very simple script that adequately fulfilled the needs of its society. But during its three-thousand-year history, it served some fourteen other languages and cultures, too. Problems with others writing cuneiform first began when East Semitic Akkadians, a different ethnic community, invaded Sumer and rose to prominence after 2800 BC. Though Sumerian continued to be spoken and written, in cuneiform, for more than a thousand years thereafter, for cultic and literary purposes (very much like Latin 2,500 years later), texts in Old Akkadian began to appear around 2350 BC with Sargon I.[20] Since the Akkadian language was typologically the opposite of Sumerian – that is, Sumerian is mostly monosyllabic, but Akkadian polysyllabic; Sumerian is not inflected with changing word endings, but Akkadian is highly inflected – writing Akkadian with the Sumerian system resulted in ambiguity and confusion (illus. 33). Akkadian scribes used only one-tenth the amount of logograms (word signs) but over twice the amount of syllabograms and determinatives. In other words, they were forced to prioritize writing's phonetic function while still using the old Sumerian logograms for many things – with their old Sumerian values and also an additional Akkadian value (as Japanese did with Chinese some three thousand years later).

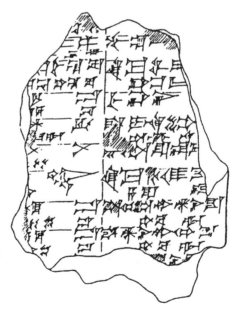

33 Bilingual Sumerian-Akkadian 'dictionary' from c. 1750 BC, used to teach Akkadian pupils to write Sumerian.

This created *polyvalence* – signs holding many values – of epidemic proportions. Why did the Akkadians not simplify? They appeared to be bound to tradition and a self-imposed efficiency. Perhaps most importantly, they were constrained by the inertia of an intransigent system, a phenomenon of writing found throughout its history. Akkadian was written until about AD 100, mainly as a literary language. As a spoken language, it competed with, and merged into, Babylonian and Assyrian, considered by some scholars to be later, separate, linguistically distinct stages of evolved Akkadian.

After 2000 BC, Babylonian speakers from southern Mesopotamia and Assyrian speakers from northern Mesopotamia continued writing in cuneiform. The Babylonians had reduced the number of signs to about 570; of these, only some two to three hundred were in everyday use.[21] The Assyrians re-introduced many archaic signs and created even more complexity, thus thwarting simplification. Most neighbouring languages adopted the Sumero-Babylonian (Sumerians' and Akkadians') sign shapes and syllabary. However, some languages borrowed only the idea of the clay wedge to write, and elaborating their own 'cuneiform' using wholly independent shapes and values. Cuneiform was used for writing Amorite proper names, Kassite glosses or complete texts in related Semitic languages, such as Eblaite, Canaanite and Aramaic.[22] Wholly unrelated languages used cuneiform, too: Hittite, Elamite, Hurrian and Urartian (some also include Hattic, the non-Indo-European predecessors of the Hittites).

For example, the Hittites of eastern Anatolia (today part of Turkey), speaking an Indo-European language, borrowed the cuneiform signs and syllabary around 1900 BC with double Sumerian and Akkadian values, and then added their own values to these. Thus, each Hittite sign had three possible readings: Sumerian, Akkadian or Hittite, depending on context. Though the Hittites also wrote in the Babylonian (Akkadian) language, most of their ten-thousand-tablet library, discovered in 1906 at the Hittite capital, Hattushash (modern Boğazköy), appears in the Hittite language, though using the foreign cuneiform script. Hittite was ill fitted to the Akkadians' already ill-fitting system: consonant clusters, in particular, were difficult to convey using syllabic signs. The Hittites introduced some new syllabic signs to help, but this merely stuck more vowels into clusters where they did not belong. This, along with other factors, makes the decipherment of Hittite texts difficult today.[23] However, for Hittite scribes working within the system on a daily basis, it was doubtless sufficient for all immediate needs.

Between about 1450 and 1250 BC, Semitic scribes of Ugarit on Syria's northern coast wrote wholly phonetic cuneiforms without logograms or determinatives. Their writing is a hybrid creation: consonantal alphabetic using the physical technique of Mesopotamia's cuneiform.[24] That is, the outer form (script) – wedges on soft clay – is cuneiform, but the inner form (writing system) is alphabetic, borrowed from Canaan (see Chapter 3). Ugaritic cuneiform was also used in Ugarit to write Akkadian and Hurrian, two related languages (illus. 34). Of interest here is that one script – Mesopotamian cuneiform – could be 'cannibalized' to convey a wholly different writing system, in this case a linear alphabet.[25]

Cuneiform was used also in Elam (south-west Iran) to write Akkadian, a language foreign to the Elamites, who spoke neither Sumerian nor a Semitic tongue (see below and illus. 37).[26] The Elamites were forced to effect great changes to the system they borrowed in order to accommodate their language. They wrote syllabically as a rule, and by the end of the second millennium BC they had reduced the syllabary to 113 different syllabic

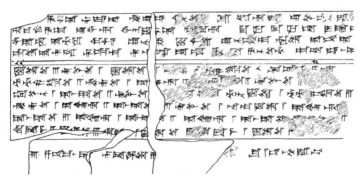

34 Among the world's oldest 'musical texts' (lyrics and instructions for performance) is this Hurrian cuneiform tablet, composed *c.* 1400 BC, unearthed near Ugarit.

cuneiform signs read mostly with Sumerian-Akkadian values; some held a new Elamite value. Only 25 logograms were used, some comprising Sumerian loan words. Only seven determinatives were used, but these extremely frequently. For example, the single horizontal (later perpendicular) wedge identified all place names and some other nouns; later, it became virtually a word boundary marker.[27]

Old Persian, like Hittite an Indo-European language, was written in cuneiforms as of the first millennium BC, mostly between 550 and 350. King Darius' monumental inscription at Bisothum – in Old Persian, Elamite and Neo-Babylonian – furnished the 'key' to cuneiform's decipherment and the reconstruction of these languages.[28] Darius' Old Persian scribes effected the most drastic simplification of the borrowed Near Eastern script (illus. 35). They reduced the cuneiform inventory to only 41 signs of both syllabic (*ka*) and phonemic (/k/) values. Thus, Old Persian cuneiform is 'half syllabic, half letter writing'.[29] It appears to be on the fence between the Babylonians' cuneiforms and the Levantines' consonantal writing, a hybrid solution using only four logograms and 36 syllabo-phonemic signs written in wedges. Of particular significance is the fact that Old Persian also conveys the individual long and short vowels /a/ (pronounced AH), /i/ (EE) and /u/ (OO) that the Ugaritic system had conveyed a thousand years earlier.

With cuneiform writing, 'literature' – from the Latin *litteratura* ('alphabet, grammar') – commenced. The world's oldest literary texts appear on Sumerian clay tablets: poems (hymns, laments, attributes and activities of the gods) and quasi-epic 'tales' (the five-poem Gilgamesh cycle of *c.* 2700 BC, written down hundreds of years later; the two poems of Enmerkar; and the two poems of Lugulbanda). However, more than 75 per cent of the 150,000 cuneiform inscriptions excavated so far in Mesopotamia are book-keeping and administrative records, the earliest of these being predominately lists of goods, people, payments and such.[30] In time, legal documents emerged, as well as religious and astronomical texts, even medicinal treatises and recipes. Scribes compiled the world's first dictionaries: lists of words, ordered according to pronunciation, sign form and meaning. The latest datable cuneiform tablet is an astronomical

1. *D(a)-a-r(a)-y(a)-v(a)-u-š(a)* 2. *x(a)-š(a)-a-y(a)-ϑ(a)-i-y(a)*
3. *v(a)-z(a)-r(a)-k(a)* 4. *x(a)-š(a)-a-y(a)-ϑ(a)-i-y(a)* 5. *x(a)-š(a)-a-y(a)-ϑ(a)-i-y(a)-a-n(a)-a-m(a)* 6. *x(a)-š(a)-a-y(a)-ϑ(a)-i-y(a)*
7. *d(a)-h(a)-y(a)-u-n(a)-a-m(a)* 8. *Vi-i-š(a)-t(a)-a-s(a)-p(a)-h(a)-y(a)-a* 9. *p(a)-u-ç(a)* 10. *H(a)-x(a)-a-m(a)-n(a)-i-š(a)-i-y(a)* 11. *h(a)-y(a)* 12. *i-m(a)-m(a)* 13. *t(a)-č(a)-r(a)-m(a)* 14. *a-ku-u-n(a)-u-š(a)*

Dārayavauš xšāyaϑiya vazrka xšāyaϑiya xšāyaϑiyānām xšāyaϑiya dahyunām Vištāspahya puça Haxāmanišiya hya imam tačaram akunauš

35 Inscription from the palace of Persepolis, *c.* 500 BC, in Old Persian cuneiform: 'Darius, the great King, the King of Kings, the King of the countries, son of Hystaspes, the Achæmenid, who built this palace'. Below the transcription (with numbers added) are edited transliterations.

almanac from Babylon describing the positions of the planets for AD 74–5.

Cuneiform continues to enrich us even now: in 1975, over fifteen thousand cuneiform tablets were discovered at Ebla (Syria) which once comprised the official library that had burnt around the year 2300 BC. It will take scholars at least a century to read and assess this enormous wealth of information. In use for about three thousand years – the same length of time that our complete alphabet has been known – cuneiform is today appreciated as one of humankind's premier scripts.

PROTO-ELAMITE

Perhaps a derivative of an older script that also inspired Indus Valley writing, the partly pictographic Proto-Elamite script of *c.* 3000 BC, still undeciphered, was impressed on soft clay to convey the language of Elam in south-western Iran on the Persian Gulf. Specimens of this script have been discovered from Susa, Elam's ancient capital, to Shahr-i-Sokhta on the Afghan border some twelve hundred km to the east.[31] At the end of the fourth millennium BC, Mesopotamians and the inhabitants of the Iranian Plateau were communicating regularly for a variety of reasons, foremost among them trade. There is no doubt that the idea of systemic phoneticism, as in Egypt, came to the Iranian Plateau from Sumer: the Proto-Elamite script, written with reed-stylus wedges on soft clay, uses the same numerical notation as proto-cuneiform, and at least one sign is shared. Some fifteen hundred tablets in the still unidentified language and script of the Proto-Elamite culture have been published in the century since the culture's discovery (illus. 36).[32] Most of these tablets have been unearthed at Susa, east of Babylon.

Some fifteen hundred signs inflated the Proto-Elamite inventory, indicating that the writing is logographic. Many of the signs are abstract, displaying a conscious preference for the geometric over the pictorial. All documents are written linearly from right to left, reading from top to bottom, as with the contemporary Sumerian proto-cuneiform script. There is no formal arrangement into columns of writing. It seems that each text commences by introducing its purpose, then naming the acting person or institution. This is followed by discrete entries which include a logogram of persons (institutions) or quantified commodities or perhaps both. The text concludes with a

36 Proto-Elamite tablet from Susa, c. 3000 BC.

37 Bi-script dedication of Puzur-Inšušinak of Susa, in Akkadian cuneiform and linear Elamite, c. 2200 BC.

numerical notation in Sumerian fashion.

It is clear that the tablets are administrative documents, more accounting records than linguistic texts.[33] The largest text comprises seven lines and treats of sheep delivered as taxes to Susa's central administration. Other texts appear to deal with the distribution of seed corn by the same administration at planting time. In general, Proto-Elamite 'literature' constitutes the book-keeping of local agricultural production.

It is possible that Proto-Elamite inspired the linear Elamite script of eight hundred years later, c. 2200 BC (illus. 37). Linear Elamite displays some signs whose values can be read, and because of this scholars have attempted to establish links with isolated Proto-Elamite signs. However, the connection between Proto-Elamite and later linear Elamite is still unclear. A major stumbling block to further analysis is the inability to reconstruct the Elamite language of the Iranian Plateau. And it is uncertain whether the Proto-Elamites were using the same language as the later Elamites.[34] As of the second millennium BC, Elamites wrote in Akkadian cuneiform (see above).

INDUS VALLEY WRITING

The world's most prominent undeciphered writing is that of the Indus Valley, though considerable advances in our understanding of this system have been achieved in recent years.[35] Possibly in use from *c.* 3500 to 1700 BC, the 'Indus Valley script', as it is called, with no known relation, was forgotten for nearly four thousand years until its discovery by European archæologists in the 1870s. The remarkable Indus Valley civilization that elaborated this script was itself identified only in 1921.

The first evidence of eastern writing – simple 'potters' marks' or ownership graffiti on pottery from *c.* 3500 BC among the Early Harappan cultures of eastern Baluchistan and the Indus Valley – slightly predates Egypt's earliest known rebus signs (*c.* 3400 BC) and Sumer's first phonetic signs (*c.* 3200 BC). Early Harappan 'writing' appears to be a proto-form of the later complete writing used as of about 2600 BC (illus. 38). Potters appear to have marked their products with special symbols – not designs or decorations – that perhaps indicate the fabricant or contents, while graffiti on these wares seem to 'record' ownership or dedicatee.

It was during the period of cultural unification that ended around 2600 BC and involved more than fifteen hundred cities and towns that a codified and generally recognized 'Indus Valley script' emerged. Some 80 per cent of Indus Valley writing occurs as seals or seal impressions. The rest appears on clay and faience tablets, bronze tools and utensils, bone and ivory rods and miniature tablets of copper and steatite. Minute writing was done on bone pins, terracotta bangles and gold jewelry. Though most Indus writing is barely more than one cm in height, in a side room of the northern gateway at Dholavira an inscription was found whose signs are over 30 cm in height: if this was a public sign, it implies general literacy.

Some 4,200 script-bearing objects have so far been unearthed, their inscriptions brief in accordance with the script's customary use – it is assumed – as a summary identifier. The usual seal inscription has two or three signs in a line and five signs in total (illus. 39). The longest Indus Valley inscription comprises twenty signs in three lines; an inscription of thirteen signs was unearthed in 1998. Prominent on many inscribed seal stones are accompanying contour pictures – these are not part of the script – of animals (tigers, buffaloes, elephants and so forth) and anthropomorphic figures, whose meaning and pur-

38 Dating from 2800–2600 BC, this Harappan inscribed sherd (one corner of which is shown) was one of several discovered by archæologists in 1999 which confirmed that the development of writing in the Indus Valley had begun earlier than previously believed.

39 Some Indus Valley seal inscriptions, 2500–2000 BC (reading from right to left).

pose remain unknown. There are no known Indus Valley texts on tombs, statues, walls or other constructions. No clay tablets nor papyrus texts have been found, though both would be expected with this writing system. It is also significant that none of the Indus Valley signs resemble either Egyptian hieroglyphs or Mesopotamian cuneiforms. However, some do resemble those of the Proto-Elamite script.

It is mooted that seafaring Indus merchants might have witnessed writing being used among western trading partners.[36] The complete writing that emerged with the Indus civilization only around 2600 BC seems to have elaborated its signary from Early Harappan symbols, indicating a protracted local development. The Indus civilization thrived between 2500 and 1900 BC from Pakistan to north-west India, its chief centres including the cities of Mohenjo-Daro (near modern Karachi) in the southern Indus region and Harappa (near modern Islamabad) in the northern Indus region. Boasting advanced town planning, the Indus people enjoyed a level of civilization comparable to that of their contemporaries in Egypt and Mesopotamia. It is

40 A Mohenjo-Daro
seal inscription,
c. 2500–2000 BC.

to this remarkable Harappan Phase that most inscribed seals, pottery and other artefacts belong (illus. 40).

The Indus repertoire comprises between 400 and 450 signs, with many alloglyphs – slightly different signs holding the same phonetic values. These depict human and animal figures as well as geometric shapes and symbols. Not all of these signs had to be in use simultaneously or universally: Harappa's own signing of seals and tablets seems to have changed over time, for example. Writing followed from right to left, as with early cuneiform. However, some of the longer inscriptions are boustrophedonic – 'as the ox ploughs', reversing direction with each line. It appears to be a logosyllabic system, like Sumerian.[37]

It is assumed that the Indus Valley signs were used primarily for commercial purposes: stamping bales of commodities with a mark of identification, for example. A possible clue to what the seals might signify lies in the seals of Near Eastern trading partners: personal names and titles of office, the latter often including names of divinities. This writing appears to have been closely associated with the ruling élite and with the merchants of the Indus Valley's leading centres. As a town-based system, writing was used to validate and solidify economic authority. It possibly also legitimized the élite's religion as being powerful and worthy of veneration.[38]

When this élite lost authority around 1900 BC, the archæological record shows that the Indus Valley script was abandoned at all northern sites. It survived until about 1700 BC only at the remote southern centre of Daimabad. Until recently, it was believed that the people(s) writing their language(s) with the Indus Valley script were forced out of their towns and cities by invaders who then remained. If these invaders were Indo-Aryans, the theory proposed, then the underlying language of the Indus Valley script might possibly be Proto-Dravidian, the ancestral tongue of the large Dravidian language family now marginalized to Baluchistan, Afghanistan and southern India.[39] However, archæological evidence for this invasion has not been forthcoming. It seems instead that the fluctuations of the Indus River might have caused floods which destroyed the civilization's agricultural base, leading in turn to the disruption of trade and economic ruin. A complete decipherment of the Indus Valley script seems unlikely 'unless radically different source material becomes available'.[40]

Once elaborated, the idea of systemic phoneticism – that speech can be graphically reproduced through a limited system of signs – flourished among humankind's earliest high civilizations. Each regional development took a separate path, one that best met local needs. The fundamental differences underlying two of the most important cultures are mirrored in their respective writing systems: while Mesopotamian cuneiforms reveal abstracted utilitarianism, Egyptian hieroglyphs 'convey a codified elegance'.[41] In Mesopotamia, the 'hardware' determined the 'software': the use of hand-held clay encouraged a system of wedge-writing whereby picture and symbol were forced to yield more and more to sound; this phonetic elaboration then permitted other languages – not even remotely related to Sumerian – to borrow and adapt this writing. But in Egypt, the 'software' determined the 'hardware': rebus writing was best effected on surfaces that accepted ink or engraved writing; this remained the Nile's exclusive system, prompting alphabetic simplifications at an early date. The cuneiform script was widely borrowed and adapted; the three Egyptian scripts were not.

However, Egypt's consonantal alphabet in time became the complete alphabet. Cuneiform writing ended around two thousand years ago; Egypt's consonantal hieroglyphs, though unrecognizable, are still being written. The contrast also obtains with writing materials: for millennia, wedges impressed with a reed stylus on soft clay competed with ink brushed on papyrus; ink won, and remains the basis of printing today.

In its eastern isolation, the Indus Valley script developed and perished, inspiring no-one and vanishing past human recollection. This, too, is the fate of many writing systems and scripts.

There are many ways that writing is borrowed. One can borrow:

- only the idea of writing;

- the idea of writing and its orientation (e.g., linear, right to left, in vertical columns);

- the writing system (logographic, syllabic, alphabetic);

- the writing system and its script;

- parts of a writing system to enrich an extant system;

- parts of a script; and so forth.

Virtually all writing systems and scripts consist of one or more of the above. Once a borrowed writing conveys a different language, adaptations or conversions are required. The most common adaptations are changes in sign inventories, excluding unnecessary sounds and including new sounds. Borrowers can also add mixed functions in order to accommodate an ill-fitting system, as Akkadian did with Sumerian cuneiforms. To make writing quicker and easier, borrowers can even elaborate other kinds of scripts – like the hieratic the Egyptians devised as a quicker way to write hieroglyphs.

Classifying writing systems and scripts can help to achieve an informative overview, each classification providing alternative perspectives. Classifying is not an easy task, as most writing systems and scripts have borrowed from multiple levels in the hierarchy of component features (illus. 41). There are many ways to classify: by typology (whether logographic, syllabic or alpha-

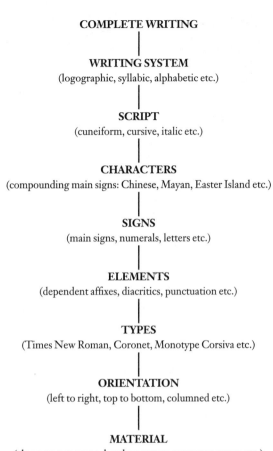

COMPLETE WRITING

WRITING SYSTEM
(logographic, syllabic, alphabetic etc.)

SCRIPT
(cuneiform, cursive, italic etc.)

CHARACTERS
(compounding main signs: Chinese, Mayan, Easter Island etc.)

SIGNS
(main signs, numerals, letters etc.)

ELEMENTS
(dependent affixes, diacritics, punctuation etc.)

TYPES
(Times New Roman, Coronet, Monotype Corsiva etc.)

ORIENTATION
(left to right, top to bottom, columned etc.)

MATERIAL
(clay, papyrus, stone, bamboo, paper, computer screen etc.)

41 A hierarchy of writing's component features.

betic), genealogy, chronology, geography or otherwise. There is no 'best' way to classify writing systems and scripts; there is only a 'most useful' classification for an explicit purpose. Some ways of classifying can be misleading. For example, typological classification remains controversial, because all complete systems comprise a combination of semantic (sense) and phonetic (sound) signs. And genealogical classification remains ambiguous, since most systems are mixed; multiple borrowing and frequent innovation often produce a superficial similarity to unrelated systems.[42]

42 Main centres of writing before 1000 BC: 1. Mesopotamian cuneiform;
2. Egyptian hieroglyphic and hieratic writing; 3. Proto-Elamite and the Elamite
cuneiform; 4. Indus Valley script; 5. Egyptian consonantal alphabet; 6. Sinaitic
and Canaanite proto-alphabets and the Byblos syllabary; 7. Hittite cuneiform
and Anatolian syllabary (Luwian); 8. Ugaritic alphabetic cuneiform; 9. Early
Greek syllabaries; 10. Chinese logograms.

Many writing systems and scripts flourished before 1000 BC
in different parts of the world (illus. 42). All but two – Egyptian
(and its derivatives) and Chinese – are now extinct and lack
descendants. Writing systems and scripts actually perish with
far less frequency than the languages they transmit. Cuneiform
writing continued millennia after the Sumerian language's
demise. Latin has long been extinct as a living language, yet its
script, a descendant of Egyptian, is today's most common one.
Throughout history, the ultimate fate of writing systems and
scripts has been determined more by economics, politics, religion and cultural prestige than by the immediate requirements
of language and writing.

As soon as Mesopotamia's phonetic writing had reached the
Nile, Egyptian scribes converted the idea into something quite

different in order to accommodate their contrary language. Part of their solution lay in a small set of signs reproducing only consonants. By around 2200 BC, they were infrequently writing – independently of hieroglyphs – only in these consonantal signs. This custom added a new dimension to humankind's relation to talking art. It would fundamentally change the course of writing in the West.

THREE

Speaking Systems

'My little fellow has opened his hand,' a proud father in Mesopotamia told his son's teacher more than three and a half thousand years ago, 'and you made wisdom enter there: you showed him the fine points of the scribal art.' Acknowledged to be the pathway to wisdom itself, writing soon spread throughout the ancient Middle East, its most active champions and innovators being the Semitic peoples. Their innovations occurred during an era of shifting powers. By 2200 BC, when the first systematized pictographic syllabaries and proto-alphabets were emerging, the Akkadians of Mesopotamia had lost dominion over vassal tribes. Their empire was crumbling. This allowed unaccustomed freedoms for West Semitic peoples of the eastern Mediterranean coastline who, in turn, acquired sudden wealth and experienced increased growth. They began to establish new trading routes, entering Egypt and returning to Canaan – that part of Palestine between the Jordan River and the Mediterranean (Palestine, Israel) – with new Egyptian ideas, which rapidly superseded older Mesopotamian customs. By the time of the Southern Babylonian renaissance of *c.* 2080 BC, Canaan had become even more closely linked culturally with Egypt, whose influence now diffused throughout the Levant and into the Ægean, realm of the Greeks and other peoples, as well. (As of the reign of Pharaoh Sesostris III – 1878–1841 BC – the Sinai Peninsula and southern Palestine actually came under Egyptian rule.) This was the era of the cosmopolitan Canaanite culture, with its integrated system of international economies and diplomacy, a time of great wealth and active trade.

From *c.* 2000 BC to 1200 BC, two main writing systems dominated this region. First, Mesopotamian syllabic writing had inspired syllabo-logographic writing; however, the Canaanite system rejected Mesopotamian cuneiform as its script, using pictorial signs – similar to those of the Egyptians – instead in order to spell out *in-di-vi-du-al* syllables of a word. Second, Egyptian consonantal writing, also on a pictorial base, inspired proto-alphabets. Both systems were highly influential and widespread. In fact, they were opposites, and only one would survive.

Initially, writing had been 'an instrument of power in the hands of small groups of priests, soothsayers and scribes serving deified monarchs'.[1] It was the perfect tool for social ascendency, the expression of a small élite's ideology. With the diffusion of writing following consonantal writing's elaboration in particular, however, writing could no longer remain the monopoly of the rich and powerful. It now served everyone: reading and writing could easily be learnt in a short time by many. Furthermore, the simple system was eminently suited to borrowing by foreign languages, often requiring only minimal conversion.

By the second century BC, the last surviving syllabo-logographic writing, that of Cyprus, had succumbed to its more powerful competitor – the complete alphabet. The victor still empowers us today. Indeed, the alphabetic idea that was first elaborated more than four thousand years ago in Egypt, Sinai and Canaan now appears to be replacing most other writing systems of the world as one of the most conspicuous manifestations of globalization.

THE SYLLABIC WRITING OF BYBLOS

Canaan comprised the international crossroads of major powers: Egypt, Mesopotamia, Anatolia and the Ægean. As linguist Florian Coulmas has asserted,

> The ensuing cultural multiplicity, the many languages that came into contact with each other, as well as the knowledge of the existence of different writing systems such as Egyptian, Assyrian and Hittite must have created the ideal conditions for experimenting with new possibilities and simplifications.[2]

Merchants, before anyone, would have acknowledged the economic need to simplify inherited scripts in order to liberate themselves from the class of scribes and to effect their own book-keeping.[3] Semitic writing, after adapting earlier writing systems, broke away from these, its two separate systems apparently emerging simultaneously – perhaps shortly before 2000 BC. The Semites used the rebus principle to create a limited, codified, standardized syllabary of pictorial signs – that is, one sign for each *pu, mo, ti* and so forth – in order to constitute a syllabo-logographic system. They eventually saw this system – one that served its users well for many centuries, and that was also borrowed by the non-Semitic peoples of Anatolia and the Ægean – succumb to the system from Egypt, the consonantal alphabet.

A syllabary is a particularly defective writing system for languages that, in their basic structure, are not CV – that is, consonant + vowel, like *p + u = pu*. This is especially true for languages with many consonantal clusters, groupings like *mpt* (as in English 'exempt'), *skt* (/riskt/ for 'risked') or *rts* ('hearts'). Many syllabic systems display great economy of expression, too, in which no distinction is made, for example, between consonants that are voiced/unvoiced (*bin/pin*) or aspirated/unaspirated (*which/witch*). This creates defective phonological (pertaining to the sound-system of a language) reproduction. To be sure, it fulfils the needs, in an immediate context, of users fully familiar with the system and its limited vocabulary. But such writing is difficult to read outside this context.

When first discovered, some syllabic writing – like ancient Crete's Linear B based on Linear A – was thought to be evidence of a people having borrowed a foreign script for a language ill suited to this borrowing. Now, it is appreciated that syllabic writing as a system – not as a script – was used by several different ethnic groups (Semites of Byblos, Anatolian Luwians, Greeks of the Ægean and Cyprus) to convey their respective language(s) using indigenous signs and/or sign values (illus. 43) – that is, their own script. It is the syllabic system itself, and not implicitly a given syllabary of signs, that is difficult to use for many languages. This difficulty, perhaps more than anything else, led to syllabic writing's giving way to alphabetic writing,

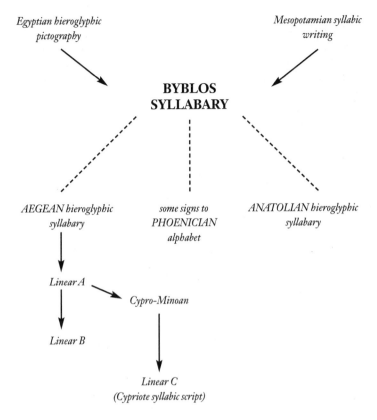

Egyptian hieroglyphic
pictography

Mesopotamian syllabic
writing

**BYBLOS
SYLLABARY**

AEGEAN *hieroglyphic
syllabary*

some signs to
PHOENICIAN
alphabet

ANATOLIAN *hieroglyphic
syllabary*

Linear A

Cypro-Minoan

Linear B

*Linear C
(Cypriote syllabic script)*

43 A possible genesis of the early syllabaries.

which is much easier to use in the West.

Byblos was one of the Western Semites' earliest centres, with thriving trade with Egypt and points north and west already in the third millennium BC. There are two ages of Byblos texts: a few Bronze Age (before 1200 BC) inscriptions on stone and metal written in a pictorial script termed 'pseudo-hieroglyphic' since its signs resemble Egyptian hieroglyphs (illus. 44), and the many Phoenician inscriptions in the Byblos dialect that used the Phoenician alphabet and dates from the Iron Age (after 1200 BC). The Bronze Age script displays too many signs – some 114 – for an alphabet but fewer than the Egyptian and Meso-potamian writing systems. This suggests that the script is a simple syllabary: a limited number of signs reproducing entire

44 The obverse (above) and reverse (below) of a spatula from Bronze Age Byblos in Canaan, inscribed with the Byblos 'pseudo-hieroglyphic' syllabary.

syllables, most of them apparently of a CV structure.[4]

This supposed syllabic system appears to be the marriage of the syllabic idea from Mesopotamian cuneiform with the 'pictographic' or pictorial idea from Egyptian hieroglyphs. Putting these together, the scribes of Byblos devised a simplified system based on the rebus principle.[5] More than twenty of the Byblos signs appear to be direct Egyptian borrowings, possibly pronouncing the Egyptian items using West Semitic words: in other words, 're-analyzing' the phonetic values of the borrowed signs in order to allow their indigenous identification. The elaboration of the Byblos syllabic script can perhaps be dated to the Early Bronze Age (before 2000 BC), as recently deciphered texts indicate.[6] However, not all scholars agree with this early date.[7] In the later Iron Age, with the greater frequency of consonantal alphabetic – that is, non-syllabic – writing, some of the Byblos signs appear also to have been used to write what had become, at Byblos too, the Phoenician linear alphabet.[8]

THE ANATOLIAN SYLLABIC SCRIPT

In the *Iliad* (24:602–17), Homer sings of Achilles' regarding the Anatolian stone inscription near Smyrna as Niobe and her relations, who had therein been turned to stone by Zeus – though at the time Homer sang this, around 800 BC, the Anatolian syllabic script was probably still in use. Over a thousand years earlier, a grouping of various ethnic and linguistic affiliations had entered eastern Anatolia, eventually to found what came to be called the Hittite Empire. Coming from Mesopotamia, they were already writing in a borrowed Sumerian-Akkadian cuneiform (see Chapter 2). As of the fifteenth century BC, some of these peoples began using an indigenous script sometimes called 'Hittite hieroglyphic'.[9] All of the known texts – except for one-word Urartian glosses on storage jars, and several names of deities in Hurrian at a Hittite shrine – convey the Luwian language, an early Indo-European tongue.[10]

Some scholars, imitating Homer, tend to regard the earliest Anatolian hieroglyphs as 'pictographs' depicting scenes or as 'ideograms' transmitting ideas. But most now accept that the Luwians' hieroglyphic script is syllabo-logographic in its concept. It appears so different from the Hittites' later Sumerian-Akkadian cuneiform writing that it was probably inspired by the much earlier system used by trading partners from Canaan – specifically from Byblos. However, only the principle of syllabo-logographic writing was borrowed from Canaan, not individual signs or conventions. Consistent with their Canaanite origin, many of the recognizable syllabic values are indisputably rebus-based: *ta*, for example, is from *targasna-* ('ass, donkey'). One tends to accept that all signs in the system originated as indigenous rebuses. All rebus signs identified thus far relate specifically to Luwian, so there seems to be little doubt that the Anatolian syllabic script was originally devised to convey the Luwian language.[11]

The script was apparently reserved for special inscriptions. Most were effected in bas-relief on stone tablets or chiselled in stone or rock walls, but seal engravings and impressions on clay or lead are also known (illus. 45).[12] The writing is found throughout a large region of Asia Minor and Syria. It was evidently elaborated specifically in order to express the local culture, something the borrowed foreign ensemble of Sumerian-Akkadian cuneiform apparently could not impart.[13] It is one of the world's purely 'monumental' scripts (and comparable in this sense to early Mesoamerican scripts) in that its main purpose was not commu-

45 Ninth-century-BC Luwian relief carving in the Anatolian syllabic script, from Carçemiş, Turkey.

nication but propaganda. The Anatolian syllabic script was first and foremost an indigenous expression of the Luwian franchise.

It seems that most signs originated pictorially, as they reproduce animals, plants, human figures, body parts and everyday objects. Fascinatingly, even numerals, such as I I I I, are used rebus-fashion: Luwian *mauwa-*, or 'four', is the sign for *m* or *ma* or *mi* – just as if we were to write '4ever' or '4bidden'. Many of the signs were later standardized, rendering their underlying objects unrecognizable. This suggests a long written tradition.

Reading from the top downwards, every other line of text reverses direction. Usually, an inscription comprises a series of horizontal panels, with the heads of the figures, as in Egyptian writing, always facing the line's beginning. Lines are frequently written with horizontal line dividers. There are no word breaks. If signs are 'grouped' vertically, these groupings are also read from top to bottom. (Sign sequencing and positioning are prioritized according to æsthetics, not speech.) There are some 220 signs in all, many of these being logograms used as determinatives to specify a particular word's pronunciation, as in Egyptian. Signs can be either logographic (word signs) or phonographic (sound signs); many are both. In contrast, Hittite's cuneiform syllabary only comprises about 60 signs, similar to the number of syllabograms in the various Ægean syllabaries. Similar to these latter, too, is the Anatolian syllabic script's failure to distinguish between voiced and unvoiced (b/p) and unaspirated and aspirated (p/ph) consonants. Final consonants, and all consonant clusters, use 'empty' vowels: *asta* is *á-s(a)-ta* – again, just as in the Ægean syllabaries. And pre-consonantal /n/ is not indicated in the spelling: *anda* is *à-ta*, for example, exactly as in the Ægean. There is great economy of expression in this system, resulting in a severely defective reproduction of actual Luwian speech.

Anatolia's mixed syllabo-logographic script survived until the seventh century BC.

ÆGEAN AND CYPRIOTE SYLLABARIES[14]

Indo-Europeans from the plains of Eastern Europe, the Greeks had evidently already occupied the mainland and islands of the Ægean, including Crete, by the middle of the third millennium BC. Around 2000 BC, following their consolidation of power on Crete, new wealth from trade with cosmopolitan Canaan allowed the creation of a complex palace economy, with major centres at Knossos, Phaistos and other Cretan sites – Europe's first high civilization, the Minoan. Trade with Canaan had evidently also brought Greeks into contact with Byblos' pictorial syllabic writing, whose underlying principle the Minoans borrowed. Now, Cretans could also write their Minoan Greek language using a small corpus of syllabo-logographic signs representing *in-di-vi-du-al* syllables. The signs themselves and their phonetic values – nearly all V (*e*) or CV (*te*) – were wholly indigenous: what the rebus signs, all originating from the Cretan world, depicted, one pronounced in Minoan Greek, not in a Semitic language. (Minoan Greek appears to have been an archaic sister tongue of the mainland's Mycenæan Greek.)

Three separate but related forms of syllabo-logographic writing emerged in the Ægean between *c.* 2000 and 1200 BC: the Minoan Greeks' 'hieroglyphic' script and Linear A, and the later Mycenæan Greeks' Linear B. Minoan Greeks apparently also took their writing at an early date to Cyprus, where it experienced two stages: Cypro-Minoan (evidently derived from

46 Baked clay label, *c.* 1600 BC, inscribed on its obverse (left) and reverse (right) with the Cretan 'hieroglyphic' script.

Linear A) and its daughter Linear C, the 'Cypriote Syllabic Script'. All Ægean and Cypriote scripts are clearly syllabo-logographic, as the objective identity of each rebus sign would have been immediately recognizable to each learner and user. It seems that determinatives were never employed in any of the Ægean or Cypriote scripts; however, logograms additionally depicted most spelt-out items on accounting tablets. All Ægean and Cypriote scripts, but for these separate logograms, were completely phonetic.

Crete's 'hieroglyphic' script is the patriarch of this robust family, its inspiration perhaps derived from Byblos via Cyprus around 2000 BC (illus. 46). As its name implies, this script used pictorial signs to reproduce the syllabic inventory of the Minoan Greek language, here used in rebus fashion as at Byblos. This writing occurs on seal stones (and their clay impressions), baked clay, and metal and stone objects, most of these discovered at Knossos and dating from 2000– 1400 BC (the script was concurrent with Linear A). There exist about 140 different signs in all – that is, 70 to 80 syllabic signs and their alloglyphs (different signs with the same sound value), as well as logograms: human figures, parts of the body, flora, fauna, boats and geometrical shapes. Writing direction was open: from left to right, from right to left, with every other line reversed, even spiral. That this script also included logograms and numerals suggests that it was initially used for book-keeping, among other things, until its replacement in this function with its simplification, Linear A. Thereafter, like

47 Side A of the baked-clay Phaistos Disk (diam: 16 cm), in the most elaborate variety of the Cretan 'hieroglyphic' script. Beginning at the bottom two 'fields' and reading from right to left: *e-qe ku-ri-ti | de-ni qe* or *Ekue, Kurwitis Deneoi-que* – 'Hear ye, Cretans and Danaans'. This is Europe's first literature and the world's earliest printing with movable type.

Anatolian hieroglyphs, the Cretan hieroglyphic script appears to have assumed a ceremonial role in Minoan Greek society, reserved for sacred inscriptions, dedications and royal proclamations on round clay disks.

This latter use is indicated by ancient Crete's celebrated Phaistos Disk (illus. 47). Of the many different varieties of Cretan hieroglyphic script – it appears that each locality used its own – that on the Phaistos Disk, dating from *c.* 1600 BC and displaying the most elaborate rebus signs of any of the varieties – is the most extraordinary.[15] Comprising Europe's first literature, it also represents the world's earliest document printed with movable 'type' (here, bas-relief punches impressed into soft clay).

The hand-sized disk, found in 1908 at the palace of Phaistos on Crete's southern coast, contains 241 Cretan hieroglyphic signs in 61 divided groupings on both sides (31 + 30). Its 45 discrete syllabic signs are written from right to left, spiralling inwards, apparently conveying a 'mobilization proclamation' in Minoan Greek.[16] Several writing conventions similar to those of the Anatolian hieroglyphs appear to be used on the Disk, evidently the same as those used for all varieties of Cretan hieroglyphic writing. That is, neither voice nor aspiration is distinguished, so one sign does service for *b/p*, *g/k* or *d/dh*, for example. (However, /d/ is distinguished from /t/.) One sign is used for both /r/ and /l/, too. Consonant clusters are written with 'empty' vowels. Both /s/ and /n/ are not written before a consonant or at the end of a word. Consonant + /w/ deletes the /w/. And diphthongs /ai/, /ei/ and /oi/ are written only with /i/.

It appears that the same conventions obtain with Linear A, the standardized stylization of the many varieties of Cretan hieroglyphic syllabograms that was invented soon after the hieroglyphs. (Proof that Linear A conveys the same Minoan Greek language lies in the word *ku-ro*, identified on accounting tablets as meaning 'sum': this would be Minoan Greek *krōs*, cognate to mainland Greek *krās* meaning 'head, limit, extremity' – etymon of English 'cranium'.) As an accounting script, Linear A occurs almost exclusively on clay tablets, though some rare bone, stone, metal and terracotta artefacts bear this script (illus. 48). Many Linear A signs can easily be traced back to their hieroglyphic sources. Others are less transparent, some not at all. Linear A apparently arose out of the need to create – with the enlarged palace economy that followed expansion into the Egyptian market under Pharaoh Sesostris III *c.* 1850 BC – an easier and quicker way to record palace transactions and inventories than that allowed by time-consuming hieroglyphic writing, much as hieratic cursive developed out of Egyptian hieroglyphs. Linear A became the functional writing system of the Minoan 'thalassocracy' on Crete and in the Cyclades, and was also used at Crete's trading outposts as far afield as Avaris in Egypt. It remained in use until about 1400 BC.[17]

Linear B, derived directly from Linear A, may first have been written *c.* 1550 BC on the Greek mainland by the Danaans, the

48 Linear A: (left) an early text from Phaistos, *c.* 1700 BC; (right) spiral ink inscription inside a cup found at the Knossos palace, *c.* 1500 BC.

Greeks of Argos (Peloponnesus), to convey the Mycenæan Greek language. The Danaans evidently perceived their tongue to be sufficiently different from Minoan Greek – at least in syllabic transcription – to justify local adaptation. (However, nearly every Mycenæan syllabic sign retains its Minoan Greek value, meaning that each depicted object was still pronounced in Minoan Greek fashion or that, by then, sense had been wholly superseded by sound.) After 1450 BC, when mainland Danaan society was fusing with Minoan society, Linear B was also being written at Knossos on Crete concurrently with Linear A. Eventually, Linear B replaced Linear A altogether, as Mycenæan Greek replaced Minoan Greek among palace scribes, and was written at the Cretan palaces at Knossos and Khania and at the mainland centres of Mycenæ, Thebes and Pylos.

Like Linear A, Linear B comprises some 120 signs, half of them syllabograms (five vowels and 54 CV combinations of twelve consonant series), the rest logograms. The latter are usually commodity 'identifiers', as most Linear B texts are accounting tablets giving only a spelt-out name, logogram and number (illus. 49). Some inscriptions, without logograms, also exist on stone or metal objects. Almost every Linear B sign can be traced back to a Linear A sign, usually displaying only slight modification in its shape. Linear B apparently retained most of Linear A's

49 The first Linear B accounting tablet ever published. From Sir Arthur Evans's initial report on ancient Cretan writing in *The Athenæum*, 18 May 1900.

writing conventions, too. However, Linear B wrote diphthongs /ai/, /ei/ and /oi/ using only the first vowel of each (Linear A used the /i/ sign for all three). Also, with a consonant + /w/, the /w/ is retained as a separate syllable (in Linear A, only the consonant is given). In these and other ways, Linear B slightly reduced Linear A's ambiguity. Linear B's writing is larger in size and more carefully executed than Linear A's, a sophistication resulting from the passage of time. Linear B writing continued throughout the sphere of Danaan influence until about 1200 BC, when Ægean society collapsed for reasons that are still unknown.[18]

With its earliest exemplar dating from about 1500 BC, the Cypro-Minoan script of Cyprus – written in Semitic fashion by pressing the stylus into soft clay, not by drawing – used some 85 syllabic signs closely styled, like Linear B, after its Linear A model (illus. 50). The first fragments of this script were discovered in the 1930s.[19] The Cypro-Minoan script was in wide use on Cyprus from the fourteenth until about the twelfth century BC. It appears that Cypro-Minoan conveys a very early Hellenic dialect of Cyprus.

Its apparent daughter script, Linear C or the 'Cypriote Syllabic Script', was elaborated almost immediately after Cypro-Minoan's demise, indicating a nearly seamless transition from one syllabic script to the other. The earliest identifiably Greek inscription using Linear C is found on a bronze spit from Kouklia (Old Paphos) dating from the eleventh century BC. Linear C, sharing many signs with Linears A and B, was used extensively from the seventh century BC until about 220 BC as a consciously archaic script on monuments (in Early Cypriote Greek), in legends on coins and in contracts on bronze tablets (in mainland Greek) (illus. 51). With the exception of being written from right to left in Semitic fashion, its conventions usually follow those of Linear A and B. However, diphthongs /ai/, /ei/ and /oi/ are written out in full – Linear A had used only /i/ for all three, whereas Linear B had written /a/, /e/ and /o/. Also, all syllables in Linear C ending in *r/l* or *s/z* or a final *m/n* are written with two syllabograms, not one as before (the one having failed to convey these specific consonants). In this way, among the several Greek syllabic scripts predating the Greek alphabet, Cyprus' Linear C achieved the least ambiguity within a writing system that could convey Greek speech only poorly. Linear C is the last descendant of a robust family of scripts that was nearly two thousand years old by the time Linear C expired.

With the exception of Cyprus, by about 1100 BC the Greeks had lost writing entirely. Approximately one or two centuries later, they borrowed writing again from the Canaanites, who by this time were called Phoenicians. But this was now a wholly different system, one much better suited – after conversion – to convey Greek speech: the alphabet (see Chapter 4).

51 Linear C bronze tablet from Cyprus, early 5th century BC, conveying a contract in Greek between the city-state of Idalion and a physician's family.

Perhaps after contact with the Minoans' earliest hieroglyphic writing, around 2000 BC, far to the north-west, the inhabitants of the central Balkans, descendants of the Vinča culture, may have inscribed the so-called 'Tartaria tablets' (see illus. 7). However, the true age of these Balkan 'inscriptions' is still unclear.

THE PROTO-ALPHABETS OF EGYPT AND CANAAN

Concentrating on speech alone, phonography – a writing system that represents sounds by individual signs – reduces the number of signs to a minimum: they are more easily learnt and borrowed. This reductionism enables a rather exact reproduction of speech, too, thus encouraging a script's use by many different languages. Words are no longer complete pictures or *in-di-vi-du-al* syllables but graphic sequences of sound signs conveying separate points of articulation. They comprise *letters* of an alphabet.

With few exceptions, letters hold no meaning in themselves. Their meaning – their sound value – emerges only when paired with one or more other letters to yield a word. However, even an alphabetic script, such as that of English, makes use of many ideograms, logograms and symbols to complement or supplement the phonetic component: numerals (1, 2, 3), mathematical symbols (+, =), punctuation (. , ! ? : for pause, intonation, distinction in meaning), and other important signs like £, $, †, %, & and @. As all alphabet scripts include such signs, they constitute mixed scripts, not 'pure' alphabetic scripts. Yet in each, the phonetic component predominates.

An alphabet is not a 'higher step' in an 'evolution' of writing, but merely another method of reproducing speech. As it happens, employing an alphabet is statistically more efficient for most languages than Egyptian hieroglyphs, Mesopotamian cuneiform syllables or Chinese characters. The same alphabet can be shared by many languages, as it is easily adaptable by attaching a small set of extra marks, points or signs to existing letters: examples include French *à, ê, é, ï, ô* and so forth.

The earliest alphabet appears to have been elaborated in Egypt over four thousand years ago. It was consonantal – that is, only consonants were written, not vowels. This is because the Egyptian language, like most Hamito-Semitic tongues, prioritizes consonants in its morphology (word construction). It uses a limited number of easily recognizable consonantal 'skeletons' within which the four major vocalic phonemes in Hamito-Semitic – /a/, /i/, /o/ and /u/ – vary to supply grammatical functions. It is much easier for most languages to be read in consonants (top line) than in vowels (bottom):

W cn rd cnsnnts, bt nt vwls
e a ea ooa, u o oe

This is true even for entire language families like Indo-European and Semitic. But it is not true for all. Tahitian, for example, could perhaps be read only in vowels, never in consonants.

Momentous in the long history of writing is the fact that with the first consonantal alphabets began the age of the Survivors. All writing today – but for a few East Asian systems – occurs in descendants of the earliest proto-alphabets from Egypt and Canaan.

Already in the third millennium BC, the Egyptians had elaborated a way to express consonants, the Old Egyptian 'consonantal alphabet' (see illus. 21). However, for many centuries this

52 Egyptian alphabetic writing: (above) one of several Kahun inscriptions, this one, on a small block of wood from *c.* 2000–1800 BC, perhaps gives the name of a tool's owner, *Ahitob*; (below) one of two alphabetic inscriptions (*c.* 1900 BC) discovered in 1998 at Wadi el Hol between Thebes and Abydos.

was used only in conjunction with hieroglyphs and determinatives. Also, there was much redundancy and polyvalence. This alphabet comprised an extremely complicated system of signs that was understood only by trained experts. By around 2200 BC, Egyptian scribes had apparently realized that they could simplify their writing enormously if they eliminated 'nonessentials'. So they reduced the entire writing system to the size of the Egyptian language's consonantal component – in other words, they began to write using only their consonantal alphabet, and nothing else. Semitic trading partners and guest workers observed this, and brought the device and its signs back to Canaan to write their language(s), too. A thousand years later, the Greeks borrowed the same device and signs from the Phoenicians, descendants of the Canaanites, and added vowels to create the complete alphabet, the system used throughout most of the world today.

It has been known for nearly a century that the Egyptians also wrote using only the consonantal alphabet. Several inscriptions at Kahun, dating from *c.* 2000–1800 BC, were found and described in the early 1900s (illus. 52).[20] In 1998, two similar alphabetic inscriptions dating from approximately 1900 BC, carved into a natural limestone wall at Wadi el Hol along an ancient route from Thebes to Abydos, were discovered. Older than the oldest proto-alphabetic inscriptions from the Sinai

Peninsula, such Egyptian archetypes indicate that exclusive alphabetic writing was occurring at this early date with some frequency, suggesting two or three centuries of prior use. Alphabetic writing was not a mere spoke in hieroglyphic writing's wheel: it could be a separate wheel itself.

Neither Greeks nor Phoenicians 'created' the alphabet, then, as many have alleged. Egyptians *distilled* the alphabet from their hieroglyphic system, which, since the third millennium BC, had used consonantal 'letters' to help sound out words.

Some scholars believe that Semitic-speaking mercenaries, miners and merchants first developed the alphabet in an Egyptian context, simplifying the hieroglyphs and standardizing these simplifications into a small repertoire of consonantal alphabetic symbols. There is no doubt that Semitic peoples residing in Egypt were soon using the idea of exclusive consonantal writing, as well as many of the Egyptians' signs. They gave the Egyptian 'pictures' Semitic names, thus changing the phonetic values of the Egyptian consonantal alphabet. They elaborated new signs, too, using the acrophonic or 'first-consonant' principle.[21] As with Egyptian, one sound was limited to one sign. Fewer than 30 letters in all were necessary to convey written speech fully in the Semitic languages.

Playing a pivotal role in the transition from the Egyptians' proto-alphabet to the Semitic *abjad*, or consonantal alphabet, was the (still undeciphered) Proto-Sinaitic script of *c.* 1800–1600 BC.[22] This was first identified in various sites on the Sinai Peninsula, whence its name. Many Proto-Sinaitic letters match Egyptian letters and logograms (see illus. 28), but with Semitic acrophonic values substituted for the depicted objects: 'waves in water', *n* in the Egyptian consonantal alphabet, had become *m*, for example, reproducing the initial consonant of Semitic *mayim* (our Latin alphabet's *m* is a direct descendant, still showing the 'waves'). The Proto-Sinaitic script shows at least 23 discrete signs – almost half of them clearly borrowed from Egyptian. It was commonly written in either columns or horizontal lines but, unlike Egyptian, from left to right. Letters face every which way, with no clear orientation, though each Proto-Sinaitic text is internally consistent (illus. 53). Proto-Sinaitic was not a 'missing link' between Egyptian writing and a

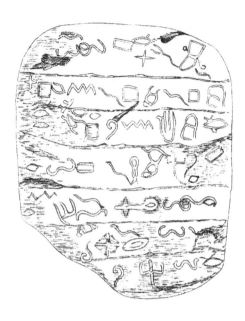

53 Proto-Sinaitic, *c.* 1850 BC: 'I am Hatšepšumoš, Superintendent of the mineral-rocks and of the sacred region ...'

full Semitic consonantal inventory; it was merely an early off-shoot of a nascent system.[23] This ancestor of the Semitic alphabet still in use today was devised to convey the consonants of a Proto-West Semitic language (illus. 54).[24]

A later development, the Canaanite proto-alphabet of the Middle Bronze Age was also pictorial, linear and consonantal, conveying one consonant per sign. The economy and flexibility of this new way of writing at the centre of trade between the peoples of Egypt, Babylon, Anatolia and the Ægean ensured its rapid development and diffusion. Egyptian scribes may have been the alphabet's distillers, but Canaanite scribes were its distributors. The oldest alphabetic writing in Canaan occurs on the Gezer Jars (discovered in Israel) from the sixteenth century BC; slightly younger inscribed artefacts have been found at Lachish, Shechem, Tell el-'Ajjul and other sites (illus. 55).[25] These inscriptions may be in one script or several related ones; they still cannot be read. Such texts occurring before 1050 BC – that is, Bronze Age linear-script texts from Canaan – are collectively known as Proto-Canaanite or Old Canaanite; after 1050 BC, they become Phoenician. All ancient North Semitic scripts – Phoenician, Canaanite, Aramaic – represent consonantal alphabets of fewer than 30 letters.[26]

Scribes traditionally elaborate on inherited fundamentals. By around 1450 BC, Ugarit – modern Ra's Shamra on Syria's northern coast, in the Bronze Age the periphery of Canaanite influence – was also writing in a consonantal alphabet (see Chapter 2). Ugarit was an important trading centre that used ten languages and five scripts, most important of which was Mesopotamia's Sumero-Akkadian cuneiform, which was East Semitic in origin (whereas most Ugarites spoke a West Semitic tongue). Perhaps for linguistic as well as for economic and cultural reasons, the scribes of Ugarit chose to innovate in a unique way, borrowing – apparently from Canaanites in the south – the idea of consonantal alphabetic writing while continuing to practise this with Mesopotamian-like cuneiform wedges on clay (see illus. 34).

The Ugaritic consonantal alphabet comprised a unique series of 30 cuneiform combinations, effected as simply as possible (including single wedges in differing orientations to convey Ugarit's most frequent consonants, /g/, /ʔ/ and /t/) in order to represent 30 different consonantal sounds. This became the Ugarit scribes' preferred method of writing. Its consonantal inventory reproduces the West Semitic linear consonantal alphabet but includes, astonishingly, three long and short vowels as well – the /aː/, /iː/ and /uː/ that allow maximum salience in Semitic languages. Ugaritic *abecedaries*, or alphabet lists, on several preserved tablets also recognizably follow, if only in part, the traditional order of the letters (as the Latin alphabet follows the order 'a, b, c' and so forth) of the West Semitic linear alphabet, an order evidently canonized in Canaan by the middle of the second millennium BC.[27] (This same order was later inherited, with respective changes, by Greek and Arabic.) Since 1929, more than a thousand tablets of tax accounts, commercial transactions and further state documents have been found in the Ugaritic alphabetic script, as well as religious and literary texts written with only 27, rather than 30, consonantal cuneiform wedges.

Within 50 years – between 1225 and 1175 BC – Bronze Age societies collapsed, ending more than three hundred years of prosperity. The mighty Hittite Empire perished; most Ægean centres, including Troy, were destroyed; Crete's culture crumbled; the great trading centres of Tarsus, Ugarit, Alalakh and Ashkelon were annihilated; Egypt's New Kingdom prosperity

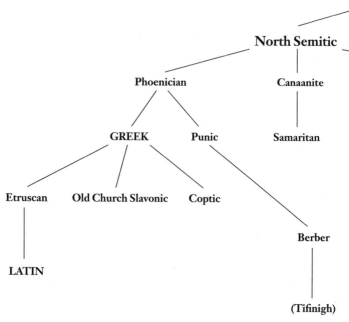

54 Ancient scripts derived from Proto-West Semitic (abridged).

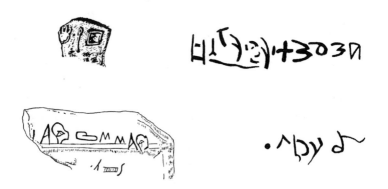

55 Proto-Canaanite alphabetic writing from the mid-second millennium BC: (above, left to right) potsherd inscription from Gezer and inscription from Lachish; (below) plaque from Shechem and inscription from Tell el-'Ajjul.

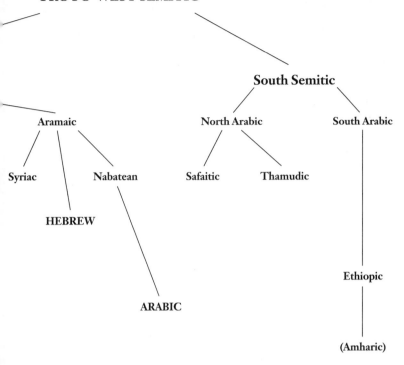

PROTO-WEST SEMITIC

South Semitic

Aramaic   North Arabic   South Arabic

Syriac   Nabatean   Safaitic   Thamudic

HEBREW

Ethiopic

ARABIC

(Amharic)

lay in ruins. All this was caused by Ægean 'Sea Peoples' or Philistines, probably Viking-like Danaans (Mycenæan Greeks) who had begun fighting among themselves and were now terrorizing the Dardanelles and expanding into the Levant, establishing colonies where they exerted strong cultural influence. They forever changed the face of the Ægean, Anatolia, Cyprus and the Levantine coast, including Canaan (thereafter called Palestine after them). Ugarit's cuneiform alphabet seemingly was abandoned overnight. Only one derivative alphabet eventually won out in the period of chaos that followed – the one used by the West Semites of Byblos: Phoenician.

The *abjad*, or linear Semitic script, flourished and diffused in two separate forms, both apparently daughters of varieties of the Canaanite proto-alphabet.[28] As early as 1300 BC, South Semitic, with 28 consonants, had already split from North Semitic. By *c.* 1000 BC, North Semitic's Phoenician consonantal alphabet was fully developed, with only 22 consonants (its language had dropped several consonantal phonemes). The Phoenician alphabet was used for about a thousand years, mutating into Punic, which was written by descendants of Phoenician colonists in the western Mediterranean until the third century AD.

The Canaanites of the Bronze Age had become the Phoenicians (literally 'dealers in purple') of the Iron Age. The Phoenicians did not suddenly emerge as a people, but were the original Semitic inhabitants of the coastal centres Byblos, Tyre, Sidon, Beirut and Ashkelon. By *c.* 1050 BC, they had supplanted the foreign Danaans as rulers of Mediterranean ports, once the power of these 'Sea Peoples' had waned. This brought sudden freedom for the Phoenicians, who sent out trade expeditions and then established commercial centres everywhere along the eastern Mediterranean.

For these commercial centres, a new and better-suited script was needed – a simplified consonantal alphabet. Phoenician writing is West Semitic writing 'proper' (illus. 56).[29] It offers the oldest legible text in any West Semitic language: the epitaph on King Ahiram's sarcophagus from *c.* 1150/1000 BC. Having replaced Byblos's syllabic writing, the Phoenicians had converted the pictorial alphabet of their Bronze Age Canaanite ancestors into a streamlined non-pictorial alphabet. Now, they were taking this alphabet to neighbouring areas in order to write several North-West Semitic languages. Though the outward shape of this new script differed at each centre, each was based on Phoenician. All Western alphabets derive from this Phoenician script. Ancient Greeks called their own alphabet *Phoiníkia grámmata*, or 'Phoenician letters'. Phoenician remained the preferred script throughout the Levant between 1050 and 850 BC. During this period, it displayed an unstable

56 One of the most famous Phoenician inscriptions, the Meša' Stele from the land of the Moabites, 842 BC: 'I am Meša', son of Kemošmelek, King of Moab from Dibon …' The language is Old Hebrew.

writing direction – from left to right, from right to left, or even with every other line reversed. Only after about 800 BC was Phoenician written exclusively from right to left. It continued to be written, without vowel indication, as late as the first century BC.

The Phoenician script's most important colonial daughter was Punic, widely used among Phoenician colonists of the western Mediterranean well into the first few centuries AD (illus. 57).

57 Section of a Punic inscription from the Phoenician colony at Marseilles, France, announcing the Carthaginian tariff for sacrifices c. 300 BC.

Late Punic deleted the laryngeal components of the consonantal letters 'ālep, 'ayin, hē and ḥēt and used what remained – copying the Latin alphabet then dominating the Mediterranean – as vowel letters instead, written between consonants as we do today. This was remarkable for Semitic writing, which traditionally recognizes only consonants.

An ancient Berber language, or more than one, is preserved in the Berber script(s): Numidian or 'Old Libyan'. Like Semitic and Egyptian, Berber languages are a subfamily of Afro-Asiatic. They are spoken across North Africa from western Egypt to

58 The so-called 'Massinissa Inscription from Thugga', a Punic (above) and Numidian (below) bilingual dating from the Second Punic War (218–201 BC): 'This temple the citizens of Thugga built for King Massinissa …'

Morocco. The ancient Numidian script appears to have derived from Punic (illus. 58).[30] Emerging from Phoenician colonization in Berber North Africa, it was perhaps elaborated as early as the sixth century BC; however, the earliest datable inscriptions come from the second century BC. The Berber script appears on Celtiberian coinage in Spain as of the first century BC, and possibly also in the Canary Islands. It was used throughout the Roman occupation.

Since the 1100s AD, all Berber writing has been in Arabic script except for a few texts in Hebrew script. The Tifinigh (*ti* + Latin *Punicus* for 'Phoenician') script of the Tuareg people of North Africa preserves ancient Berber writing today. Used by both men and women for love letters, domestic ornamentation and family messages (often when women cannot read Arabic), Tifinigh is an extraordinary case of domestic script preservation.

THE ARAMAIC WRITING FAMILY

As of the tenth century BC, two further North Semitic scripts – Aramaic and Canaanite (illus. 59) – emerged. Aramaic was to become as significant as Phoenician, since it was the source not only for Hebrew and Arabic, the two most widely used Near Eastern scripts three thousand years later, but probably also for the hundreds of scripts of the Indian subcontinent and beyond.

At first, Aramaic speakers of the northern Levant, southern Anatolia and northern Mesopotamia used the Phoenician script. The oldest inscriptions in the Aramaic language, still in Phoenician, date from the ninth century BC. But just at this time, Aramaic speakers were elaborating a distinct script of their own, also called Aramaic (illus. 60). As of the eighth or seventh century BC, Aramaic had become the most widely spoken tongue in the ancient Near East, the interlanguage of the entire region. It eventually became the official language of the Persian Empire (550–330 BC).

Re-introducing a practice introduced by the Semitic scribes of Ugarit many centuries earlier, writers of the Aramaic script began indicating long vowels at the end of words, then inside words, using extant consonantal letters in a supplementary

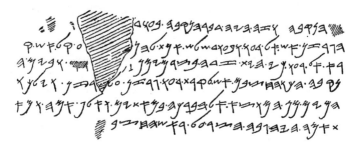

59 The so-called 'Siloam Inscription' in the Canaanite script. Discovered in 1880 at the outlet of the Siloam tunnel near Jerusalem, it memorializes the digging of a subterranean channel *c.* 700 BC.

function as special vowel signs called *matres lectionis*, or 'mothers of reading'. (Short vowels were marked only much later.) Writing only in consonants had apparently created too much ambiguity, especially for words with very short consonantal 'skeletons' that could allow many possible readings (in English, for example, consonantal *mn* could be 'man', 'men', 'moon',

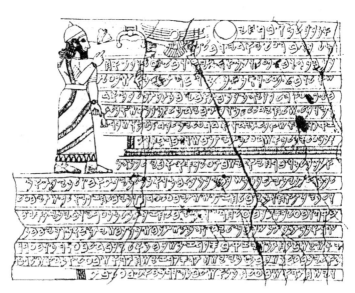

60 Upper half of the famous Canaanite-Aramaic 'Kilamuwa Inscription' recounting in Old Aramaic the tribute paid by Prince Kilamuwa, son of Khaya, King of Ya'di, to the Assyrian king Shalmaneser III (858–824 BC).

'mean', 'mane', 'mine' and so forth). In addition, the limited vocabulary of early inscriptions was being superseded by a more complicated vocabulary requiring a more exact reproduction of speech. So Aramaic writers began indicating long vowels. Eminently useful, this practice soon spread to writers of the related Canaanite script. (Southern Semitic peoples would continue to write only in consonants, however.)

As the influence of the Aramaic language waxed with the Persian Empire's rising star, the Imperial Aramaic script became the West's principal type of writing. It even replaced Assyrian cuneiform, with ink on skin or papyrus now preferred over wedges in soft clay. The Age of Clay was slowly coming to an end, never to return. The Aramaic script became so widespread and influential that it survived even the collapse of the Persian (Achæmenid) Empire itself. Political conditions continued to support the script's stability and uniformity for some time. Aramaic writing was taken to Iran, then to south and Central Asia. However, by the end of the third century BC, it was mutating into new scripts. In the West, the Nabatæns elaborated their own form of it (which later developed into Arabic). In the Syrian desert, the Palmyrans did the same. In northern and southern Mesopotamia, several derivatives emerged.[31] Also emerging from Aramaic was Hebrew, the script of the Jewish nation.

Among Canaanite Hebrews around 850 BC, the Phoenician consonantal alphabet had already inspired the Old Hebrew script, principally documented in religious literature (illus. 61). Its secular use ceased when a linear Hebrew *abjad* was written during the 'Babylonian Captivity', the exilic period of the Jews (597–539 BC). At that time, Old Hebrew was replaced by a variety of the Aramaic script which itself had been greatly influenced by Old Hebrew. (Old Hebrew continued in use, for special purposes, until AD 135; it was the model for the Samaritan script of the first century BC that is still used by Jews in some sacral contexts.[32]) By the fifth century BC, most Jews were using the Aramaic script, which they standardized by regularizing each letter into a square frame – hence the name *kĕtāb merubbā'*, or 'square script'. By the first century BC – as in the Dead Sea Scrolls (illus. 62) – the script was fully standardized. Later, two varieties emerged: round-lined Sephardic (Oriental-

Gezer	Monumental	Cursive	Book hand	Coin script	Samaritan	Modern Hebrew
ꓘ	ꓘ F ꓔ	ꓘ ꓘ ꓘ	ꓨ ꓨ ꓨ	ꓘ ꓘ ꓘ	ꓘ ꓦ ꓥ	א
ꓭ	ꓭ ꓭ ꓩ	ꓯ ꓯ ꓲ	ꓴ ꓱ ꓱ	ꓭ ꓴ ꓭ	ꓭ ꓭ ꓭ	ב
	ꓶ ꓔ ꓦ	ꓶ ꓶ ꓶ		ꓶ ꓶ ꓶ	ꓔ ꓔ ꓔ	נ
ꓷ	ꓷ ꓵ ꓷ	ꓵ ꓵ ꓵ	ꓷ ꓷ ꓷ	ꓶ ꓷ ꓵ	ꓷ ꓵ ꓵ	ד
ꓴ ꓦ ꓴ	ꓴ ꓦ ꓴ	ꓴ ꓴ ꓴ	ꓴ ꓴ	ꓴ ꓴ ꓴ	ꓵ ꓵ ꓴ	ה
ꓬ ꓬ	ꓬ ꓮ ꓬ	ꓬ ꓬ ꓬ	ꓬ ꓓ ꓓ	ꓓ ꓮ ꓥ	ꓵ ꓮ ꓴ	ו
ꓕ	ꓖ ꓖ ꓖ	ꓱ ꓱ ꓴ	ꓵ ꓴ	ꓭ ꓕ ꓳ	ꓐ ꓯ ꓐ	ז
ꓐ ꓭ	ꓗ ꓗ ꓗ	ꓳ ꓳ ꓳ ꓳ	ꓗ	ꓒ ꓗ ꓳ	ꓗ ꓗ ꓗ	ח
	ꓳ ꓳ ꓶ	ꓜ ꓜ ꓢ		ꓭ	ꓭꓭ ꓖ	ט
ꓚ ꓱ	ꓘ ꓚ ꓴ	ꓕ ꓴ ꓤ	ꓕ ꓤ ꓤ	ꓴ ꓕ ꓦ	ꓩ ꓩ ꓜ	י
ꓨ	ꓬ ꓬꓬ ꓬ	ꓬ ꓬ ꓬ	ꓴ ꓬ	ꓬ ꓬ ꓘ	ꓬ ꓬ ꓴ	כ
ꓥ	ꓴ ꓴ ꓴ	ꓲꓲꓲ	ꓴꓴꓴ	ꓕꓴꓦ	ꓴꓴꓴ	ל
ꓮ	ꓬ ꓼ ꓬ	ꓬ ꓬ ꓜ	ꓬ ꓬ	ꓴ ꓬ ꓬ	ꓬ ꓬ ꓴ	מ
	ꓴ ꓬ ꓒ	ꓬ ꓶ ꓬ	ꓬꓬꓬ	ꓱ ꓬ ꓳ	ꓲ ꓬ ꓰ	נ
ꓵ	ꓵ ꓕ ꓴ	ꓩ ꓣ ꓩ		ꓴ ꓴ	ꓴ ꓴ ꓮ	ס
ꓳ	ꓳ ꓴ ꓭ	ꓳ ꓳ ꓳ	ꓮ	ꓳ ꓚ ꓵ	ꓳ ꓳ ꓴ	ע
ꓲ	ꓲ ꓶ ꓶ	ꓶ ꓲ ꓶ	ꓲ	ꓲ	ꓢ ꓶ ꓶ	פ
ꓴꓴ	ꓱ ꓰ ꓭ	ꓜ ꓜ ꓭ	ꓱꓲ	ꓬ ꓸ ꓴ	ꓬ ꓴ ꓬ	צ
ꓷꓷ	ꓒ ꓒ ꓒ	ꓰ ꓕ ꓒ	ꓰ	ꓒ ꓒ ꓔ	ꓷ ꓒ ꓒ	ק
ꓯꓣ	ꓯ ꓯ ꓷ	ꓷ ꓯ ꓯ	ꓷꓷ	ꓷ ꓯ ꓷ	ꓷ ꓷ ꓯ	ר
ꓪꓪ	ꓪ ꓪ ꓪ	ꓪ ꓪ ꓪ	ꓪ ꓪ	ꓦ ꓪ ꓪ	ꓪ ꓴꓴ	ש
ꓫ ꓘ	ꓫ ꓫ ꓴ	ꓫ ꓫ ꓫ	ꓫ ꓫ	ꓴ ꓴ ꓫ	ꓳ ꓴ ꓫ	ת

61 Stages of the earliest Hebrew alphabet.

62 Text of the prophet Habakkuk on a leather Dead Sea Scroll (c. 170 BC) in an early stage of the Square Hebrew script. In the penultimate line, the third word from the right margin reads 'YAHWEH' in an older Hebrew script as a vestigial honorific usage.

Spanish) and angular Ashkenasic. Square Hebrew became the script for all Jewish texts, secular and sacral. During the Middle Ages, it survived only in sacral use, but in the 1800s Jewish writers began using it again for profane purposes. It is the modern script of the state of Israel.

Square Hebrew remains very close to the Aramaic script of the first few centuries BC, as our own capital letters are very close to the Latin alphabet of the same period. The Hebrews inherited vowel marking from the Aramaic script, and extended the principle to further reduce ambiguity. Syrian inscriptions first showed the use of diacritics – special dashes and dots grouped around consonants – to indicate vowels. This probably prompted the Hebrew inclusion of diacritics, too, alongside Aramaic long-vowel marking to do the same thing.[33] However, already in the last few centuries of the first millennium BC, Hebrew scribes were using more than one diacritical system. Used today to mark vowels in poetry, children's books and especially holy texts, the 'Tiberias System' of Hebrew diacritics was elaborated at the important port of Tiberias in Palestine over eleven hundred years ago (illus. 63).

Though formally still a consonantal alphabet, Hebrew, with its inherited consonants that also mark long vowels and its own

בְּרֵאשִׁ֖ית בָּרָ֣א אֱלֹהִ֑ים אֵ֥ת הַשָּׁמַ֖יִם וְאֵ֥ת הָאָֽרֶץ׃ וְהָאָ֗רֶץ
הָיְתָ֥ה תֹ֙הוּ֙ וָבֹ֔הוּ וְחֹ֖שֶׁךְ עַל־פְּנֵ֣י תְה֑וֹם וְר֣וּחַ אֱלֹהִ֔ים מְרַחֶ֖פֶת עַל־פְּנֵ֥י
הַמָּֽיִם׃

bə-rē'šiþ bārā' älōhim' eþ ha-ššāmajim wə' eþ hā-'āräṣ. wə
hā-'āräṣ hājəþā þōhū wā-ƀōhū wə hošäχ 'al-pənē þəhōm,
wə rūăḥ 'älōhim mərahäfäþ 'al-pənē ha-mmājim.

63 Genesis 1:1, 2 in the modern Square Hebrew script using the 'Tiberias
System' of diacritics: '[1] In the beginning God created the heaven and the earth.
[2] And the earth was without form, and void; and darkness was upon the face of
the deep. And the Spirit of God moved upon the face of the waters.'

elaborated diacritics indicating other vowels, is in many ways
vocalically more precise than most modern Latin alphabets.[34] It
even maintains the graphic distinction, lost in modern spoken
Hebrew, between long and short vowels. (British English displays vowel length only by default, as in 'cot' versus 'cart'.) The
Hebrew script is thus archaic, with many redundancies. As an
example, /i/ can be written either as consonant *jodh* or as a dot
under the preceding consonant; some writers do both. In everyday use, as with Arabic, the Hebrew script is two scripts in one:
one highly marked, showing each vowel; the other highly
reduced, leaving vowel identification to context alone.[35] Today,
Hebrew remains heavily dominated by consonants which, as in
all Semitic scripts, constitute the very foundation of writing.

The Nabatæn Arabs used the Aramaic language as a special
cultural second tongue. They also wrote in the Aramaic script
between the first century BC and third centuries AD (illus. 64).
The Nabatæns were a gathering of nomadic Arab tribes living
in a region stretching from the Sinai Peninsula to northern
Arabia and eastern Jordan. In the Hellenistic era following
Alexander the Great's conquests, they formed a kingdom that
lasted from around 150 BC until conquest by the Romans in 105
AD; their capital was the peerless rock city of Petra. Their
Nabatæn form of Aramaic writing became the immediate
parent of Arabic writing.

Like Hebrew, Arabic is an important religious script whose
significance, longevity and expansion are owed to its veneration

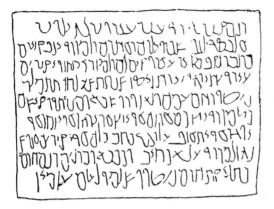

64 A Nabatæn inscription from 1 BC: 'This is the tomb which 'Aidu, son of Kuhailu, son of Elkasi, built for himself and his children …'

as a vehicle of faith.[36] North Semitic's youngest member, it was elaborated in the fourth century AD (illus. 65) – that is, before Islam. Once it was chosen to convey the Koran in the seventh century, its hegemony in the region, and beyond, was assured. Today, the Arabic consonantal alphabet is read and written on the Arabian Peninsula, throughout the Near East, in western, Central and South-East Asia, in parts of Africa and in all areas of Europe influenced by Islam (illus. 66). The Arabic script has been adapted to more languages belonging to more families than any other Semitic script, including Berber, Somali, Swahili (illus. 67), Urdu, Turkish, Uighur, Kazakh, Farsi (Persian), Kashmiri, Malay, even Spanish and Slavonic in Europe.[37] When borrowed, Arabic letters were never dropped, but new or derived letters frequently were added to reproduce sounds not included in the Arabic inventory. Arabic facilitates this process by distinguishing between some letters only by varying the number of dots written with each; this function can then easily be extended by foreign tongues needing new letters compatible with Arabic's fundamental appearance.[38] Arabic is one of the world's great scripts, and will doubtless survive for many more centuries.

Like all Semitic scripts, Arabic uses a consonantal alphabet commonly indicating word roots, but with a richer inventory of

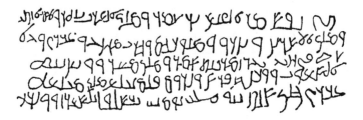

65 This inscription from Namara in Syria, dated AD 328, reveals a transitional stage from Nabatæn to Arabic, especially in its use of ligatures (lines linking letters).

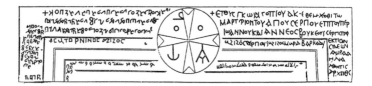

66 Trilingual in Greek (upper right), Syriac (upper left) and Arabic (bottom) from AD 512, the earliest dated inscription in the Arabic script.

بُوَانَ ذَكَتَابِ دِ رِنْخَ

بِنَعْرِاج كُكُتْنُكَيَ بَرَوَهِي نَدَعْ اِلِ اِبْغُوِ

شَنَابَ كَتِدَ كَتَابَ ثَمَكَ شَحَرُوفِ

كُوَ نِعَيْنَ تَعَلَّنْدِ يْتِنِ يُكْسُوَ حِيْل

نَثَمَاءِ مَأْتَدِ يْتِنَ هَيَ يَنَتَمِيْنَ مَكُسَدِ يَ يَدَرَ

مُكُوِيلِ وَاكَ

سعيد بن هلال البو علي

٢١ نُفَمْبَر ١٩٤٧ م

67 Swahili-language letter written from right to left using an adapted Arabic consonantal alphabet with full diacritics above and below the consonants to show all the vowels.

	Nabatæn	Neo-Sinaitic	Early Arabic	Eighth century	Kufic	Early Naskhi	Modern Naskhi
'							
b							
g (ǧ)							
d (ḏ)							
h							
w							
z							
ḥ(h)							
ṭ(z)							
y							
k							
l							
m							
n							
s							
'(ġ)							
(p)f							
ṣ(d)							
q							
r							
sh-š							
t (ṯ)							

68 From ancient Nabatæn to modern Naskhi, the Standard Arabic script.

28 basic letters and additional augmentations, some created by adding a dot under existing letters (illus. 68). (A '29th' letter is the ligature of *lām* and *'ālif*.) Arabic also inherited the long-vowel use of some consonants and the special diacritics to signal other vowels. However, vowels in Arabic are consistently indicated only in the Koran and in poetry. All other texts use only consonantal writing, with diacritics assisting occasionally in ambiguous readings. The use of *'ālif* for long /a:/ is an Arabic innovation. Short /a/, /i/ and /u/ make use of derived forms of simplified consonants: for /a/, a horizontal bar over the consonant; for /i/, a similar bar under the consonant; and for /u/, a small hook over the consonant. If a tiny circle is written above a consonant, this means no vowel accompanies the consonant. All but six Arabic letters occur in four different shapes, each determined by the letter's position in a word: independent (the neutral or standard shape), initial, medial or final (illus. 69).[39]

Arabic's enormous geographical expansion generated a great variety of local Arabic usages, much as the Latin alphabet was doing throughout Western Europe at the same time. However, the Arabic script was so intimately associated with the Koran and its commentaries that it developed an inherent conservatism – the script hardly changed at all, while the language using it changed dramatically. Schools were allied with religious conservatism, and so a chasm grew between written and spoken Arabic.[40] Though now distinct, the two forms are regarded as varieties of one language.

The South Semitic script that had split from North Semitic as early as 1300 BC originated in the Arabian Peninsula. This southern linear *abjad*, which expired in the first millennium AD, served as the model for daughter scripts conveying North Arabic (Syrian) and Abyssinian (Ethiopic) languages. Its two most important members are South Arabic and Ethiopic. The South Arabic script, like North Semitic writing, is highly symmetrical, with pronounced angularity.

The inscriptional Ethiopic script (not syllabic Ethiopic, a different script) initially lacked vowel letters. The Ethiopic inscriptions are in Ge'ez, the language of Ethiopia's Christian church in the first centuries AD. In the fourth century AD, scribes began innovating systematic alternations in consonants' shapes

Name	Initial	Medial	Final	In isolation	Sound value
'elif			ـا	ا	;
bā	بـ	ـبـ	ـب	ب	b
tā	تـ	ـتـ	ـت	ت	t
ṯā	ثـ	ـثـ	ـث	ث	ṯ
ǧīm	جـ	ـجـ	ـج	ج	ǧ
ḥā	حـ	ـحـ	ـح	ح	ḥ
ḫā	خـ	ـخـ	ـخ	خ	ḫ
dāl			ـد	د	d
ḏāl			ـذ	ذ	ḏ
rā			ـر	ر	r
zā			ـز	ز	z
sīn	سـ	ـسـ	ـس	س	s
šīn	شـ	ـشـ	ـش	ش	š
ṣād	صـ	ـصـ	ـص	ص	ṣ
ḍād	ضـ	ـضـ	ـض	ض	ḍ
ṭā	طـ	ـطـ	ـط	ط	ṭ
ẓā	ظـ	ـظـ	ـظ	ظ	ẓ
'ain	عـ	ـعـ	ـع	ع	:
ġain	غـ	ـغـ	ـغ	غ	ġ
fā	فـ	ـفـ	ـف	ف	f
kaf	قـ	ـقـ	ـق	ق	ḳ(q)
kāf	كـ	ـكـ	ـك	ك	k
lām	لـ	ـلـ	ـل	ل	l
mīm	مـ	ـمـ	ـم	م	m
nūn	نـ	ـنـ	ـن	ن	n
hā	هـ	ـهـ	ـه	ه	h
wāw			ـو	و	w
jā	يـ	ـيـ	ـي	ي	j
lām-elif			ـلا	لا	lā

69 The modern Naskhi, or Standard Arabic, consonantal alphabet: an inventory of positional forms.

in order to indicate any of seven different vowels, forming a CV syllable of the *abugida*, the Ge'ez syllabary. In this way, the later Ethiopic script became a complete alphabet (illus. 70). Ethiopic's vocalization is unique among all Semitic scripts. One scholar has suggested that this developed through contact with India's Kharosthi script, which operates on the same principle –

	+ă	+ū	+ī	+ā	+ē	+ě or without vowel	+ō
h	ሀ	ሁ	ሂ	ሃ	ሄ	ህ	ሆ
l	ለ	ሉ	ሊ	ላ	ሌ	ል	ሎ
ḥ	ሐ	ሑ	ሒ	ሓ	ሔ	ሕ	ሖ
m	መ	ሙ	ሚ	ማ	ሜ	ም	ሞ
š	ሠ	ሡ	ሢ	ሣ	ሤ	ሥ	ሦ
r	ረ	ሩ	ሪ	ራ	ሬ	ር	ሮ
s	ሰ	ሱ	ሲ	ሳ	ሴ	ስ	ሶ
q	ቀ	ቁ	ቂ	ቃ	ቄ	ቅ	ቆ
b	በ	ቡ	ቢ	ባ	ቤ	ብ	ቦ
t	ተ	ቱ	ቲ	ታ	ቴ	ት	ቶ
ḫ	ኀ	ኁ	ኂ	ኃ	ኄ	ኅ	ኆ
n	ነ	ኑ	ኒ	ና	ኔ	ን	ኖ
'	አ	ኡ	ኢ	ኣ	ኤ	እ	ኦ
k	ከ	ኩ	ኪ	ካ	ኬ	ክ	ኮ
w	ወ	ዉ	ዊ	ዋ	ዌ	ው	ዎ
‛	ዐ	ዑ	ዒ	ዓ	ዔ	ዕ	ዖ
z	ዘ	ዙ	ዚ	ዛ	ዜ	ዝ	ዞ
j	የ	ዩ	ዪ	ያ	ዬ	ይ	ዮ
d	ደ	ዱ	ዲ	ዳ	ዴ	ድ	ዶ
g	ገ	ጉ	ጊ	ጋ	ጌ	ግ	ጎ
ṭ	ጠ	ጡ	ጢ	ጣ	ጤ	ጥ	ጦ
p̣	ጰ	ጱ	ጲ	ጳ	ጴ	ጵ	ጶ
ṣ	ጸ	ጹ	ጺ	ጻ	ጼ	ጽ	ጾ
ḍ	ፀ	ፁ	ፂ	ፃ	ፄ	ፅ	ፆ
f	ፈ	ፉ	ፊ	ፋ	ፌ	ፍ	ፎ
p	ፐ	ፑ	ፒ	ፓ	ፔ	ፕ	ፖ

70 Ethiopic script: To consonants already possessing a short /a/ value, regular series of marks in respective positions are attached to signal other vowels, thus forming a complete alphabet.

that is, each letter represents a consonant + /a/, with diacritics for other vowels – and predates Ethiopic's innovation by several centuries.[41] Also suggestive of a borrowing (but not from Kharosthi) is the fact that Ethiopic, alone among Semitic scripts, reads from left to right. The Ethiopic script today preserves the long-extinct Ge'ez language of Ethiopia's Christian church. Over the past seven hundred years, the Amharic language has developed in Ethiopia to become the country's official tongue, during which time the Ethiopic script has been adapted to convey Amharic – yielding the Amharic script – and several other indigenous languages.

THE INDIC SCRIPTS OF INDIA AND SOUTH-EAST ASIA

The hundreds of past and present scripts of the Indian subcontinent and their numerous Asian and Pacific derivatives – the world's richest treasury of scripts – cannot be sufficiently described, indeed even listed, in a brief history of writing. Were this work in five volumes, Indic scripts would fill three of them. Nonetheless, over 50 per cent of India's population remains illiterate, and hundreds of minority languages there still have no script. Oral transmission has commonly been preferred in this region. The Brahmins, India's priestly class, long viewed writing as inferior to speech. Perhaps for this reason, among others, writing did not commence on the Indian subcontinent until about the eighth century BC. (Indus Valley writing had been extinct for a thousand years, having left no descendants.) Once writing began, oral transmission continued for many centuries. Finally, the art of writing flourished to embody great literature in a variety of languages and scripts – though restricted to small groups of practitioners and generally devoid of the honour and prestige writing commanded nearly everywhere else.

India displays one of the world's 'richest and most varied literary traditions ever'.[42] Since the creation of the Indian state in the mid-1900s, there have been many calls for the adoption of a single script that all Indians could read. This call has been in vain. Indeed, according to one Indian scholar, 'today a new script is created in India almost once in three months.'[43] If anything, this reveals writing's socio-symbolic significance: much more than a tool to record speech, writing is the emblem of the social franchise. This fact is better exemplified in India than anywhere else.[44]

Indian folklore credits elephant-faced Ganesh, the god of wisdom, with the invention of writing: it is said that he broke one of his tusks to use as a pencil. Scholars, on the other hand, are in general agreement that Semitic writing was the direct source for writing on the Indian subcontinent, probably the Aramaic script that dominated the Middle East in the first millennium BC. Though fragments of earlier Indian writing are known, the first longer documents are the famous edicts of King Asoka from *c.* 253–250 BC, which were carved on stone pillars or rocks throughout Hindustan. The two earliest Indian scripts – Kharosthi and Brahmi – both appear in the Asoka inscriptions. In them it is already clear that the writing is not native. Indeed, no script was ever 'created' from scratch on the Indian subcontinent. Though the region can proudly claim more than two hundred scripts, they derive entirely from the single Brahmi script, which itself derived from a Semitic source (illus. 71).

Reading from right to left, the Kharosthi script was apparently inspired in northern India by Aramaic, which was the interlanguage and script of a region that stretched from Syria in the west to Afghanistan in the east (illus. 72). In Kharosthi, each letter conveys *Ca* (that is, a consonant + vowel /a/) unless another vowel is specified – just as in the later Ethiopic script – in which case it is then indicated by its respective diacritic attached to the consonantal letter. Though some scholars see this as a syllabary, its consonantal framework identifies it as an *abudiga* system, whereby each composed character represents a consonant to which a specific vowel attaches; remaining vowels are represented by a consistent modification of each consonant sign. (The name *abudiga* is actually Ethiopic, after the first four consonants and first four vowels of this script's traditional order.) Commonly used throughout north-west India in the first few centuries BC, Kharosthi in time succumbed to the ascendent Brahmi script.

Subsequent Indic scripts were intentionally modelled only

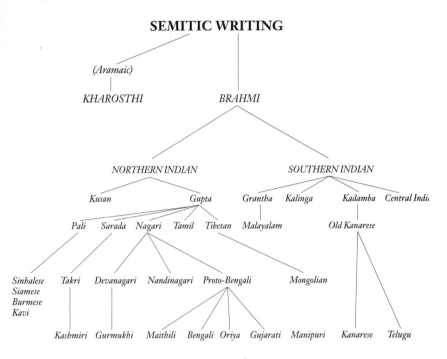

SEMITIC WRITING

(Aramaic)

KHAROSTHI   BRAHMI

NORTHERN INDIAN   SOUTHERN INDIAN

Kusan   *Gupta*   *Grantha*   *Kalinga*   *Kadamba*   *Central India*

Pali   *Sarada*   *Nagari*   *Tamil*   *Tibetan*   *Malayalam*   *Old Kanarese*

Sinhalese   *Takri*   *Devanagari*   *Nandinagari*   *Proto-Bengali*   *Mongolian*
Siamese
Burmese
Kavi

Kashmiri   *Gurmukhi*   *Maithili*   *Bengali*   *Oriya*   *Gujarati*   *Manipuri*   *Kanarese*   *Telugu*

71 A family tree of a few of the most important Indic scripts.

after Brahmi, ancestor of all Indic writing but Kharosthi. Brahmi originated in the eighth or seventh century BC and was already in widespread use by the fifth century BC (illus. 73). Similarly borrowed from Semitic writing, Brahmi comprises a very similar system to Kharosthi's, also following the *abudiga*. It appears that Indian scribes consciously redesigned the Semitic writing they borrowed according to well-understood phonological principles.[45] The Indians were antiquity's finest linguists; the West did not begin to approach their level of linguistic sophistication until the early 1800s – in some cases the early

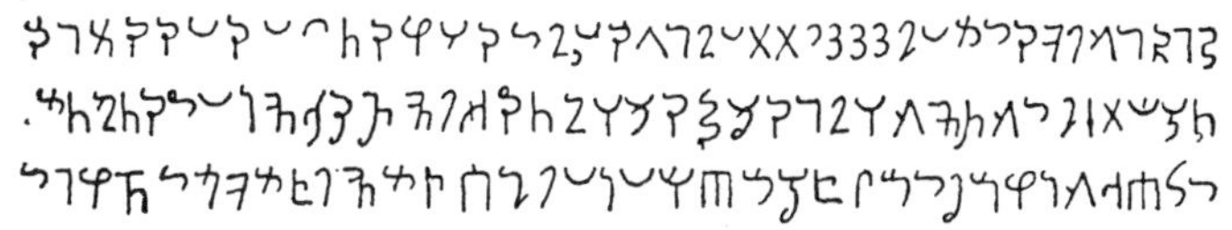

ᔍᑕᕽ � ᐁ ᓂᒋ ᕽ ᐊ ᕽ 686 ᕑᓂ ᑅᕽ ᐊᕐᒋ ᐁᕽᕽᒃ ᐃᑊᔍ3333 ᓂ ᕽᕽᕽ686ᐱᕽᐱᕽᐱ ᕽᒃᕽ
ᕽᒃᒃᕽ686686ᕽᐃᑕᔍᓂᑕᕝ686ᑕᕽᑕᐱᕽᒃᕽ686ᕽᒃᐱᔍᐱᕽᕽᒃᕽᐁᕽᒃᕽᒃᑕᕽᒃᑅ686
686ᕽᒃᕽ686686ᑕᕽᕝ686ᕽᒃᕽᑕᕽᒃᕽᑊ686ᐁᕽᑕᐁ686ᐱᕝ686ᑅ686686ᕽᒃᕽᐁᕽᐁᕽᑕᑅ686ᕽᒃ686

72 Inscription in the Kharosthi script, 3rd century BC.

73 Brahmi script from the Asoka inscriptions, *c*. 253–250 BC:
'This is a decree of King Piyadasi, beloved of the gods ...'

1900s.[46] Ancient Indian scribes classified their letters according
to places of articulation (a surprisingly 'modern' practice): first
vowels and diphthongs, then consonants (with 'default' /a/), in
the exact back-to-front order as in the human mouth – gutturals,
palatals, cerebrals (palatals), dentals, labials, semivowels and
spirants. It appears to confirm the fundamental equality of writing systems that the Indians, possessing such linguistic insight,
did not abandon their 'cumbersome' system for a streamlined
alphabet once they encountered Greek writing. That is, they
maintained their system because it best conveyed the full repertoire of Indic sounds.[47] The 'graphic syllable' of their *abudiga*
system of consonant + diacritic seemed, at least to Indian
scribes, to yield more salient phonetic information than a mere
letter. So in all derivative scripts, Indic writing remained consonantal alphabetic.

Brahmi's consonants possess an inherent /a/ unless they display an attached diacritic indicating that another vowel is to be
used instead (illus. 74). Initial vowels – that is, /a/, /i/, /u/ and /e/
beginning a word – have their own separate letters, also known
as 'syllabic vowels'. The simple consonantal 'skeletons' one is
accustomed to finding in Semitic scripts are here complicated
by the Indic languages' greater repertoire of C (consonant) and

	BRAHMI (3rd century BC)	Cave temples (c. AD 100)	Gupta (c. AD 380)	Cursive Gupta of Central Asia	Tocharian script	Siddhamatrka	DEVANAGARI	MODI
a								
i								
u								
e								
o								
ā								
ka								
kha								
ga								
gha								
ṅa								
č								
čha								
ja (=ǧa)								
jha (=ǧh)								
ñā								
ṭā								
ṭhā								
ḍa								
ḍha								
ṇa								
ta								
tha								
da								
dha								
na								
pa								
pha								
ba								
bha								
ma								
ya								
ra								
la								
va								
śa								
ṣa (ša)								
sa								
ha								

74 The Brahmi alphabet and some derivations.

V (vowel) structures, which demand the identification of specific vowels: V, CV, CCV, CCCV, CVC, VC and other syllabic possibilities. Brahmi is commonly written from left to right, as in the Asoka inscriptions, though the earliest Brahmi inscriptions, like most Semitic scripts, are written from right to left. No-one knows why Brahmi scribes suddenly reversed their writing direction over two thousand years ago.

Two of the world's major language families are conveyed by Brahmi-derived scripts: the native Dravidian tongues, spoken today chiefly in southern India, and the Indo-European, Sanskrit-derived languages of northern India and parts of south-west India. Around two thousand years ago, Brahmi writing branched into two main script families: Northern Indian and Southern Indian (see illus. 71), each comprising many different scripts. All used the same Brahmi principle of vowel indication through diacritics, and many were very alike in appearance. However, being able to read one did not facilitate reading another: though the underlying writing system was almost identical, the shapes of letters and diacritics were not.

Northern Indian comprises those scripts that stretch from north-western India to South-East Asia, and includes the scripts of Nepal, Tibet and Bangladesh. An early branch of this, as of the fourth century AD, was the Gupta script, Brahmi's first main daughter. Gupta spread with the mighty Gupta empire of northern, central and western India, from the early fourth to the late sixth century AD. The Gupta alphabet became the ancestor of most Indic scripts (usually through later Devanagari). There were four main subtypes of Gupta, each derived from the original Gupta alphabet: eastern, western, southern and Central Asian. Central Asian Gupta further branched into Central Asian Slanting Gupta (with its Agnean and Kuchean variants) and Central Asian Cursive Gupta, or Khotanese.

Beginning around AD 600, Gupta inspired the important Nagari, Sarada, Tibetan and Pali scripts. Nagari, of India's north-west, first appeared around AD 633. Once fully developed in the eleventh century, Nagari had become Devanagari, or 'heavenly Nagari', since it was now the main vehicle, out of several, for Sanskrit literature (illus. 75).[48] Devanagari's alphabet comprises 48 letters: thirteen vowels and 35 consonants, their

व्यवहारान्नृपः पश्येद्विद्वद्द्विर्ब्राह्मणैः सह ।
धर्मशास्त्रानुसारेण क्रोधलोभविवर्जितः ॥ १ ॥

vyavahārān nṛpaḥ paśyed vidvadbhír brāhmanaiḥ

saha dharmaśāstrānusāreṇa krodhalobhavivarjítaḥ

75 Devanagari, the main vehicle for Sanskrit literature: 'The ruler shall examine the trials together with learned Brahmins in accordance with the law, free of ire and passion.'

order fixed since ancient times by Indian grammarians (illus. 76). There are many writing conventions a student must learn: different vowel forms for initial or medial positions; nasalization; muting of the 'default' /a/; weak aspiration; and other details, especially the use of ligatures, which are highly complex and numerous, particularly in Sanskrit.[49] As with all Indic scripts, Devanagari is written from left to right. Because of its special writing conventions, word division only needs to be shown at particular junctures. That is, the customary horizontal bar linking all consonantal letters is broken in certain instances: when a word ends on a vowel, diphthong, nasal or weak spirant; or when words begin with a consonant. Otherwise, all words are written together. Word division is only marked through what is known as *sandhi*, which Sanskrit scribes took great care to distinguish: prioritizing the sentence over its constituent words, scribes marked 'breath groups' (as professional singers do today). A sentence's end was marked with I; a complete passage of text ended with I I (see illus. 75).

In time, Devanagari became India's principal script. It also became one of the world's most important, as it was used to convey many other languages of the region, such as Hindi (illus. 77), Nepali, Marwari, Kumaoni and several non-Indo-Aryan languages. Devanagari failed to become India's sole script perhaps because of the region's long disunity. Subsequently, it became the parent of, among other scripts, the Gurmukhi

Vowels		Consonants			
✳	✚				
श्र / अ	— a	क k ग ख k-h ग g घ g-h ङ ṅ (gutturals)		प p फ p-h ब b भ b-h म m (labials)	
श्रा / आ	ा ā				
इ	f i	च c छ c-h ज j झ / ज्ञ j-h ञ ñ (palatals)		य y र r ल l व v (semivowels)	
ई	ी ī				
उ	ु u				
ऊ	ू ū	ट ṭ ठ ṭ-h ड ḍ ढ ḍ-h ण ṇ (cerebrals)		श ś (or ç) ष ṣ स s ह h (spirants)	
ऋ	ृ r (or ṛi)				
ॠ	ॄ r̄ (or ṛī)				
ऌ	ॢ ḷ (or ḷi)				
ए	े e	त t थ t-h द d ध d-h न n (dentals)		: ḥ • ṃ or ṁ	
ऐ	ै ai				
ओ	ो o				
औ	ौ au				

✳ form in initial position   ✚ form in medial position

76 Devanagari's consonantal alphabet as used in Sanskrit literature.

which the Sikhs elaborated in the 1500s in order to write their Punjabi language (illus. 78). Today, Devanagari survives in India alongside some ten other major scripts (including the Latin and Perso-Arabic alphabets) and about 190 others of lesser significance.

Another important member of Northern Indian derived from Nagari (not from Devanagari) is Proto-Bengali. Proto-Bengali generated the Bengali script (illus. 79) that has been used over more than five hundred years to convey a number of significant languages: Bengali, Assamese (which added four letters) (illus. 80), Manipuri (illus. 81), Maithili (illus. 82), some Tibeto-Burmese languages and the Santhali group of languages (West Bengal, Bihar and Orissa). Orissa's Oriya language elabo-

ग्यारह बजे वहां पहुंचा था और पौने तीन बजे अवकाश पा यह
सन्देश लाया हूं कि कमला अपनी भाभी माया के साथ आयेगी।
उसकी मां तो रजनी भाभी के घर पर थी। उसके भाई बिहारी-

77 Hindi.

ਉੱਲੂ ਵਲ ਵੇਖਿਆ ਈ ਨਾ ਜਾਏ। ਉਸ ਨਾਲ ਅੱਖਾ ਈ ਨਾ ਮਿਲਾਈਆਂ ਜਾਣ।
ਪਿਛੇ-ਤੇ ਨ ਤੁਰਦੇ ਤੁਰਦੇ ਸੀੜੀਆਂ ਤੋਂ ਕਾਗਜ ਚੁੱਕੇ ਜਾਣ…। ਜੇ ਉੱਲੂ ਉੱਡ
ਕੇ ਖਾਏਗਾ ਵੀ ਜਾ ਦੰਦੀਆਂ ਵੱਢੰਗਾ ਤਾਂ ਵੀ ਮੂੰਹ ਤਾਂ ਬਚ ਈ ਜਾਏਗਾ। ਲੱਕ

78 Gurmukhi.

বদলে রইলো এই ঘড়ি। একটু অদ্ভুত ঘড়ি। এই ঘড়িটাই শব্দ ক'রে
তাল দিতো গানের সঙ্গে-সঙ্গে। একটা যন্ত্র ঘুরিয়ে দিলে প্রত্যেকটি
টিকটিক আওয়াজ রীতিমতো জোরে তবলার বোলের মতো টকটক

79 Bengali.

অলপ্তর বনমালীর কিসনকান্ত প্রকাসর
কাবরে বড়মান অমবীয়া- অমরর আহীসকালে
এই গিয়াি লিখি অটিপালো—। এই গিয়াি অপলার সামৱে

80 Assamese.

৯৬ সৌৱ্য৯৬ ৭৬মে দ্রালী ৬ল্ড ৰ্ণা৬মআ।
সৱ্য দ্রল দ্রাৱ সৱ্য৯ঙৱে মৰ্জ্ঞ সৱ্যকৰ্ড ৬ৰ্ণৱে

81 Manipuri.

কোনামনবমকঁঞ্জনহুরেসাতে কি গহিমপুরেবাকাসমকরনকৌচ্ছনজেবা
রবুধনমৱগ্রিমসমজেহমরহিমাশামসমহমম্রদীযতঅনওগ্রনম্বা

82 Maithili.

ଜେଠକ ବେଳେ ଭାହାର ବଡ଼ ପୃଥ ସେଉରେ ଥିଲ୍ଲ ।
ପୁଣି ଅସୁ ୨ ଭାର କଠରେ ପ୍ରବେଶ ହୋଇ ନାଥ ଓ ବାଧ୍ୟର

83 Oriya.

ગાંધીયુગમાં આપણા વિવેચનનું લક્ષ્ય પાછળથી કાવ્ય પરથી
ખસીને કવિ તરફ ગયેલું લાગે – ખાસ કરીને ઉમાશંકરમાં. કવિની
સાધના, કવિની શ્રદ્ધા, કવિના સર્જનવ્યાપાર – આ બધા વિશે

84 Gujarati.

85 Kaithi.

rated its own script based on the Bengali script (illus. 83). The
Gujarati (illus. 84) and Kaithi scripts (illus. 85), conveying
Gujarati and Bihari, are closely related to the Bengali script;
however, Devanagari is now used to write Bihari instead.

Sarada was another Gupta daughter that yielded the Takri
script. In turn, this generated the Kashmiri script of Kashmir.

A further Gupta daughter, Pali script, was parent to the many
scripts (Siamese or Old Thai, Burmese, Kavi, Sinhalese and
others) that were specifically elaborated for writing Prakrit languages – any one of the vernaculars of northern and central
India, arising from or connected with Sanskrit – involved with
Buddhism. As Buddhism expanded, so did the many Pali scripts.
There are no Pali scripts in India today. The several that survive
are to be found in the Buddhist countries of Central and South-
East Asia, as well as in the Indonesian islands, where they have
provided a model for many new scripts. The Siamese or Old
Thai script uniquely developed a method for indicating phone-
mic tone.[50] Because the Thai language changed after writing's

introduction, some consonants in the script became superfluous: these 'extra' letters were subsequently turned into tonal letters. Thai also has four diacritics that attach to a consonant's right 'shoulder' to convey tone. (If the consonant already has a vowel diacritic, then the tone indicator is written above this.) Successive vowels are common in Thai but not in Indo-Aryan languages, and so these are accommodated using special marking. And silent letters that retain the historical spelling – no longer pronounced, like the *a* in English 'bean' – also receive a diacritic, as if we were to write 'bea*n'.

Another Pali script was Kavi. This developed with several new scripts in the Indonesian islands in the wake of prolonged religious and cultural influences from India. Kavi prevailed in Java between the ninth and fifteenth centuries. Modelled after Siamese, it chiefly served Javanese speakers, the islands' largest linguistic community. Kavi was written with the Indic conventions for indicating vowels. However, the Javanese variety of Kavi has introduced some fascinating features: special signs used in the writing of correspondence signal the writer's rank in relation to the addressee (that is, higher, equal, lower; Javanese Kavi is the only Indic script to codify social relationships); punctuation marks denote new paragraphs; and capitals are used to write each letter of proper names.[51] There are several Kavi-derived scripts in the region (illus. 86). Kavi also generated the only scripts in pre-contact Oceania: the Macassar-Buginese scripts in Celebes (perhaps through the Batak script of Sumatra), and the now-extinct Tagala and Bisaya scripts of the Philippines, which were first encountered by Westerners in 1521.

A further Pali script, Sinhalese of southern India, Sri Lanka

86 Written on bamboo strips in the 1800s, this Kavi-derived Rejang script from South Sumatra conveys the Malay language.

ගැනීමයි. එවිටයි සාහිත්‍ය කලාවෙන් කළ හැකි කළ යුතු සංස්
කෘතික විප්ලවය සාර්ථක වන්නේ. සම්ප්‍රදායිකව ආරක්ෂා
කළ යුත්තේ ඇත්ත වශයෙන්ම අධික ආර්ථික දියුණුව නිසා

87 Sinhalese.

ག་ཞན་གྱི་བུ་བ་མི་ཤེས་ཀུང་

དེ་དང་དེ་ལས་སྒྱུད་པ་སྦྱང་

88 Tibetan.

and the Maldives, is based on Pali conventions but is also heavily
influenced by the Malayalam script of Southern Indian (illus.
87).

Another important Northern Indian member perhaps
derived directly from Gupta – and thus a sister script to Nagari,
Sarada and Pali – is Tibetan (illus. 88).[52] However, the Tibetan
language wears this foreign Indo-Aryan script most uncomfort-
ably. The script retains the Indic consonantal alphabet with diacritic attachments to indicate vowels – but with only one vowel
letter, the /a/, which is the same as the system's own 'default' /a/.
This /a/ letter is then used to attach other diacritics in order to
indicate further vowels. Because the Tibetan language has
changed greatly since *c*. AD 700 (when the script was first elaborated from Gupta) while the script has remained almost
unchanged, Tibetan is extremely difficult to read today. Its
greatest problem is that it marks none of the tones of its tonal
language. Though Tibetans have long tried to adapt written
Tibetan to spoken Tibetan, high illiteracy has been the price of
failing to achieve this. Tibetan schools in Tibet, by governmental decree, now teach only the Chinese script and in the Chinese
language.

There are two main Mongolian scripts, both alphabetic:
Phags-pa and adapted Uighur. Phags-pa represents a remodel-
ling of the Tibetan script by Grand Lama 'Aphags-pa-blo-
gros-rgyal-mthsan in 1260, by decree of the Mongol emperor

89 Modern Mongolian.

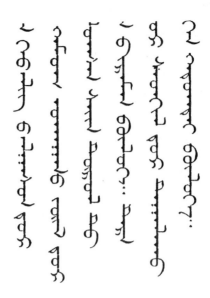

of China Kublai Khan. Uighur is ultimately of Aramaic origin; Mongolian scribes borrowed some signs and marks from Tibetan to remodel Uighur in the 1300s in order to create a more serviceable alphabet, called Galik. The modern Mongolian script (illus. 89), written in vertical columns from left to right, emerged out of this.

The Southern Indian scripts chiefly convey the subcontinent's principal native language family, Dravidian, just as the Northern Group generally, but not exclusively, represents the intrusive Indo-Aryan branch of Indo-European, which arrived in the region *c.* 1900 BC. Southern Indian is not as large or influential as Northern, its scripts transmitting Tamil, Telugu, Malayalam, Kanarese and others. Already two hundred years before Nagari's elaboration, varieties of more than five different Southern scripts were being written. The early Kadamba script was the model for the Old Kanarese, which itself inspired several scripts with large regional importance in southern India. Around AD 1500, the later form of this, Kannada (illus. 90), and Telugu (illus. 91) began to develop into their modern recognizable scripts – southern India's two most important ones.

Another consequential Southern Indian script was Grantha. Some eight hundred years ago, it served as the model for the

ಹೋಗು ನೀನೇನು ಮಾಡುತ್ತಿ."

ನಾನು ಊರಲ್ಲಿ ತುಂಬ ಅಸ್ಮಿವಂತ ಮುದುಕ. ನನ್ನ ಒಬ್ಬನೇ ಮಗ ಇವನ ಕೈಗುಣದಿಂದಲೇ ಬದುಕಿದ್ದ. ಆ ಸಂತೋಷ ಒಂದು ಕಡೆಗೆ. ನನ್ನನ್ನು

90 Kannada.

ఎకా గ్రహస్తాశ దొగ్-జాణ ఫ్లాత లశిల్ల |
తాంతులె ప్రైశం సాను శవ్లణగెల్య బావ్సు శడె

91 Telugu.

രതിയുടെ ഉഷം കുറിഞ്ഞു. കാരണമില്ലാതെ ശരീരം
വിറച്ചു. നെഞ്ചിൽ ചുഞ്ചെൽകൊക്ക കൊളത്തി വലിക്കെ
ന്ന ആനുഭവം. എന്താരള്ളപ്പെട്ട മനഷ്യനാണിയാം.

92 Malayalam.

சுதந்திர புருஷர்களாய் இந்த மண்ணில் வாழ்ந்த மூன்றோர்
களின் நினைவு தோன்றி அவர்களைப்போல் நாமும் சுதந்திரப்
பிரஜைகளாய் வாழ வேண்டும் என்ற தீவிரம் நமக்கு

93 Tamil.

Malayalam script, which conveyed Malayalam as well as the
Sanskrit of southern India (illus. 92). (Today, in the south, it
conveys only Malayalam, but in the west also Telugu.) Grantha
had already generated the Tamil script around AD 750; it is func-
tionally similar to the scripts of Northern Indian, perhaps
through Nagari. The writing of traditional Tamil is known for
its simplicity and ease of reading; the writing of modern Tamil is
fraught with difficulties (illus. 93).[53] The old written language of
Tamil did not need to indicate aspirated consonants like /ph/ or
spirants like /f/, and so its repertoire of about 20 letters was
small. (In contrast, Old Kanarese had about 40 letters, and
Malayalam 53.)
    Northern and Southern Indian share the original Brahmi

principles of consonantal signs with obligatory diacritics to indicate vowels. Differences lie only in the individual languages the single system is conveying, each with varying needs. All Indic scripts differ externally much more than they do internally, like one large family all wearing different clothes. The inner form of writing, the consonantal alphabetic system, links them genetically; the outer form of writing, the hundreds of different scripts, separates them socially. People generally identify with graphic externals – a letter's shape – before anything else. Entire systems are seldom perceived.

Most of the Indic scripts have not been named here – those of Brahmi origin that have conveyed hundreds of languages for over 2,400 years. This writing has touched a large portion of humanity. At the beginning of the third millennium AD, the region maintains the world's greatest diversity of scripts. Simplification and reduction – doubtless even widespread replacement – will inevitably come as a result of globalization. However, change will perhaps take longer here than elsewhere.

The era of the earliest writing systems was followed by writing's accelerated diffusion and diversification. Syllabic writing was practised for many centuries in Byblos, Anatolia and the Ægean. Consonantal alphabetic writing gradually spread, first from Egypt, then from the Levant, to eventually replace syllabic writing altogether. Consonantal alphabetic writing went on to convey, with a major conversion of the system, the languages of the Indian subcontinent and those of Central and South-East Asia. But this was only in part because the structural principle underlying the consonantal alphabet – the representation of consonantal phonemes – allowed one to borrow easily. It is seldom the efficiency of a writing system or script that determines its longevity and influence, but rather the economic power and prestige of those using it. Writing and its rise and demise foremost comprised the power barometer of ancient societies: Phoenician to Aramaic to Arabic traced a seventeen-hundred-year history of waxing and waning fortunes in the Middle East. A powerful society's writing system – the consonantal alphabet – will mark history, while a weak society's will perish.

Still, consonantal writing is not always a comfortable cloak. It might eminently suit Semitic frames, but non-Semitic languages requiring equal representation of consonants and vowels have found it wanting. No writing system is intrinsically 'better' than another, even those of powerful and rich peoples. Most preliterate peoples have borrowed and then adapted writing, as we have seen. For many, a major innovation to the system itself has been necessary in order to make it into usable writing. The three classes of writing – logographic, syllabic and alphabetic (and their transitional and mixed usages) – are each maximized by a particular language, society and era.[54] As in the natural sciences, the success or survival of a system does not entail superiority but adaptability.

Such a situation led to the last major innovation in the history of writing, a gift of the Greeks – the complete alphabet, evidently adaptable for everything from alpha to omega.

FOUR

From Alpha to Omega

'The Phoenicians who came with Kadmos,' wrote Herodotus in the fifth century BC of the legendary Phoenician prince of Tyre and brother of Europa, '… introduced into Greece, after their settlement in the country, a number of accomplishments, of which the most important was writing, an art which, I believe, had been unknown to the Greeks until then.' While the Greeks received consonantal alphabetic writing from the Phoenicians, syllabic writing had been known to them long before this (see Chapter 3). Since Kadmos had lived, as Herodotus also alleged, approximately 1,650 years earlier – that is, when the syllabic writing of the Phoenicians' ancestors had arrived in Hellas – perhaps the historian was recalling a legend relating to the Greeks' first borrowing of writing rather than the second.

Of course, Egyptians rather than Greeks or Phoenicians were apparently the first to represent single consonants with only one sign corresponding to each consonantal phoneme in their language. (A phoneme is a speech-sound considered in respect of its functional relations in a linguistic system, like *b* and *p* in English *bin* and *pin*.) This brilliant way of writing – one, and only one, sign for each consonantal phoneme – spread to Sinai and Canaan and revolutionized writing in terms of flexibility and economy. One no longer needed to learn hundreds of signs; usually, fewer than 30 'letters' (signs in an alphabet) were needed to convey the consonantal phonemes of any given language. In this way, writing became available to everyone.

The innovation, as particularly developed and documented in the North Semitic scripts, spread rapidly, becoming the ancestor of three geographically and linguistically diversified developments.[1] Phoenicians inspired the Aramaic script, which, in turn, inspired the hundreds of scripts of southern and South-

East Asia (see Chapter 3). Further, the Phoenician-inspired Aramaic script also motivated the scripts of Mongolia and the Manchu empire, with secondary influence from distantly related Indic-derived scripts. But before all these, Phoenicians had inspired the Greeks. And it was through the Greeks' borrowing and splendid adaptation of the Phoenicians' consonantal alphabet that the 'complete' alphabet – one awarding vowels a status equal to that of consonants – emerged. (Only the linguist's phonetic alphabet is complete, but it is too ponderous for everyday use.)

THE GREEK ALPHABET

All scholars agree that the Greeks received their 'Phoenician letters' directly from these peripatetic merchants of Tyre, Sidon, Byblos, Ashkelon and other rich Levantine ports who, after the fall of the 'Sea Peoples', dominated Mediterranean trade. However, not all agree when and where this borrowing occurred. Recent claims that the Greeks 'invented' the alphabet for the sole purpose of writing down Homer are fanciful. The related claim that the collapse of the Mycenæan civilization in the thirteenth century BC caused all Greeks to lose the art of writing for many centuries[2] is simply untrue: the Greeks of Cyprus transformed their Cypro-Minoan writing into Linear C shortly after this date. They then borrowed Phoenician writing, which they used concurrently with Linear C.

This latter borrowing evidently came as a result of close contact with Phoenician merchants whose alphabetic writing Cypriote scribes recognized as being quicker and easier for accountancy than syllabic writing. This opinion is urged by certain phenomena of early Cypriote alphabetic writing: these exhibit usages only scribes accustomed to syllabic writing would display. Though the exact date of the Greeks' borrowing of the Phoenician alphabet is unknown, the general consensus of Classicists is that it occurred around the tenth century BC, at the very latest around 850 BC.[3] The opinion voiced already in 1906 by Edward Maunde Thompson, Director and Principal Librarian of the British Museum, still holds a century later: 'The Greeks learned the art of writing from the Phoenicians at least as early as the ninth century B.C.; and it is not improbable that they had acquired it even one or two centuries earlier.'[4]

So a seamless writing tradition has always empowered the Greeks, who never did lose writing completely and who, having acquired writing *c.* 2000 BC from the Levant, have been writing ever since. No other Indo-European people has possessed writing for so long.

This also means that early Greek-speaking communities experienced two borrowings of writing, and of two different systems, too, both from the Levant. Around 2000 BC, the Minoan Greeks of Crete borrowed Byblos's idea of syllabic writing (but not their individual signs, nor their Semitic values). Then, around 1000–900 BC, Cypriote Greeks borrowed the Phoenicians' idea of alphabetic writing (this time including the signs as well as their Semitic values). Alphabetic writing then diffused among the Greeks of the Ægean – first via Rhodes and Crete, then by way of Euboea – from *c.* 850–775 BC. This syllabic-to-alphabetic development displays increasing vocalism in Greek writing, similar to what the Indian subcontinent was soon to experience. The vocalic development of both regions contradicted their Semitic source, which continued to remain essentially consonantal.

The Greeks' second borrowing of a Levantine writing system represented a 'primary transmission', in that the act generated an entirely new form of writing which then, through 'secondary transmission',[5] diffused throughout Greek-speaking communities. It was this secondary transmission that in time created the rich local varieties of the early Greek alphabet witnessed by the archæological inventory. The many local adaptations in the alphabet fortuitously coincided with the historical dynamics of Greek re-expansion, mainly through the Euboeans, who at once began taking the new alphabet far beyond Hellas' shores.[6] Particularly in the early eighth century BC, Euboeans blazed the trail for Greece's mercantile expansion, carrying their characteristic form of the Greek alphabet with them as they established trading colonies from Syria in the east to Ischia near Naples in the west.[7] The Euboean script was an eighth-century elaboration, a more modern relation of those older Greek forms of the alphabet used, for example, on Crete, Thera and Melos which remained closer to the Phoenician prototype.

The Greeks were the first in history to represent vocalic phonemes systematically and consistently. (With their *matres lectionis*, the Aramaic scribes achieved the same several hundred years later, followed by the Hebrews with their vocalic diacritics; see Chapter 3.) What is more, they awarded each Greek vowel a sign just as if it were a consonant, and then wrote these signs either alone or bound together with a consonant. By using consonants and vowels together in this way, they reproduced speech more faithfully than any system devised before or since. Thus the Greeks achieved the first 'mapping' of a language's relevant sounds. And though they wanted only to convey their own particular dialect of Greek using the new Phoenician writing, the scribes of Cyprus came up with an innovation that, usually with only minor adaptations, could convey any language on Earth. In this way, the Greeks 'perfected' alphabetic writing, within given limitations.

With their borrowing of syllabic writing *c.* 2000 BC, the Greeks had had to elaborate a whole new set of pictorial syllabograms based on Minoan Greek names for things according to the rebus principle. Now, with alphabetic writing, the Cypriote Greeks took over the alphabetic idea and the Phoenician signs themselves, since these were letters, not pictures. That is, a sign's sound was important, not its meaning. Because this was so, the Greeks even adopted the Old Phoenician names for each sign, and in their traditional Semitic sequence, too – *'ālep*, *bēt*, *gīmel*, *dālet* and so forth – but pronounced as Greek *alpha*, *bēta*, *gamma*, *delta*. The significance of each name was unimportant. It sufficed that these were the names of letters.

In other words, the Greeks did what many had done millennia earlier in similar circumstances: borrow someone else's system and then adapt it to the immediate needs of the local language. Some five hundred years earlier, the scribes of Ugarit were already using the three long and short vowels /a/, /i/ and /u/ to 'complete' their consonantal alphabet. The Greeks' consonant-and-vowel alphabet was simply another variant of this. The Phoenicians themselves were already using an alphabet that was 'complete' for their own needs and thus, as such, represented an advanced alphabetic script (illus. 94). Nonetheless, in view of its simplicity and adaptability, the Cypriote Greeks' contribution must be regarded as the last major innovation in the history of writing.

Why did the Greeks effect changes? Because, as linguist Florian Coulmas noted discerningly, 'The Semitic alphabet applied to a non-Semitic language could not be used to represent the sounds of that language without significant adaptations.'[8] Unlike the Phoenicians' Semitic language, Greek uses vowels and consonants equally as bearers of information. Vowels had already been inherent in the Greeks' earlier syllabic writing, which the Cypriote scribes would certainly have appreciated. These scribes now created vowels out of the Phoenicians' own alphabet. When recited in 'litany' fashion using the full names of each letter, this alphabet contained sounds similar to known Greek vowels, but fronted by consonants the Greeks either did not perceive (as these sounds did not exist in Greek) or chose to ignore in order to exploit their vocalic, rather than their consonantal, value.[9] The reinterpretation of the Phoenician letters probably occurred 'automatically as a consequence of the learning of the letter-names and the acrophonic principle by speakers of a language with a non-Semitic phonological system'.[10]

Semitic phonology – the system of a language's significant sounds – was indeed very different from Greek. All Phoenician words begin with consonants, but many Greek words begin with vowels. Greek-speaking scribes were in fact forced to effect major changes merely in order to pronounce the names of the Phoenician letters, whose meanings were now gone. Some consonantal letters whose sounds were not needed for Greek as spoken around 1000 BC were borrowed, then, only for the vowels in their name. In this way, the 'weak consonantal' or 'semi-vocalic' sounds of the Phoenician letters were each heard, or simply chosen to be used, as pure vowels instead of consonants or semi-vowels. So Old Phoenician ʾālep, the glottal ʾ, became Greek A, the alpha. Old Phoenician hē was interpreted as Greek E. (The /h/ was not marked, though often present in Greek; much later, this became a diacritic, when needed.) Old Phoenician yōd, the y- sound, became Greek I. And Old

Phoenicia c. 1000–900 BC	Crete c. 750 BC	Athens c. 700 BC	Ionia c. 400 BC	NAME / VALUE /
𐤀 'ālep/ʔ/	A	⟨alpha⟩	A	alpha/a, ā/
𐤁 bēt/b/	⟨bet⟩	[none]	B	bēta/b/
𐤂 gīmel/g/	Λ	[none]	Γ	gamma/g/
Δ dālet/d/	Δ	[none]	Δ	delta/d/
𐤄 hē/h/	⟨he⟩	⟨he⟩	E	epsilon/ɛ/
Y wāw/w/	⟨waw⟩	[none]	[none]	(digamma/w/)
I zayin/a/	I	|	I	zēta/z/
𐤇 ḥēt/h/	⟨het⟩	⟨het⟩	H	ēta/æ/
⊗ ṭēt/ṭ/	⊗	[none]	Θ	thēta/tʰ/
𐤉 yōd/j/	⟨yod⟩	⟨yod⟩	I	iōta/i, ī/
𐤊 kāp/k/	⟨kap⟩	⟨kap⟩	K	kappa/k/
L lāmed/l/	Λ	⟨lamed⟩	Λ	lambda/l/
𐤌 mēm/m/	⟨mem⟩	M	M	mu/m/
𐤍 nūn/n/	⟨nun⟩	⟨nun⟩	N	nu/n/
𐤎 ṣāmek/ṣ/	[none]	[none]	Ξ	xi/ks/
⊙ 'ayin/ʕ/	⊙	O	O	omikron/o/
𐤐 pē/p/	⟨pe⟩	⟨pe⟩	Γ	pi/p/
Z ҫādē/sᵖ/	M	[none]	[none]	(san/s/)
φ qōp/kᵖ/	φ	[none]	[none]	(qoppa/k/)
𐤓 rēš/r/	⟨res⟩	⟨res⟩	P	rhō/r/
W šīn/ś, s̀/	[none]	⟨sin⟩	Σ	sigma/s/
+ tāw/t/	T	T	T	tau/t/
	Y	Y	Y	upsilon/y, ȳ/
			Φ	phi/pʰ/
		X	X	chi/kʰ/
			Ψ	psi/ps/
			Ω	ōmega/ɔ/

94 The Phoenician consonantal alphabet's borrowing into Greek, each letter represented by only one of several possible variants.

Phoenician *'ayin*, the glottal ', became Greek O. The earliest Greek alphabetic writing already shows all these forms.

Greek Y for /y/ (like in French *tu*) was taken from elsewhere, as this sound is not present in Old Phoenician; in later centuries, Greeks distinguished Y from ου (as in English BOOT) – just as Modern French distinguishes *u* from *ou*. However, the Y was also the Old Phoenician *wāw*, the /w/ that, in altered form, later became the Early Greek 'digamma' or /w/ (which was eventually dropped from the alphabet as the Greek language changed).

In addition, the Greeks added three new signs taken most likely from earlier Cypriote writing. These conveyed the frequent Greek consonantal sounds not present in Old Phoenician: φ for /ph/, originally a *p* + *h* sound (as in 'top hat'); X for 'kh'; and ψ for the double consonant /ps/.[11] Also, vowel length was phonemic in Early Greek – that is, a short vowel significantly contrasted with a long vowel in some words. So, on the way from the earliest inscriptions to Classical Greek, the two most frequent long vowels were each awarded a special letter: Ω for long /o:/ (by opening up the bottom of Greek short o), and H for long /ɛ:/ (from Old Phoenician *ḥēt*, which is pronounced with a long /e:/ or AY sound).

At its inception, the Greek alphabet probably was fairly complete in its inventory. Still, writing it remained pretty much a 'primitive' business (illus. 95). For many centuries, there was no standardized Greek orthography. There was also no distinction between capital and small letters, no punctuation and no word separation, and every region followed local conventions – sometimes using local letters of their own. The earliest Greek inscriptions are written in Semitic fashion from right to left, or in boustrophedon, 'as an ox plows', alternating direction with each new line. By the sixth century BC, however, most scribes preferred to write from left to right on each successive line. This method eventually replaced all others.

The three main groups of early Greek alphabetic writing comprise the archaic alphabets of Crete, Thera and Melos; the Eastern alphabets of the Ægean, Attika and Asia Minor's western coast; and the Western alphabets of western Greece and the Sicilian colonies. Throughout most of this period, Greece comprised a motley assemblage of independent city-states, not a

95 The Dipylon Jug (*c.* 730 BC), discovered near Athens' ancient western gate, bears the earliest inscription in Greek letters: 'to him who dances most delicately'.

kingdom or unified nation. By the middle of the fourth century BC, however, all competing versions of the Greek alphabet had been discarded for the single Ionian alphabet, one of the Eastern scripts from Ionia (today's western Turkey). This alphabet had everywhere assumed preferential status among Greek scribes, who were now writing Classical Greek (Attic, based on the language of Athens) (illus. 96). Primarily because of the Ionian Homer's *Iliad* and *Odyssey*, Ionian had already become the prestige script for the Classical Greeks of Athens who, in 403–402 BC, had made the Ionian alphabet compulsory in all Athenian documents.

At the time of Herodotus (fifth century BC), books consisted of papyrus scrolls, some more than twenty m long. By then, the animal skins of earlier centuries had become an ethnological curiosity. Several leather documents (any skin tanned with agents like acacia pods or oak bark become leather) written in

Egyptian hieroglyphs from about 2500 BC have survived. In early antiquity, skins were popular as a writing material throughout western Asia, Iraq and Persia. Only the non-hair side was available for writing, so a scroll format emerged – rolls of connected leather sheets written on one side. As Herodotus wrote in *The Histories*: 'The Ionians also call papyri *skins*, a survival from antiquity when papyrus was hard to get, and they did actually use goat and sheep skins to write on. Indeed, even today many foreign peoples use this material.' (Of course, in the first millennium AD, animal skins – in their processed form as parchment and vellum – again became the preferred writing material, as Christian writers favoured vellum; see Chapter 7.) For many centuries, Greek, Etruscan and Roman writing was done on stone, leaves, bark, linen, clay and pottery, wall spaces, precious metals, lead, bronze, wood and sometimes animal skins. However, most writing occurred on tablets coated with wax – Greek *pínaksoi* or *déltoi* and Latin *ceræ* or *tabulæ* – and on sheets of papyrus, throughout classical antiquity readily available from Egypt's vast resources. These then formed rolled or, very rarely, individually leafed and bound books: Greek *bíbloi* and Latin *libri*.

Histories of writing usually concentrate on formal writing, often called 'book hand'. However, most formal scripts – as was the case with Egypt's hieroglyphics – eventually elaborate quicker and simpler ways of writing common things, reserving the book hand for special purposes. These simpler scripts are often cursives, or flowing scripts, and much more has been written in such cursives than in book hands. Greek cursive writing dates from at least the third century BC, most of it on papyri (illus. 97). It is evident that one stroke per letter was the normal intention; sometimes, letters were connected, forming a ligature. Cursive Greek writing became the everyday script used on papyri, wax tablets, ostraca (potsherds for writing), graffiti and other things (illus. 98). Inscriptions on stone monuments and metal and clay objects of every kind were written almost exclusively in book hand.

Greek and Latin palæography – the study of older writing and inscriptions – identifies no original distinction between majuscules (large or upper-case letters) and minuscules (small

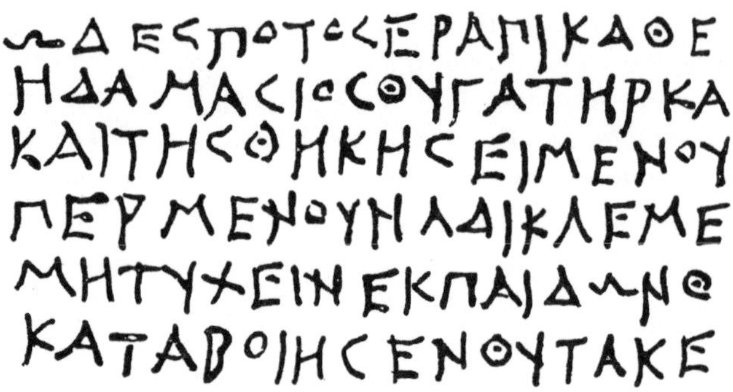

ΛΔΕΣΠΟΤΟΣΕΡΑΠΙΚΑΘΕ
ΗΔΑΜΑΣΙΟΣΟΥΓΑΤΗΡΚΑ
ΚΑΙΤΗΣΘΗΚΗΣΕΙΜΕΝΟΥ
ΠΕΡΜΕΝΟΥΗΛΔΙΚΛΕΜΕ
ΜΗΤΥΧΕΙΝΕΚΠΑΙΔΛΝΘ
ΚΑΤΑΒΟΙΗΣΕΝΟΥΤΑΚΕ

96 Classical Greek: the so-called 'Papyrus of Artemisia' – who here invokes against her child's father – from the first half of the 3rd century BC, one of the earliest surviving examples of Greek literary or book hand.

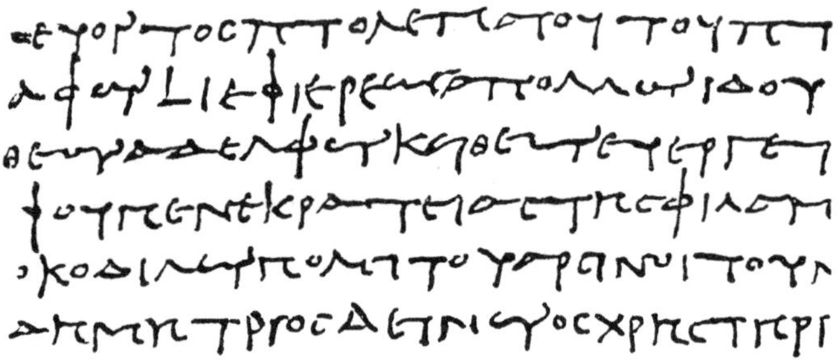

97 Early Greek cursive: the will of Demetrius, son of Deinon, 237 BC.

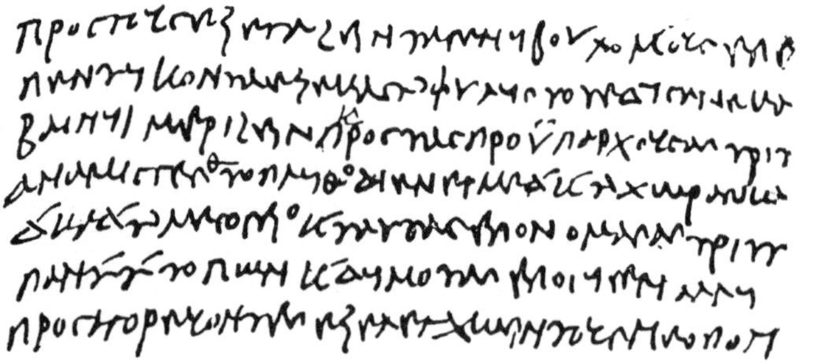

98 Later Greek cursive writing: a copy of Aristotle's *Constitution of Athens*, *c.* AD 100.

or lower-case letters). Early Greek and Latin writing occurred only in majuscules, of which there were two kinds. Capitals, the oldest form of Greek alphabetic letters, use strokes meeting at angles to avoid curves, unless these are required for identification; capitals are the standard letters for monumental and other formal inscriptions. Uncials allow curves, more easily written on soft material such as papyrus. In early Greek papyri, the uncial is the ordinary letter form. Uncial writing, closely resembling modern capitals but more rounded, was especially popular between the fourth and eighth centuries AD in manuscripts that almost exclusively used parchment and vellum.

Because of Greece's military (Alexander the Great), economic and cultural influence, the Greek alphabet became the prototype for the 'complete' (that is, fully vowelized) alphabets that emerged in Europe in the following centuries. These eventually diffused, almost exclusively through Greek's granddaughter alphabets Latin and Cyrillic, throughout the entire world – a process still going on over two thousand years later (illus. 99).

In first-millenium-BC Asia Minor (today's Turkey), the Greek alphabet inspired an impressive number of non-Greek

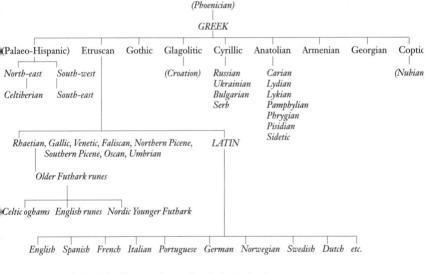

99 An abridged family tree of some Greek-derived scripts.

100 Armenian *notrgir* writing, AD 1616.

peoples to elaborate their own Anatolian alphabets: Carian, Lydian, Lykian, Pamphylian, Phrygian, Pisidian (of the Roman period) and Sidetic.[12] Nonetheless, these scripts failed to acquire lasting significance because of the region's declining economic fortunes followed by several major invasions.

The Armenian monk St Mesrob (*c.* 345–440) is said to have elaborated the Armenians' first script *c.* AD 405 – Armenian is a separate branch of the Indo-European superfamily of languages (to which Greek and Germanic, which includes English, also belong). Based on the Greek alphabet, the Armenian script originally consisted of around 36 mainly capital letters. By the 1200s, Armenian *notrgir*, or cursive writing, had been developed, then replacing writing in capitals (illus. 100).

St Mesrob is also credited with devising the Georgian alphabet in the early 400s AD – Georgian is a Caucasian, not an Indo-European, language – as well as the Albanian alphabet. (Such multiple attributions suggest that Mesrob's role was apocryphal.) The ecclesiastical Georgian script used 38 letters; over time, several styles of writing Georgian developed, with varying numbers of letters (illus. 101). The *mkhedruli*, or 'lay hand', which began as a medium for non-sacral texts, is Georgian's most frequently employed script, still in use today.

In Egypt (see below), the Greek alphabet inspired the Coptic alphabet that replaced one of the world's oldest writing traditions. In the Balkans, Greek generated the Glagolitic and Cyrillic scripts, which eventually generated the Russian script,

101 The Georgian ecclesiastical hand from a book of prayers, AD 1621.

among others. And Greek inspired several scripts on the Italian peninsula, the most important being the Etruscan, which in turn inspired the Latin script – the world's most successful.

MEROÏTIC AND COPTIC

Meroïtic was the language and script of the Africans of the 'Kingdom of Kush', whose capital was Meroë (today Sudan's Begrawiya).[13] Around 250 BC, Meroïtic scribes borrowed Egyptian hieroglyphs, or used Egyptian-derived signs, in order to write their language in an alphabet of 23 letters, each conveying one of either three vowels or fifteen consonants, an initial /a/ and four special syllabic signs. The first datable Meroïtic text is the hieroglyphic temple inscription of Queen Shanakdakhete (c. 180–170 BC). Meroïtic writing occurs on rocks, papyri, ostraca, pottery, statues, stelæ, temple walls, altars, shrines and offering tables.

The simplicity of the system indicates a Semitic origin, as it appears to follow the same Aramaic rules that later, via Nabatæn, yielded Arabic (see Chapter 3). Meroïtic's external script may have been Egyptian, but its internal system was actually Semitic in nature. There are in fact two Meroïtic scripts.

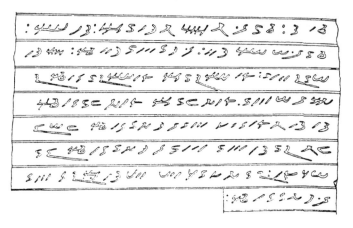

102 Meroïtic linear cursive writing: 'O ... Isis! O ... Osiris! Here lies the noble Tameye ...'

The seldom-used Meroïtic hieroglyphic writing, like the Egyptian hieroglyphs it copied, was pictorial and reserved only for royal or sacral purposes. Meroïtic linear cursive, like the Egyptian demotic writing it used as its prototype, was written in all other situations and eventually replaced the hieroglyphs altogether (illus. 102).[14]

The hieroglyphs were usually written in columns, the cursive script in horizontal lines reading from right to left (as with all Semitic writing). Similar to Indic writing, however, is Meroïtic's possession of a consonant automatically paired with the vowel /a/, the 'default' vowel, unless it is followed by the letter /i/, /e/ or /o/.[15] That is, if no vowel is written after a consonant, then /a/ is to be read in that position. At the beginning of words, a separate letter /a/ is used – since it cannot automatically be paired with a consonant as *Ca* (consonant + /a/). The frequent syllabic combinations *ne*, *se*, *te* and *to* have their own special letters, and the letter /e/ is also used to mark the lack of a vowel following a consonant. Some common closing consonants, like /s/ and /n/, are not always written, their presence understood to be self-evident (as in the Ægean syllabic scripts). In Meroïtic cursive writing, /i/ is usually ligatured to its preceding consonant.

More than a thousand Meroïtic texts have been documented from a wide region south of Egypt. Unfortunately, as with

Etruscan, though the texts can be transliterated (converted into the readable letters of our Latin script, for example), only a few words are translatable. This is because the Meroïtic language the script conveys is still largely unknown, being neither Afro-Asiatic (as are Egyptian and Semitic) nor apparently related to any subsequent language of the region. Therefore, most inscriptions cannot be read. Meroïtic cursive continued to be used for writing the Meroïtic language until about AD 325, when the Meroïtic empire collapsed. It then was used to convey Nubian languages for a short time. After the fifth century AD, Meroïtic cursive, too, was defunct.

As of Alexander the Great's conquest of Egypt in 332 BC (Alexandria, that magnificent centre of trade and learning, had been founded early in 331 BC), the Greek language and script, empowering commerce and inspiring written culture, greatly influenced writing in Egypt. Well into the first few centuries AD, indigenous Egyptian writing (hieroglyphic, hieratic and demotic) and Greek were used side by side successfully. However, ever more documents in the Egyptian language began to appear in the Greek alphabet. A new script emerged with the proselytizing by Christian, Gnostic and Manichæan missionaries in the fourth century AD. These individuals translated the Bible and other scriptures using a modified Greek alphabet that conveyed the everyday Egyptian vernacular or 'Coptic' – from the Arabic name *Qubti*, or 'Egyptian', which derives from the Greek *Aigúptios*.[16] Greek writing apparently continued to be used in Egypt for commercial and official business until shortly after the Arab ingress of AD 639/40. Today, Coptic mainly designates the Egyptian language and script from the fourth to the tenth century AD.

The Coptic script comprises 32 vowels and consonants: 25 from the uncial Greek script of the time, and seven from Egypt's own demotic script. The demotic signs were used because many of the Greek letters failed to have a corresponding sound in Coptic phonology. Especially in Old Coptic, the number of demotic borrowings varied according to dialect. In the writing of the standardized Sa'idic dialect of Coptic, for example, six demotic signs were used (illus. 103).[17]

Old Coptic was customarily written from right to left, in

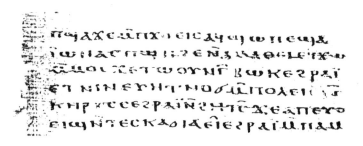

103 Papyrus Coptic Bible in the Sa'idic dialect, early 4th century AD.

Semitic fashion. However, later Standard Coptic was written from left to right, in Greek fashion.[18] Syllables with sonant letters – /r/, /l/, /m/, /n/ and so forth – often neglected to mark their accompanying vowels; in Sa'idic Coptic, however, such missing vowels were indicated by a stroke above the sonants. Like its contemporary Greek source, Coptic did not separate words or provide punctuation. A few diacritics marked letters in special positions: a circumflex ^ over a vowel, for example, showed that it constituted a separate syllable (though this practice was not introduced until after the seventh century AD).

Though Islam's victory in the seventh century brought the Arabic language and script to Egypt, Coptic writing continued into the ninth century as a normal working script.[19] The Coptic language and script endured among Egyptian Christians into the 1200s, and even later in some locales. After this, however, it became solely a liturgical language and script – that is, it was used only in the Christian ritual of Egypt's Coptic Church (surviving today, in limited use, in the liturgy of the Coptic Orthodox Church).

To the south along the Nile, the Nubian Church borrowed the Coptic alphabet and adapted it for the local language. Among other changes, Nubian added three new letters based on signs (with their values) from cursive Meroïtic. The Nubian Church then used this to write liturgical books in the everyday language of Nubia.

The Greek alphabet's most significant borrowing occurred on the Italian peninsula. Around 775 BC, Euboean colonists from Greece established a colony at Pithekoussai, west of Naples; this was Greece's first foothold in Italy. Cumæ was established later. From these two bases, Greek culture began to influence the Etruscans of central and northern Italy, who in time became the chief intermediaries between the Greeks and other Western European peoples. Among the Etruscans' most important cultural borrowings was the Greek alphabet, which they used to write their language for the first time. Today, Etruscan remains largely unknown – it is unrelated to any known tongue. As Giuseppe Della Fina, Director of the Archæological Museum in Orvieto, has put it, 'Trying to understand Etruscan from the few examples we have has been like trying to learn Italian from looking at gravestones. Each new text dramatically increases our chances of one day deciphering the ancient language.'[20]

It was on a Euboean foundation that the Etruscans built. The Euboean-Etruscan alphabet that emerged from this process was borrowed in turn by, among others, the Romans to write their Latin language (illus. 104). This explains why today's Latin alphabet differs so greatly from modern Greek writing.

The earliest known Etruscan inscriptions date from the seventh century BC (illus. 105). Some thirteen thousand Etruscan inscriptions are known, most of them discovered north of Rome along the western half of the Italian peninsula in what was ancient Etruria. Many of them are funerary, recording dates and names of people and places (illus. 106). In Italy, Etruscan writing is second only to Latin in amount of documentation; it was Italy's prevalent form of writing until *c.* 200 BC, when Etruria was assimilated into the Roman Empire.[21]

The Etruscan language differed greatly from Greek.[22] For one thing, it had no voice/voiceless contrast in its stop consonants – so it was not necessary to distinguish /b/ from /p/, /d/ from /t/, or /g/ from /k/. (Eventually, the Etruscans dropped /b/ and /d/ from their alphabet.) There was also no /o/ (which they also dropped). The Phoenician *ḥēt* sign kept its old value *h*, though Greek began using this sign for H, or *ēta*, a vowel. X was

Euboean	Etruscan	Early Latin	Latin
c. 700 BC	c. 600 BC	c. 500 BC	c. 100 BC
			A
	( )		B
			C
	( )		D
			E
(<Y)			F
			G (< C)
			Z (↓)
			H
thēta	th	[none]	[none]
			I
			K
			L
			M
			N
xi		[none]	[none]
	( )		O
			P
	sh	[none]	[none]
			Q
			R
			S
			T
			U, V
			X
			Y (< Y)
	ph	[none]	[none]
	(>x)	[none]	[none]
	f	[none]	[none]
			Z

104 Euboean Greek's borrowing into Etruscan, with Latin derivatives.

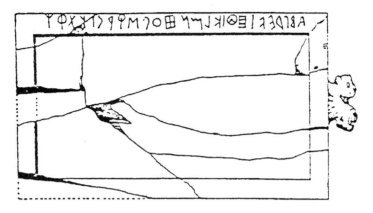

105 The Marsiliana Tablet, an Etruscan-model (Greek) alphabet on an ivory writing tablet found at Marsiliana d'Albegna, Italy.

106 Etruscan inscription on the 5th-century-BC Vetulonia Stele from Vetulonia in Tuscany, Italy.

the double consonant /ks/, not Greek /χ/ or 'kh'. There were three different ways to write /k/, depending on environment: C for /k/ before /a/; ϙ for /k/ before /u/; and Γ for /k/ before /i/ and /e/. The Euboean *gamma* sign C was employed for most uses of /k/, since the Etruscans had no /g/. (During the fifth century BC, northern Etruria occasionally used K for /k/ before /a/.) Various sibilants – that is, /s/, /z/, /š/ (sh) and so forth – reflected local Etruscan usage. The voiceless stops (/p/, /t/, /k/) alternated with the aspirates (/f/, /θ/ or 'th', /χ/ or 'kh') in several Etruscan words: the sounds /k/ and /χ/, for example, were frequently interchanged in inscriptions; however, after liquids and nasals – /l/, /r/, /m/, /n/ – only /χ/ is written, never /k/. Original /f/, written as F + Phoenician *ḥēt* to reproduce /wh/, was replaced during the sixth century BC by the new letter 8, added at the end of the Etruscan alphabet. Etruscan Z was always voiceless /ts/.[23]

The age-old Semitic names of the letters, borrowed by the Greeks, were not continued by the Etruscans.[24] Instead, they named the vowels after their actual sounds, and the consonants after their sounds plus the Etruscan neutral vowel /e/, or AY – so T was *te* (TAY), P was *pe* (PAY) and so forth. The special letters K and ϙ were *ka* (KAH) and *ku* (KOO) owing to their restricted usage, while C was normal *ke* (KAY). Spirants – consonants that prolong sound, like *f*, *v* and so forth – were named by their pronunciation with a vocalic utterance: so S was 'sss', L was 'lll' and so on. Later, the vowel /e/ was prefixed to these spirants in analogy to the consonants. In this way, S became /es/ and L became /el/, as we still call them today. X was /eks/ and not /kse/ because an initial /ks/, contrary to Greek, did not occur in Etruscan (it is assumed). All 21 Etruscan names for the letters of the alphabet – based not on the acrophonic principle of object-words but on sound alone – in time became, with two exceptions, the Roman names. Eventually, due to regular sound changes over the centuries, they also became our English names: *a*, *b*, *c* and so forth.[25]

The direction of written Etruscan was generally from right to left, in the older Euboean and Phoenician fashion. However, a few late Etruscan inscriptions follow Latin's left-to-right direction. There was no word separation until the sixth century BC, when scribes customarily used one or two dots to separate individual words.

107 Oscan inscription from Pompeii, 1st century BC.

Much is still to be learnt about Etruscan writing, which ceased being used in the second century BC when the Romans' Latin language and script prevailed. Significant finds are still being made. In 1999, a bronze tablet bearing 32 lines of Etruscan text was unearthed by a building contractor in Cortona, Tuscany. Dating from *c.* 300 BC, it is known as the Tabula Cortonensis, and is one of some ten surviving texts of significant length. Contributing 27 new words to a known vocabulary of some five hundred terms, this tablet appears to be a property contract between two families.

The Etruscan alphabet was also used by non-Etruscans over a wide region of Etruria, Campania and Emilia. Etruscan writing additionally inspired the alphabets of the non-Roman peoples of Italy, with the exception of southern Italy and Sicily, where the Greek alphabet prevailed. However, all Etruscan-derived scripts – Latin (see below), Ligurian, Lepontic, Rhætian, Gallic, Venetic, Faliscan, Northern Picene, Southern Picene, Oscan (illus. 107) and Umbrian – conveyed, in contrast to enigmatic Etruscan, recognized Indo-European languages.

LATIN

About a century after Rome's founding in 753 BC, the Romans borrowed both the Etruscans' writing system and their script from the dominant Etrurian culture in the north. The Romans appropriated the paraphernalia of writing, too, along with their Etruscan names: *stilus*, a writing implement; *cēra*, wax (for tablets); *ēlēmentum*, a letter of the alphabet; and Greek-Etruscan *diphtherā*, skin (as a writing surface). Latin's oldest monumental inscription – boustrophedonic lines on the Lapis Niger in Rome's Forum – dates from the second quarter of the sixth century BC. As with each borrowing of writing throughout history, the Romans adapted their host script in order to accommodate Latin's particular requirements. This process took many centuries (see illus. 104).

At the time of the borrowing, the Etruscans were still writing *b* and *d*, and so the Romans were able to use these letters for the relevant Latin sounds. The Etruscan alphabet's three different /k/ letters were taken over as well; for these, the Romans wrote C, K and Q (for ꟼ). However, the K, redundant for Latin, was reserved for special archaic words. Some voiced uses of C, similarly left over from Etruscan practice, were also retained, such as the abbreviation 'C.' for the name Gaius. And the Romans began using Q only as the special sound /kw/ when /k/ came before /u/, writing this as QV (we maintain this practice today, writing *qu-*). The double consonant (cluster) /ks/ was simply X. And the Romans kept Etruscan Z in the seventh position of the inherited alphabet, though Latin possessed no /dz/ sound.

The Latin vowels were not particularly marked for length: each A, E, I, O and V could be either short or long, depending on context. The letters I and V were also used to designate the semi-vowels /j/ (the *y*-sound) and /w/ (illus. 108).

In the third century BC, Rome's first headmaster of a private school, Spurius Carvilius Ruga, observed that the Roman alphabet needed a /g/, so he took the Etruscan C and gave it a hook – G – to supplement their alphabet with this sound. In this way, Ruga 'voiced' the Roman C with a single stroke, displaying his recognition that the only difference between the two sounds was a voiceless (C)/voiced (G) contrast – a sophisticated insight into language's internal structure, which, at this time in history, was shared only by Sanskrit grammarians in India. Ruga then inserted this new letter G in seventh position in the Roman alphabet, removing the useless Z and banishing it to the end,

108 Early Latin inscription on the lid of the Ficoroni Cista, a 4th-century-BC bronze toilet box from Præneste, Italy: 'NOVIOS•PLAUTIOS•MED•ROMAI•FECID / DINDIA•MACOLNIA•FILEAI•DEDIT•' ('Novios Plautios made me in Rome / Dindia Macolnia gave [me] to her daughter').

which is why we have 'a-b-c-d-e-f-g', ending with 'z', today. The ordered replacement – not simple supplementation – reveals how canonical the order of the alphabet was perceived to be by Romans of the third century BC.[26]

A century later, once Rome had conquered Greece, the immense influx of Greek culture and words into Roman everyday life prompted the borrowing of two sounds that had been missing from the Latin language: /y/ (as in French *tu*) and /z/ (from earlier Greek /dz/). The first had already been borrowed from Greek via Etruscan as V for /u/, so the later Greek shape Y of the second century BC could now simply be copied for the separate /y/ sound. Its name, *upsilon*, remained Greek. (Today, Germans still call their 'y' *Ypsilon*, and French say *y-grec* [EE-]. Why English speakers say 'y' is unclear.) The 'useless' Latin Z that Ruga had banished to the end of the alphabet was now called Greek *zēta*, the origin of Commonwealth English *zed*; North Americans, in analogy to other letters, have since changed this to /zi/ (ZEE).

The Romans' basic letter shapes were monumental capitals for inscribing stone. Latin majuscule writing had two main branches: square and rustic capitals, and uncials. Most ancient Latin manuscripts that have survived are in rustic capitals, but square capitals are probably equally old. Square capitals tend to be monumental, while rustic are actuarial – that is, the script preferred by accountants. Square capitals are thick and right-angled, their bases and tops finished with fine strokes and pendants (illus. 109). Rustic capitals are slender, with short cross-strokes and no finials (illus. 110).

QVRTSX·I

109 The peerless Latin monumental square capitals: lettering from Trajan's Column in Rome, dedicated in AD 113.

The Romans changed the mono-linear tradition, whereby all letter lines had to be equally thin or thick: Imperial Roman capitals used contrasting thinness or thickness in each letter, with the choice influenced by ink-writing using a broad nib. (A nib is the point of a pen, which in earlier times could be trimmed to any desired width). The Romans also emphasized the use of serifs – light lines or strokes crossing or projecting from the end of a main line or stroke in a letter – much more than the Greeks ever did, allowing improved legibility and generally enhancing the beauty of the script. (Trajan's Column, dedicated in AD 113, is often said to bear 'monumental Roman lettering at its finest'.) The point at which most readers of this book will be able to read one of these described ancient scripts for the first time is marked by the Romans' square capital writing, a familiar ancestor of our own writing.

Uncial writing was a modification of square capital writing (illus. 111). Here, a round hand avoided angles by using curves instead, with the main vertical strokes usually rising above or falling below the line of writing. Roman uncial writing came into use as a literary hand around the fourth century AD. From

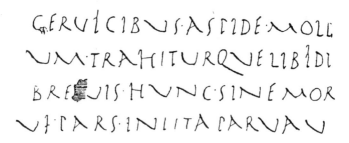

110 Latin rustic capital writing: fragment of a poem on the Battle of Actium written at Herculaneum before its destruction by the eruption of Vesuvius in AD 79.

ueneRuNTaδeumiNhospi
TiumplaRes· quibus
exponcbaTTesTiρicaNs
REGHumδT· Suaδensq·
eisδehuexlegemosiei
pRophetisamianeusr

111 Latin uncial writing: the Fulda Manuscript of the New Testament, copied
c. AD 546.

the 400s to the 700s, uncial writing was Latin's premier literary
hand.

Like the Greeks, the Romans also developed cursive writing,
though it was anything but 'flowing' and connected as the word
usually implies: Roman 'cursive' almost always maintained separate, unconnected letters. Its main characteristic was the
attempt to reduce the number of strokes per letter while maintaining legibility; as with Greek writing, nearly every letter was
reduced to a solitary pen or stylus stroke. The graffiti at
Pompeii and Herculaneum comprise some of the earliest
Roman cursive writing that has survived, most of it written
between AD 63 and 79, when both towns were destroyed by an
eruption of Mount Vesuvius (illus. 112). Roman wax tablets and
tiles also preserve cursive writing (illus. 113, 114). The everyday
writing of the Empire, Latin cursive was commonly penned in
haste. The old letters were modified in the process, eventually
yielding to minuscule (lower-case) writing centuries later. It is
assumed that Pompeii's (and other) graffiti display a form that
had already been in use between two and three hundred years
earlier. Many cursive letters can easily be misread for others, as
significant distinctions were lost in the haste of writing them.

The nature of any given communication and its desired
effect determined which style of Roman lettering was chosen
for writing. Just as we do today, the Romans appreciated that
the medium was also a significant part of the message. Styles of
lettering possessed particular cultural and social associations,
each befitting a given class or circumstance. Even a simple *CAVE*

112 Early Latin cursive writing scrawled on a plaster wall at Pompeii before AD 79: 'communem nummum … / censio est nam noster … / magna habet pecu ni[am]'.

113 Latin cursive on a wax tablet (dated AD 167) found at Alburnus Major in Dacia (Verespatak, Hungary), recording the disbanding of a burial association: 'Descriptum et recognitum / factum ex libello qui propo / situs erat …'

114 Latin cursive on a 1st- or 2nd-century-AD tile found at Silchester, England, probably used as material for a writing lesson: 'Pertacus Perfidus / Campester Lucilianus / Campanus conticuere omnes'.

CANEM ('Beware of dog') in mosaic tiles in front of a Roman residence in Narbonne in southern France reflected the social standing – or desired standing – of the house's occupants.

As with the Greeks, most writing was done on wax tablets and papyrus. (Papyrus was preferred until the second century AD, when it became increasingly rare; in France, howevever, it was still in common use in the sixth century.) Vellum – fine parchment made from the skins of calves and an uncommon writing material under the first Roman emperors – became the writing medium for the new religion of Christianity. Vellum eventually replaced papyrus altogether and, with it, the pagan world it 'represented' (if only in a metaphorical sense). The finest literary productions, written in the most sophisticated scripts, were undertaken for Homer in the Greek world and for Virgil in Rome's classical period; these were overwhelmed by the Bible, in vellum, already during the first few centuries of the Christian Church. Such writings were more highly valued and better looked after than others, and large numbers of them were produced.

Who was able to read such works two thousand years ago? By the first few centuries AD, literacy was widespread in the Roman Empire. This is the greatest lesson to be learnt from Vindolanda, a former Roman military base in northern England along Hadrian's Wall. Since 1973, some two thousand letters and documents on wooden tablets have been discovered there, attesting to writing's pervasiveness in ancient Roman society, even in this farthest reach of the Empire. Comprising the largest archive of early Roman writings unearthed anywhere, the Vindolanda literature dates from between AD 85 and 130. All inscriptions are written in ink or engraved by stylus on wax and convey the thoughts of ordinary men and women corresponding with each other on the base itself and with others far removed. The fact that such a trove, in such an isolated locale, exists at all testifies to the great amount of correspondence that must have been taking place among Romans throughout the Empire.

Writing maintained personal contact, ultimately preserving the social network and Roman culture even in primitive foreign parts. Such correspondence also secured military supplies and sanctioned orders, as well as conveying essential intelligence. In other words, writing kept the Empire functioning. More recently, other Roman sites in Britain — Carlisle, Ribchester and Caerleon in Wales, to name only three — have revealed similar caches of wooden tablets. Roman literacy is now known to have been much more widespread than was appreciated only a generation ago.

The Latin alphabet was not a structural advance over the borrowed Etruscan system. That is, it also maintained letters of equal status conveying both vowels and consonants. Of course, this was a world apart from Semitic writing, in which vowels are sometimes conveyed through optional diacritics above and below the consonantal letters. It was also quite different from Brahmi's daughter scripts from India to Indonesia, in which regular series of vowel marks were attached to, or incorporated into, the consonantal alphabetic inventory. All subsequent Latin-derived scripts share the distinctive characteristic: one letter = one sound (vowel or consonant). How each script realizes this varies from language to language, as an alphabet is not a rule but a tool.

By the first century BC, the Latin alphabet had nearly arrived at complete orthographic phonemism – that is, nearly each letter constituted a distinctive sound in Latin's sound inventory.[27] This is something that English, for example, is still far from achieving (see Chapter 8). The Latin alphabet replaced all other scripts of the Italian peninsula except for Greek, the script of culture and education, and eventually became the official script of the western half of the Roman Empire. (Greek remained the official script of the eastern half.) The Latin alphabet later became the vehicle of one of the world's major religions, Christianity, just as the Arabic alphabet became the vehicle for Islam from Spain to Indonesia at the same time. In this capacity, the Latin alphabet assumed a special role in Western society that prevented its replacement by Germanic runes or Celtic oghams during the Middle Ages (see Chapter 7).

The Latin alphabet, first because of Christianity, later because of colonization and then globalization, has spread 'further and to more languages than any other script before or after'.[28]

Peoples of the north-east and south of the Iberian peninsula (Spain and Portugal) were using four different scripts in the first millennium BC: North-east Iberian (or simply Iberian), South Iberian (or South Lusitanian), Ionic Greek and Latin.[29] The indigenous Iberian scripts and their several varieties appear to have derived from one original Palæo-Hispanic script. It is evident that this original script must itself have derived from either a Greek or a Semitic (Phoenician) prototype. However, it remains impossible to determine with certainty which of the two was the source.[30] The south-west variety of South Iberian appears, from its seeming conservatism, to be closest to the original script, perhaps emerging as early as the sixth century BC. South Iberian may then have diffused to northern Spain during the course of the next century.

All native Iberian varieties of writing display three characteristics preventing their definitive attribution to either Greek or Semitic. First, the Iberian writing system combines both alphabetic and syllabic signs – that is, all vowels and continuants (/r/, /m/, /n/ and so forth) have a letter, but each stop in the Iberian language, such as /k/, is written together with a following vowel as a separate syllabogram (*ka* sign). Second, the syllabograms, not the letters, display both chronological and geographical variation. And third, the syllabograms are labial, dental and velar but, like Etruscan, do not contrast voice; so it seems to make no difference whether one uses *b/p*, *d/t* or *g/k*. Greek and Latin inscriptions in Iberian do show a contrast, however, so perhaps the Iberians purposely chose to use a defective script for their language(s), in which context alone was expected to define the contrast.

Very few Iberian inscriptions are longer than one word. When there are several words in a text, word separation is achieved by a centred dot or colon. North-east Iberian is written from left to right (there is one boustrophedonic inscription), as one finds in later Greek and Latin. South Iberian is written from right to left, as in all Semitic scripts, suggesting that this may be the older script. The differences between the sign shapes of North-east and South reveal no perceptible pattern,

115 North-east Iberian, c. 300 BC.

ᐯ ᐱ H ◇ ᴎ ᐱ △
ᴎ · ᕐ ᐱ ᐤ ᛙ I ᴎ ᛐ
ᖴ ᐐ ᛏ I ᴎ : ᐸ ᐱ ✕ ◇
ᖴ ᐐ ᐸ ᐊ Y ᴎ : ᐯ Y ᖴ
◇ ᴎ ᐸ H ᛏ ᴎ · ᖴ ᐐ ᐺ
ᴎ

however: some are identical, while others are wholly different. Because the underlying language(s) is still unknown, it is not possible at present to offer a grammatical and semantic analysis of the Iberian inscriptions. As with Etruscan, present scholarship is generally limited to identifying proper names and recognizing limited contextual sequencing in order to ferret out possible grammatical elements.

The North-east Iberian script, in which the most inscriptions have survived, was the only script (with rare exceptions) to be used from *c*. 400–100 BC in north-east Spain and southern France (illus. 115). Its usage was uniform, suggesting a shallow time-depth and a homogeneous society using one language. Each letter in North-east Iberian possesses a minimum of two variants. The Celtiberians – the Celts who around 600 BC invaded from the north to permanently settle wide areas of Spain – borrowed this script, as well as Latin, for inscriptions in their Celtiberian language. The attending adaptations reveal phonological peculiarities: for example, *r* was distinguished from another type of *r* using a diacritic mark, while a special Greek sign conveyed a particular *s*. The Celtiberian script also reduced North-east Iberian's fifteen syllabograms to just five consonantal letters – B, Δ, T, Γ and K. These were then written using vowels, as in a normal alphabetic script.

South of this region, three scripts were employed simultaneously: North-east Iberian, South Iberian and Greek. In

Andalusia, in Spain's far south, most inscriptions are in South Iberian, with some rare examples of North-east Iberian.

South Iberian had time to branch into two script families, South-western and South-eastern. The South-west script, also called 'Tartessian', similarly conveys an unknown language. Using several letters that are different from those of the other scripts, this is perhaps the Iberian script closest to the original Palæo-Hispanic one. South-eastern Iberian shares more features with North-east Iberian, as if it comprised the medium for early diffusion.

The native Iberian scripts appear to have been abandoned in favour of the Latin script by the first century BC.

GOTHIC

East Germanic Goths rose to prominence during the Great Migrations of the fourth and fifth centuries AD.[31] Their Gothic languages are primarily known to us today through a few surviving fragments of Bible translations. It was the Visigothic bishop Wulfila († AD 383), according to three ecclesiastical historians writing a century later, who created 'Gothic letters' in order to translate the Bible into the Visigothic language. The fourth-century Greek alphabet was Wulfila's only apparent source.[32] Though the bishop's original Visigothic hand has not survived, closely related derivative scripts preserved in two later Gothic manuscripts no older than the sixth century have been preserved (illus. 116).

'Wulfila's script', as it perhaps should properly be designated, is an alphabetic script written from left to right without word separation. Spaces indicate sentences or passages, as does a colon or a centred dot (as with the Iberian scripts). Nasal suspension – that is, marking where an /m/ or /n/ should be – is sometimes indicated by a macron (a topping stroke) above the preceding letter. Ligatures are even rarer than macrons. There are frequent contractions: for example, *ius* is often used to spell 'Jesus'. Apart from rare profane relics – witness the sixth-century Latin-Gothic Deed of Naples – Wulfila's script, measured by those few inscriptions that have survived, appears to have

ATTAПNSARΦПΪΝhΙΜΙΝΑΜ·
ΥΕΙhΝΑΙΝΑΜQΦΕΙΝ·ΙΙΜΑΙΦΙΝΑΙ
ΝΑSSΠSΦΕΙΝS·ΥΑΙRΦΑΙΥΙΑGΑ
ΦΕΙΝS·SΥΕΪΝhΙΜΙΝΑGΑhΑΝΑ
ΑΙRΦΑΙ·hΑΑΙΕΠΝSΑRΑΝΑΦΑΝΑSΙΝ
ΤΕΙΝΑΝΓΙΕΠΝShΙΜΜΑΔΑΓΑ·GΑh
ΑΕΛΕΤΠΝSΦΑΤΕΙSRΠΑΑΝSSΙGΑΙ
ΜΑ·SΥΑSΥΕGΑhΥΕΙSΑΕΛΕΤΑΜΦΑΓ
SRΠΑΑΜΠΝSΑRΑΙΜ·GΑhΝΙΒRΙΓ
ΓΑΙSΠΝSΪΝΕRΑΙSΤΠΒΝGΑΙ·ΑRΑΑΠ
SΕΙΝΝSΑΕΦΑΜΜΑΠΒΙΑΙΝ·ΠΝΤΕ
ΦΕΙΝΑΪSΤΦΙΝΔΑΝΓΑRΔΙ·GΑhΜΑ̃ΗS
GΑhΥΠΑΦΠSΪΝΑΙΥΙΝS·ΑΜΕΝ·.·

116 Gothic or 'Wulfila's Script': the *Paternoster* from the 6th-century North Italian *Codex Argenteus*: 'ATTA UNSAR THU IN HIMINAM ...' ('Our Father, who art in heaven ...').

conveyed exclusively ecclesiastical texts.

The Gothic script that Wulfila devised from the Greek alphabet did not engender daughter scripts. After the sixth century AD, it was replaced almost everywhere by related descendants of Greek and Latin alphabets. Gothic's last sentinel, the ninth-century *Codex Vindobonensis* 795, was perhaps by then only an antiquarian curiosity.

THE RUNES

The runes are the Germanic peoples' only indigenous script in that, unlike Gothic, they do not copy any known alphabet. In the great Northern Saga of the Scandinavians, the invention of writing is attributed to the god Odin (West Germanic Wodan). However, the runes were clearly inspired by some Mediterranean alphabetic script. Most scholars currently prefer to regard the runes' immediate origin as lying in a North Italian, Etruscan-based script – perhaps Rhætian or Lepontic (Lugano)

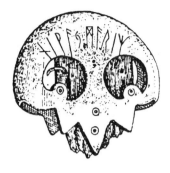

117 Among the earliest Germanic 'older Futhark' runes are the inscriptions, dating from *c.* AD 200, on either side of the end-clasp of a sword sheath discovered in a moor at Thorsberg near Schleswig, Germany.

– that was borrowed, then heavily adapted, by an unknown Germanic tribe. This probably occurred in the early first century AD, during the reign of the emperor Tiberius.

The earliest known runic inscriptions, dating from the second half of the second century AD, were already fully developed (illus. 117). Many of these have been found in southern Jutland, the southernmost part of the Danish peninsula, which also includes Germany's Schleswig-Holstein, indicating that this area may have comprised a major point of diffusion for the runes. Some five thousand inscriptions have been found so far, nearly all of them in Scandinavia, most of these in Sweden. The runes pervaded Germanic society for at least eleven hundred years, until they succumbed to the Church's Latin alphabet.

Unlike most of the world's scripts, the runes never became literary or utilitarian. As their name implies – Old Norse *rún* meant 'secret or hidden lore' – the runes remained socially restricted to a limited domain of usage: mostly memorial stones, but also rings, brooches, clasps, weapons, ivory containers and other treasured objects.[33] Because of such restricted use, the runes never contributed to the creation of a literate Germanic society. The original materials on which they were engraved, wooden sticks and bones on which a knife could best notch vertical lines, apparently determined their characteristic angularity.[34]

Though there were several different runic scripts in use from Iceland to the Black Sea, recording many different Germanic languages, these divide easily into two main chronological types: early Germanic and later Nordic. As has happened throughout history, the Germanic borrowers of the source script borrowed according to the needs of the unique phonology of their own language. They were highly selective, discarding the traditional order of the Etruscan alphabet to create a new, unique one. The first six runes in this new order gave the earliest – that is, early Germanic – runes their name: FUTHARK, the alphabet used from roughly AD 200 to 750. The 24 letters of the Futhark runic alphabet were traditionally divided into three groups of eight families called *ættir*.

Some runes are identical to Etruscan letters (or variants of Latin), while others are unique. They provide a more exact reproduction of their underlying Germanic sounds than the Etruscan or Latin alphabets could for Germanic. For example, unlike today's Latin alphabet, the runes distinguished between the phonemically separate *ng*'s in *ungodly* (*n* + *g*) and *sing* (*ng*). Wielding the foreign Latin alphabet, we now ambiguously write these two words using one digraph or letter-combination (*ng*), whereas a runic scribe would have used three separate runes (*n*, *g* and *ng*) for this task. The runic conveyance reflects the precision of a native script designed to accommodate its own tongue.

About 250 inscriptions survive in what is now designated as the 'older Futhark', runes written before the eighth century. All but 50 of these are Scandinavian, and only in Sweden and Norway does one find stone inscriptions in the older Futhark. A small number of inscriptions exist on other, smaller objects – such as brooches found in the Rhenish-Franconian area of Germany. It is possible that the language(s) of these earliest runes is not the contemporary vernacular(s), but an archaic, formalistic language (or languages) written in early Nordic and/or in East Germanic dialects. However, this possibility obtains only for the older Futhark.

Futhark inscriptions are generally standardized, the forms of the runes being everywhere nearly identical but for /k/ and /j/. Each rune had its name according to the acrophonic principle, a method evidently borrowed from the assumed North Italian source script (though the Germanic values are different): /f/ was *fehu*, or 'cattle', /i/ was *isaz*, or 'ice', /h/ was *haglaz*, or 'hail' and so forth. In this way, one rune could stand for two different things: a sound and an object.[35]

Despite the runes' standardization, their reading direction and orientation were remarkably arbitrary. Boustrophedonic lines and upside-down letters occur. Two runes could combine into a compound rune. Double consonants, like *dd* or *ss*, could be expressed with one consonant. There was seldom any word separation. As of the end of the fifth century, five stacked dots or lines could serve to separate words or mark the end of a passage.[36]

It was long assumed that the runes primarily held shamanistic value for their users and observers (most of whom were not readers); that, through their writing, wishes, blessings, even curses could follow. However, scholars now appreciate that runes served many purposes. On the Gravestone of Rö in North Bohuslän, Sweden, the following is inscribed in the older Futhark from around AD 400: 'Swabahari, with gaping wounds. I, Stainawari, painted. I, Hrar, placed the stone on the riverbank here.' Owners' names often appear on precious objects. Sometimes, even the maker's name is memorialized: 'I, Hlewagastir the Kind, made horn' is engraved on the famous Golden Horn of Gallehus from Denmark, also fashioned around 400. Despite such profane uses, literacy among early Germanic peoples would nowhere have reached those levels enjoyed by their Greek- and Latin-speaking contemporaries.

The older Futhark runes arrived in England with the Angles, Saxons and Jutes between 450 and 600.[37] England's runes were exclusively the provenance of Germanic invaders. Native British Celts never used them; indeed, they probably saw them as symbols of the German trespass. In both Frisia along the North Sea coast and in England, a new series of runes developed out of the older Futhark. English runic scribes demanded changes to the system, particularly to that part of it concerning vowels: four new runes were added, making 28 in all. (Around 800, Northumbrian scribes increased the number to 33.) The earliest Old English inscription in this new 'Futhork' alphabet comes from Caistor-by-Norwich. In the seventh century, Christian missionaries from Ireland and the Continent began 're-introducing' the Latin alphabet to England – Latin writing had been in use in most of Britain since the Roman occupation. Contrary to their Scandinavian use, the runes in 'Anglo-Saxon' England were sometimes also written on objects bearing inscriptions in the Latin alphabet.

There is no evidence that England's Christian church ever wished to eliminate the use of runes. And Christian tradition was too firmly footed on a Latin-alphabetic base ever to be conveyed wholly with them. The Church of Rome's holy scriptures and commentaries and other literary works were all in the Latin alphabet. All Judæo-Christian, Greco-Roman education in Western Europe was in the Latin alphabet. Germanic runes could never compete. The Church evidently realized this and avoided hostility.

England's last runes date from the tenth century, when even the Church was frequently using runes on gravestones, stone crosses and reliquaries. The Latin alphabet had long replaced the runes by 1066, the Norman Conquest merely reinforcing the Latin script's own earlier conquest and precluding a return to Germanic foundations.

On the Continent, Frisia's runes, very similar to England's, were last used in the ninth century. In the Rhenish-Franconian and Alamannian (South-west German and Swiss) regions, the last runes had been notched and engraved two centuries earlier, when Christian missionaries – long before they did this in England – decisively replaced Germanic writing with the Church's Latin.

Only in Scandinavia did the runes endure.[38] In fact, they experienced a new resurgence. Like England, Scandinavia had also innovated. However, this had not been an expansion but a massive simplification of the system: a third of the runic inventory had been deleted, from 24 letters down to sixteen. An individual rune was now expected to convey as many as six or more sounds. (Today's English orthography at times suffers from a similar degree of ambiguity.) In fact, the new Scandinavian alphabet held too few letters to adequately convey Old Norse phonology. By 800, this 'younger Futhark' had been fully developed, at which time a major simplification of letter forms began, one that continued for several centuries. In the tenth century, for example, dotted runes were introduced in order to remedy the simplified system's phonemic inadequacy; this made it possible to distinguish between voiced/voiceless consonants (*b/p*, *d/t* and *g/k*) and even vowels (*e/i*). Latin's growing importance in Scandinavia, however, forced the order of runes to follow the Latin alphabet: *a*, *b*, *c* and so forth.

A renaissance of rune writing accompanied the Viking expansion. Most surviving monumental runes, engraved from Nassaq on Greenland to Piræus in Greece, date from the beginning of the Viking Age up to the High Middle Ages. As of the eleventh century, with the rising influence of the Christian Church in Scandinavia, runes more frequently appeared on memorial stones, and in much longer inscriptions. Scandinavians also began writing a good deal of profane material in runes, including law codes and literary texts.

The younger Futhark runes of Scandinavia long maintained preferential status over the Latin alphabet, which was perceived as foreign. However, as of the 1200s the Latin alphabet of the rich Hanseatic League and the powerful Church began to offer at least a viable alternative. In time, the linguistic advantages of runic writing failed to be appreciated when weighed against profits and salvation. Over subsequent centuries, the runes bowed ever lower before Latin's supremacy: as had already happened in England centuries before, the vehicle for all learning in Scandinavia had become the Church's Latin. Nonetheless, as late as the beginning of the 1900s, runes were still being written in several areas of Sweden.

Today, runic writing, once the voice of all Germanic peoples, engages a mere handful of academics and hobby enthusiasts.

THE OGHAMS

Ogham (pronounced OHM), Old Irish *ogam*, is the first known writing system of the Celts of Ireland and the British Isles. Its monumental use dates from the early fifth to the seventh century AD.[39] Unlike the runes of the contemporary Angles, Saxons and Jutes in England, ogham writing is also the isles' only known indigenous script in which the borrowed idea of writing alphabetically was elaborated in a unique way. The oghams –

the letters of the ogham – enjoyed wide use from southern Ireland (the probable point of diffusion) to the Isle of Man, Scotland and Wales. Ogham writing primarily adorns tombs and memorial stones, though it also decorates wooden staves, shields and other objects.

The oghams' origin is unclear, as is their ordering principle.[40] A possible source of inspiration might have been the runes, since the Celts were maintaining active contact with rune-writing Angles, Saxons and Jutes at the time of the oghams' elaboration. As the oghams comprehend an alphabetic script, it is evident that the system originated from an Etruscan (or Latin) derivative; here again, the runes provide the most economic explanation. Also, ogham writing distinguishes between the sounds /u/ and /w/, a distinction Latin lacks but the runes maintain. The evidence for a Gælic Celt – not a Brythonic Celt (that is, Cumbric, Welsh, Cornish and Breton) – adaptation of the source script argues for an Irish elaboration: there is no /p/ sound in the ogham alphabet; this sound was absent in Primitive Irish, too, but present in all Brythonic languages. Ogham writing in Ireland displays only the oghams, which further suggests a diffusion point, whereas Brythonic Celts sometimes wrote them together with Latin.

Most scholars agree that the ogham was not a literary or utilitarian script, but represents the secret script of the Celts of Ireland and the British Isles (though Germanic oghams also exist). Even its name, again like that of the Germanic runes, suggests this: Old Irish *ogam* means a form of cryptic speech involving phonological replacement – a kind of Irish 'pig Latin'.

There are twenty letters in the ogham alphabet.[41] Like the runes, each ogham letter has a name that is acrophonic: the ogham for /b/ is Old Irish *beithe*, or 'birch', for /l/ *luis*, or 'herb', for /f/ *fern*, or 'alder' and so forth. Each is written as either straight scores or diagonal scores numbering from one to five and scored above, below or directly through either a horizontal or vertical line. Ogham's outward appearance is thus very much like that of a tally-stick or notched memory aid. Very often, this line constitutes the arris – the sharp edge formed by the angular contact of two adjacent sides – of a stone monument or wooden stave. The ogham line or arris always forms the orientational

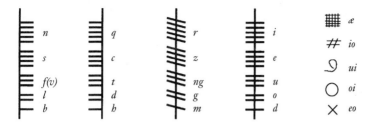

118 Ogham's five alphabetic 'families', read from bottom to top.

median of ogham writing.

The twenty tally-like signs are divided, again very much like the runes, into 'families' or groups (but now four instead of the runes' three) of five signs each (illus. 118). The first three families are consonants: one to five scores cut to the right of (family one), to the left of (family two), and diagonally across (family three) the ogham line. The fourth family holds vowels; customarily, these are scores cut directly on the ogham line, but they also appear as horizontal short scores across the line. A supplemental fifth family comprises both consonants and vowels but was later adapted to convey diphthongs and digraphs (two letters written together to make one sound, like *æ*). Ogham writing has no word separation, punctuation or other type of additional marking.

There are two ogham writing traditions, with nearly identical appearances. Active ogham writing that primarily involved the inscribing of monuments began in the fifth century (illus. 119). These monumental inscriptions customarily display oghams in boustrophedon fashion, commencing at the bottom left side of the stone and progressing over the top and down the right side. The monumental tradition ceased in the seventh century, to be followed by the manuscript tradition, which lasted into the High Middle Ages. These Scholastic oghams, as the manuscript letters are called, were written only in Irish manuscripts, horizontally from left to right in imitation of Latin writing; occasionally, they display a > sign between words. The same letter values obtained in both traditions, but the later manuscript texts include intervening Irish sound changes.

In this way, ogham writing was recalled and commented on

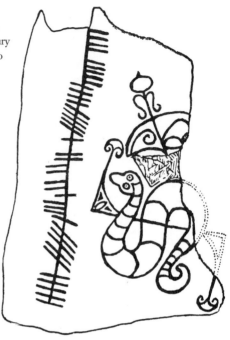

several centuries after active public use, at least in Ireland. By the High Middle Ages, however, many ogham inscriptions were already seemingly being 'neutralized' by the engraving of a Christian cross alongside. In the end, as with Germanic runes, the Church's monolithic Latin alphabet eventually outweighed the Celts' remarkable ogham writing.

THE SLAVONIC SCRIPTS

The two most important Slavonic alphabets are Cyrillic and Glagolitic (Croatian).[42] Tradition relates how King Rastislaw of Moravia wished to break free of the German-controlled Roman Church, and so asked the Byzantine Emperor for instructors who could preach in the vernacular. The Emperor sent two brothers: Constantine (later called Cyril) and Methodius. These two missionaries then broke with Roman tradition – which allowed scripture only in Hebrew, Greek and Latin – by effecting their own Old Church Slavonic translations of the Bible. In this way, the Cyrillic and Glagolitic scripts were 'created'.

The problem with this 'Constantine myth' is that it has *two* separate alphabets being 'created' at the same time to fit Slavonic needs. For a long time, it was unclear what script Cyril had traditionally been credited with 'inventing' in order to convey a Slavonic language 'for the first time'. Today, most scholars accept that Glagolitic is Cyril's adaptation – not his creation or elaboration – of an extant Slavonic script for Macedonian Slavonic.

Glagolitic has 40 letters, Cyrillic 43. Their phonetic values are nearly the same. The two scripts differ greatly in outward appearance. Perhaps this is because Cyrillic derives, but for a few extraneous letters, from Byzantine Greek uncials (capitals) of the late ninth century while Glagolitic derives from much earlier Byzantine Greek cursive letters. Apart from this purely external difference, however, the two scripts share an almost identical writing system. It appears that Cyrillic borrowed some of its letters from the earlier Glagolitic, as Glagolitic had been elaborated as early as the seventh century for reasons that are still unknown. In the 860s, Glagolitic was formalized and adapted by Constantine (St Cyril), who added certain letters to convey special Macedonian Slavonic sounds. These additional letters perhaps came from Armenian (for the consonants) and variant Greek forms (for the vowels). A generation later, in the 890s, Bulgarian disciples found St Cyril's Glagolitic script improper for ecclesiastical texts and chose Byzantine Greek uncial writing – then thought of as a more formal, dignified script – to write holy scriptures. The Cyrillic script was born. Only in later centuries were names attached to the two scripts: *glagólica* from *glagol* ('word', 'say') and *kiríllica* from Cyril, Constantine's adopted monastic name.

Glagolitic would originally have suited the contemporary Macedonian Slavonic language very well. After the ninth century, Glagolitic and Cyrillic existed side by side in Macedonia and Bulgaria (illus. 120). However, over the following centuries Cyrillic evidently caused the displacement of many original Glagolitic letters. In the 1100s, it became more dominant (illus. 121). Glagolitic's diffusion to Serbia and Bosnia had meant

120 Glagolitic script: Matthew 6:26–8 from the *Codex Zographensis*, late 10th–early 11th century.

many changes to accommodate dialectal differences. Digraphs and ligatures were introduced to convey Slavonic sounds that were missing from the borrowed Byzantine Greek alphabet. From the 1300s to the 1500s, Glagolitic found use in the liturgies of some Czech and Polish communities. After this, it diminished everywhere but Croatia, where, in the early 1800s, it took on a cursive form for official business in local administration. Today, Glagolitic survives as a liturgical script in many Roman Catholic dioceses in Dalmatia and Croatia where Slavonic (not Latin) has always been the liturgical language.

The Cyrillic script's homeland long remained Bulgaria, Serbia and Kievan Rus (illus. 122).[43] The 1700s saw major orthographic changes in the Russian form of Cyrillic writing, mainly to facilitate the printing of secular works in order to encourage greater literacy: simpler letter forms were standardized, and redundant Church variants were dropped.[44] The Great Reform of 1918, at the birth of the Soviet Union, completed the last of the major orthographic reforms, achieving the Cyrillic script that is used today in Russia and its sphere of influence, with only minor subsequent adjustments (illus. 123).

Cyrillic has become one of the world's great scripts and the bearer of a long and highly influential literary tradition. Experiencing many orthographic reforms which have caused

121 Old Bulgarian
Cyrillic inscription
from a column on the
Bjal-Brjag Church in
Preslav district,
eastern Bulgaria,
c. AD 1050.

ZHTKШHHT ZHPГ
ШYВШYΛЄXШYM
CTHKYПЄ:YNЄ:TШ
YΛCXH:ФM:ЄCTPШ
ГHNKYПЄ:YKZ:TШ
YΛCXH:ooNΔ:TШYPT
ШYNAПHΛЄZШПAN
ЄCTPYГHNKYПЄ:K:
TШYΛCXH:M:AΛXACH
KYПЄ:A:XΛШ YВPHⁿ·ᴬ·

enormous changes in its external appearance but not in its internal system, Cyrillic in time became the script of the majority of
Slavonic peoples. (Western Slavs and some Southern Slavs
either preserved or have re-introduced the Latin alphabet.)
Cyrillic writing was adopted by all Russians, Ukrainians,
Bulgarians and Serbs as the vehicle of the Greek Orthodox religion they all embraced. Thus, among these peoples Cyrillic
became the script of all learning (as had happened with the

Н ПОΝЄЖЇОΥ БШВЪЖΑΙΑΓΑΖЄΙΗ ΝΙCΖΙΠΗΤΔΠΓΑΛΗΝΙC
CΛΟΒΟΥ ΔΟБΡΟ ΓΖΠΑΒΛΑΗΝΟΥ ΠΕБЇΗΝΖΒΓΣΓΠΟΥΠΗΟΛ
ΝΗΝΟ ΗΖΛΟЖΗΝΟΥБΖΙΤΗ , ΙΑΓΗΟΙCΑΖΟΥΑЩЄ ΑΡΕΒΝΓΑ
CΛΟΒΙCΑ · ΝΙCΟΤΟΡΙΗΟ БΛΑΔΑШΑ ΗCΠΡΒΒΑ , ΗΔΑЖΙΑΟ
ΓΑΙ ΔΟΙΤΗΓΟШΑ · ΝΙCΟΤΟΡΙΗ ΥΡΤΒΟΒΑШΑ , ΗΔΑЖΙΑ
ΙCΙΑΗΙCΟΛΓΤΖ , ΙΖΙΟΥ БШВΖΙΠΡΙΕΜΑΙΝΖ ΠΑΓΟΙ
ΠΡΟΥΔΑΓΓΟ , ΑЧΗΝΝΖЖΑΝΟ ΔΓΛΟΗΠΡΟΥΑΝΟΗ · ΟΥΠ
ШΑЖΠБΖШΝΑШΑΑЖΙΒΖCΛΟΒΙΙΧΟΠΡЪΑΖΙ , ΒΕΛΗЧΙ
ΔΑΡΟΒΙΠΒΟΗ ΗΛΗБΟΥΠΗΕΠΒΙΕ · ΗΠΡΟΥΒΗΑΓΟΒΑΡΑ
ΗБΟΛΓΖΝΒΝΑΓΟ , ΔΑΡΟΒΕΠΡΟΧΛΑЖΔΑΛΠБ ΒΖΔΑΒΑΕ

122 Southern Slavonic manuscript (dated 1345) in the 'Polu-Ustáv', or Semi-
Ustáv, Cyrillic script that served as the main model for the first Slavonic
book-printing in the 1500s.

123 Modern Russian
Cyrillic: standard (above)
and italic (below) versions
of the same poem.

О любви рассказать я хотела—
Говорят: это частное дело.
Не согласна! Не стану таить!
Я считаю, любовь—это нить
Между сердцем моим и Отчизной.
Песнь любви—это здравица жизни!

О любви рассказать я хотела—
Говорят: это частное дело.
Не согласна! Не стану таить!
Я считаю, любовь—это нить
Между сердцем моим и Отчизной,
Песнь любви—это здравица жизни!

Latin script in Western Europe). With Russia's growing inter-national importance, Cyrillic was eventually recognized as the 'Russian alphabet'. It eventually replaced, at least officially, nearly all other scripts in the former Soviet Union, thus convey-ing, with varying degrees of adequacy, more than 60 different languages.

Since the collapse of the Soviet Union, a renewed interest among affected non-Slavs in writing their languages using the Arabic, Latin or some other script has become evident. This replacement script often manifests itself as the emblem of ethnic identity.

Several centuries before the Phoenicians' consonantal alphabet spread eastwards, it had diffused westwards because of age-old mercantile and cultural links between Levantines and Greeks. As a result, by the first century AD alphabetic writing had pene-trated wide regions of Western society, fulfilling most of the same functions that writing fulfils there today. No longer the sole franchise of élite accountants or powerful priests, literacy increased in prosperous centres to the point where writing now described the full range of human activity – from the most exalted (monumental and sacral inscriptions, revered prose and poetry) to the most mundane (personal letters, public signs, graffiti). By the fourth century AD, shops in Beirut's Byzantine market, for example, were identified by Greek alphabetic addresses written at their thresholds in mosaic tiles. With the

Greek alphabet in particular, writing had become an indispensable part of civilized society in most of the West. Indeed, writing had come to define, in most instances, what 'civilization' meant.

Because of its crucial role in Classical Greek society, writing has recently been proposed as having been responsible in some way for the development of the first democracies, since it early fostered general literacy. The 'Alphabet Effect' theory assumes an alphabet-inspired free West of reductionist thinkers and scientists, as opposed to the East's 'pictographic characters' that somehow produced holistic thinking. However appealing, this theory is fallacious on both points. An alphabet – be it Greek, Aramaic or Indic – has nothing to do with democracy. Widespread literacy of the scope needed for a democracy is a rather modern development that also exists in most undemocratic nations. Chinese characters might retard literacy, being so difficult to learn, but they do not prevent it. Perhaps most importantly, analytic thought is possible in any writing system, whether logographic, syllabic or alphabetic. Analytic thought is possible without writing. Society *as we know it* cannot exist without writing, granted. However, writing is an effect of society, not a cause.

The Greeks' vowelized alphabet did not change the way people thought. It did facilitate the way people wrote about what they thought. In this way, it fostered greater literacy, more discussion and thus more complex domains of thought. However, Greek writing did not spawn democracy, theoretical science or formal logic. It helped to preserve the thoughts of those who considered such things, and to train others to build upon these and similar ideas.

A great philosophical tradition also existed in China – without complete alphabetic writing. For writing in East Asia had taken a wholly different direction.

FIVE

The East Asian 'Regenesis'

Many scholars claim that the East Asian 'regenesis' of writing in the second millennium BC was an independent phenomenon. On the contrary, counter others – it was Western-inspired. The debate is an old one. The present Chinese government's cultural agenda may nourish the first explanation. However, the cumulative weight of accepted archæological evidence seems, at least at present, to suggest a Western inspiration. Complete writing never 'emerges from nowhere'. Either there is a protracted period of 'incomplete writing' that leads to complete writing, as happened in ancient Mesopotamia (see Chapter 1), or complete writing's sudden appearance signals a borrowing.

Had complete writing, similarly developed, appeared often in prehistory, the case for multiple origins of complete writing would perhaps be persuasive. However, the fact that it appears as the ultimate distillation of a long tradition of graphic mnemonics only in Mesopotamia – and from there, in local adaptations, gradually everywhere else, with the furthest regions displaying the most recent writing – encourages, many believe, the acknowledgement of the very slow diffusion of complete writing throughout the world. Having been practised in Mesopotamia and points east for some two thousand years, the idea of complete writing apparently diffused from there to north-central China, where, due to the demands of the Chinese language, writing went on to assume its unique East Asian cast.

Once developed, Chinese writing became the main vehicle for the transmission of Chinese culture throughout East Asia. Unopposed by any other form of writing, both the Chinese writing system and its *hànzi* script – the 'characters' or sinograms also known as Korean *hanja* and Japanese *kanji* – were borrowed wholesale for conveying languages so different from

Chinese as to make their reading not merely laborious but equivocal. In time, local adaptations emerged. Two of these adaptations produced systemic extremes the likes of which the world had never seen. Korea's Hankul writing is probably history's most efficient method for reproducing human speech. In contrast, Japan's two writing systems that make use of three scripts written together following arbitrary rules perhaps embody the most complicated form of writing ever devised.

Because of its regional supremacy, Chinese writing has sometimes been called the 'Latin of the Far East'. It is true that Buddhism and its Chinese language and script fulfilled in East Asia the same sort of role that Christianity and its Latin language and script did in Western Europe at about the same period. As we have seen (Chapter 4), Latin's diffusion provided the vehicle for Christianity for non-Roman Germans, Celts and other peoples. Likewise, Buddhism and its Chinese-language writings spread among non-Chinese Japanese, Koreans, Vietnamese and others. But Rome crumbled, whereas China grew more puissant until Chinese language and writing permeated East Asia. Here, Chinese language and writing were more than a past ideal, as Latin had become in the West. They were culture itself.

All East Asian writing commences, then, with Chinese writing. Chinese writing's influence, and many of its *hànzi*, its characters, live on nearly two thousand years after their borrowing by non-Chinese, despite many adaptations and subsequent changes. The history of East Asian writing is the glory of Chinese writing – and the agony of its conversion by culturally constrained peoples who, for better or worse, sometimes spoke languages Chinese writing could ill convey.

CHINESE WRITING

Oldest of all East Asian writing systems, Chinese writing seems indeed, at first blush, to have 'emerged from nowhere'.[1] Having appeared in north-central China in the second half of the second millennium BC already nearly fully developed, it became not only East Asia's most important form of writing but also humankind's principle medium of written expression. One scholar has estimated that until the middle of the 1700s AD, more books had been published in Chinese than in all other languages of the world put together.[2] Chinese writing has been in continuous use for well over three thousand years, with very little change to its system (but with great changes in the shape of individual *hànzi*, or characters). It has been, and continues to be, one of the world's greatest cultural vehicles.

The earliest Chinese writing comprises divinatory oracles on ox scapulæ (shoulder blades) and turtle plastrons (the under part of the shell or armour) dating from perhaps as early as 1400 BC during the formation of the Shang Dynasty, China's first attested civilization (illus. 124). A cache of 21 such 'oracle bones' was discovered as recently as 1971 near modern Anyang on Henan's northern border. Many scholars assume from the conventionalized appearance of China's earliest inscriptions that Chinese writing must have experienced a protracted local development. A few believe that evidence for this assumed development lies in Chinese pottery fragments, some dating from as early as 4800 BC, that bear incised marks of some kind.[3] However, these marks bear no formal resemblance to later Shang characters, so most Western scholars, at least, do not accept them as evidence of Chinese 'incomplete writing' leading to complete writing.

Others regard the sudden emergence of nearly fully developed writing in north-central China around 1400 BC as the primary argument for a cultural borrowing. As with ancient Egypt, China's 'missing developmental stage' in writing suggests a foreign prototype. This argument is persuasive, since it is the most economical one. The earliest Chinese inscriptions display the characteristic writing in columns, reading from top to bottom and from right to left, that distinguishes inscriptions on the reverse sides of Mesopotamian monuments (until about 1500 BC). Chinese writing also incorporates the Mesopotamian principle of one sign for one spoken syllable – in early Chinese writing, this was a non-standardized logosyllabary – as well as the rebus principle. Given the breadth of writing's possible manifestations, these multiple fundamental similarities surely should not be attributed to coincidence. In both generality and speci-

ficity, a mid-second-millennium-BC borrowing of Mesopotamian writing – that is, its principles and orientation – is
indicated. (Already in the early 1900s, scholars were claiming
that Chinese writing had been inspired by a Mesopotamian prototype.)[4] However, a Mesopotamian borrowing is not proven.
The signs of the earliest Chinese system conveyed, in rebus
fashion, only the Chinese language, and were themselves certainly never part of any importation. If a borrowing did occur,
then from its onset Chinese writing – like that of ancient Egypt,
the Ægean and Easter Island – wore a native cloak over a foreign frame.

The original form of Chinese writing was the *wén*, or 'unit
character'. As in Mesopotamia and Egypt, a simple sketch of a
known object prompted its pronunication. As ancient Egyptian
was a polysyllabic language, it had used the rebus principle to
compose discrete sounds in order to make up a whole word

124 Chinese 'oracle-bone' inscription (*c.* 1200 BC)
discovered near Anyang in Henan.

from several hieroglyphs (see Chapter 2). In monosyllabic ancient Chinese, however, a syllable was a *wén* that, in most cases, was already a complete word. Homophony allowed lexical expansion, whereby one pronunication then included several different ancient Chinese words. The converse, polyphony, also obtained; semantically related words were conveyed with one *wén*. For example, the 'mouth' *wén* could be used to mean 'to call out'. Both homophony and polyphony imbued early Chinese writing with 'graphic multivalence' – single *wén* with different values depending on their contextual use. This introduced great versatility into early Chinese writing.[5]

However, it also created ambiguity. The system was too loose, since context alone is insufficient to identify which reading of a *wén* is correct. In Shang Dynasty writing, there was also no standardized set of *wén*, but rather a wide variation in shapes and values. This, too, evidences a system only recently elaborated. With north-central China's rapidly centralizing society, in need of standardization once writing's requirements and potentials had been recognized, the correction of writing's ambiguity was discovered to lie in converting *wén* into compound characters.

Of the more than 2,500 *wén* in use *c.* 1200 BC – already being written with brush and ink – some fourteen hundred are identifiable as the source of later standard Chinese characters (illus. 125).[6] Shang writing remained logosyllabic, with one character conveying one word – or single monosyllabic morpheme. (A morpheme is a linguistic unit that conveys a meaning and that is not decomposable into further meaningful forms; English *writing*, for example, contains the morphemes *write* and *-ing*.) In this way, each Shang character is a logogram. There were two types of logograms in the Shang system. First, there was the *wén*, perceived, as we have seen, to permit too much ambiguity. Then, there was the problem's solution: the *zì*, or compound character, comprising two or more *wén* joined together as one sign. Herein lies the unique feature of Chinese writing. A 'phonetic' (sound identifier) or a 'signific' (sense identifier, like the Egyptian determinative but different in that it cannot stand alone) can be attached to the *wén* to help identify which word in the language is meant. The compound *zì* character is thus a

	Swamp	Fire	Thunder	Wind	Water	Mountain	Earth	Sky
1400–800 BC								
UNTIL 800 BC								
800–220 BC								
UNTIL 209 BC								
UNTIL 200 BC								
200 BC – AD 200								
c. AD 100								
c. AD 400								

125 Development of some important Shang Dynasty characters in derivative scripts.

combination of a *wén* and one of these two identifiers.

By compounding in this way, Chinese writing could express the full range of Chinese speech. Any character, no matter how complex, conveyed a single syllable that, it appears, stood for a single word. A few characters always stood for the same word, but most offered several possibilities.

However, just as with the *wén*, scribes soon gave compound *zì* characters multiple meanings and multiple sounds. Once the compounds were themselves compounded, a third level of complexity was added to the system. A solution to this new problem was to add more character components to a sign in order to identify its meaning and/or sound. (In this way, as many as six character components can now occur in one common Chinese sign – such as *yù* for 'worried', composed of six individual components. And even more than six occur in uncommon or specialist characters.)

Early Chinese writing was fairly transparent: one could generally recognize and pronounce the simple characters. In its earliest days, the system essentially represented an incomplete phonography that added significs (sense identifiers) to lessen ambiguity. But spoken Chinese changed over the centuries. Phonetics were no longer consistent, so more significs had to be added. The result was the loss of phonographic status: the relationship between the morphemes in the language and characters in the writing system was no longer transparent. In this way, Chinese writing became fully logographic (sense and sound, but mostly sound).

The logographic, or 'word-writing', nature of Chinese writing dominates the system, reproducing units of spoken Chinese. Characters convey words, not ideas or concrete objects. British philosopher Bertrand Russell once thought Chinese characters were 'ideographic', believing each 'represents an idea'.[7] This is incorrect. Chinese characters, as whole units or blocks of components, are words – or single monosyllabic morphemes – in the Chinese language, and nothing else.

Though Chinese writing is primarily syllabic, it is not a syllabic writing system due to the fact that most characters possess a signific (sense identifier). For this reason, Chinese writing has been termed 'morpheme-syllable writing', which is perhaps the best definition of the system's unique place in the world of writing.[8] Linguistically speaking, then, Chinese characters are 'morpho-syllabograms' – syllables reproducing morphemes (of which a small part, like the numerals, can be ideograms, a subset of the system). Each character is two in one: a morpheme and a syllable in which this morpheme is conveyed. There are far more characters in Chinese writing than syllables in the Chinese language, but about an equal number of morphemes. Since a person can hold only a limited number of characters in her or his mind, the syllabic component dominates. Still, sound transmission remains vague, unable to provide exact reproduction in many instances.

Like all writing systems, the Chinese thus harbours its own weaknesses. Semantic-phonetic compounds reveal a great and contradictory variety of usage: there remains no standard and consistent marking to indicate which element of a *zì* is the sense and which is the sound, either graphically or positionally. The roles of each vary, too. For example, some phonetics hold consistent syllable and tone, some vary tone, and some vary syllable and tone both. Significs are equally variable.

Whatever their values, both phonetic and signific are apparently read in the same instant by an educated Chinese adult. Less expert readers search either the first or the second for an initial clue to the correct reading. Because of this, there are two ways of reading Chinese: instantaneous 'whole-word' reading, and inductive semantic-phonetic combining. Most Chinese come to read in 'whole-word' fashion, as we do in English once we have mastered the basics and internalized the exceptions. Significs actually play a restricted role in the sense decoding of Chinese characters; phonetics are much more important in the reading process.[9] In fact, 'the phonetic element is far superior in predicting pronunciation than is the semantic element in predicting meaning.'[10] However, phonetic and signific together hold a unique 'visual key', it appears, to memorized sound and sense.

This is why it seems more appropriate to call Chinese signs 'characters'. 'Sign' reflects unity, whereas 'character' signals combinatorial flexibility (as in Mayan glyphs and Easter Island's *rongorongo*). Each Chinese character expresses the dynamics of one or more sense signs joined together with one or more sound signs, each component of their compounding to be read in any number of ways, as is the final product. Only a character, never a sign, achieves such a multi-dimensional performance.

Each Chinese character has to be learnt individually, too, as one individually learns words in a language. There are several clues to pronunciation and meaning – phonetic, signific, context and so forth – but there is no predictability. Unlike an alphabet, which provides a key to the unlimited 'opening up' of a lexicon, each Chinese morpheme-syllable is 'encoded' in the writing system and requires an individual unlocking process. The process actually appears to activate regions of the human brain different from those used by alphabetic readers (see below).

The Western Zhou Dynasty (1028–771 BC) initially brought forth a few oracle texts, but then only inscriptions on bronze

126 The *Shuo-wén* was a standardized chancellery script used chiefly around the middle of the first millennium BC; this inscription dates from the Qin Dynasty (221–206 BC).

vessels cast in clay using the lost-wax technique. The shape of the characters, later designated as the 'Great Seal Script', differed from those of the Shang Dynasty, principally because of the use of soft wax for casting. The rounded shapes were later copied on bamboo, silk and wood using ink and brush. Over the centuries, this, together with the effects of political disunity – many different scribes were using different languages and writing conventions – created a great range of regional and textual script forms (illus. 126). However, the writing system itself remained the same, despite great script variation.[11]

By the third century BC, the accumulated orthographic differences were preventing universal legibility. Qin Shi Huang-di, first Emperor of a unified China, recognized writing's usefulness in uniting disparate peoples and exploited it as a tool for political power. The Qin Empire, during its administrative and military articulation of the Middle Kingdom, chose the standardization of Chinese writing as a main vehicle to achieve its aims. During the Great Writing Reform of 221 BC, Qin's grand councillor Li Su simplified the Great Seal Script, which now became the new standard Small Seal Script, the ancient world's greatest effort at a conscious script reform intended to

127 Reading from right to left, each of the double columns holds one of the six main types of traditional Chinese writing.

effect political and social centralization. The immediate success of the latter process lay primarily in the terrifying omnipotence of the new Qin regime. It also heralded the most important demarcation in the history of Chinese writing, as Li Su's Small Seal Script engendered all subsequent Chinese scripts.

The Qin Empire soon crumbled, however. During the Han Dynasty (202 BC–AD 220), orthographic variation continued. There were many forms of writing in use: archaic Small Seal and the various clerical scripts, as well as the three styles for calligraphic writing (regular, running and cursive). These are all still in use today (illus. 127). A new trend began, standardizing syllabograms that ignored significs (the sense identifiers); this might have developed into a syllabary and then into a complete syllabic system. But scholars soon insisted on a more conscientious emphasis of each *zi*'s signific; indeed, significs become the essential part of each *zi*.

A major orthographic standardization of Chinese occurred *c*. AD 120 with the completion by Xu Shèn of his famous *Shuō wén jiě zì* ('Explaining *wén*, Analyzing *zì*'). Here, Xu Shèn established the differences between the *wén* unit characters and the *zì* compound characters; identified 540 different graphic elements (significs or semantic classifiers), yielding a basis for semantic

128 Xu Shèn's *liù shu*, or 'six writings'.

classification of each character, no matter how complex; and assigned each Chinese character to one of six (four graphic, two usage) different classes.

Xu Shèn's *liù shu*, or 'six writings', of characters best illustrate how Chinese characters are composed (illus. 128). The first class is pictographic: 'tree', 'sun' and so forth. The second class is symbolic (or ideographic), like the numerals 'one', 'two', 'three'. The third class is the compound analytic, such as 'tree' plus 'sun' yielding 'east'. The fourth class comprises the phonetic loan or rebus, as seen in *lai*, or 'a kind of wheat', which is also used for 'to come' since it was once homophonous (pronounced the same). The fifth and most important class includes the semantic-phonetic compounds – that is, characters that have a signific for sense and phonetic for sound: 'sugar' is written with the classifier 'cereal' and the phonetic *táng*. The sixth class contains *chuan chù*, or 'mutually interpretative symbols', whereby a character conveys a word of the identical or similar meaning but with a different pronunication: for example, the *yuè* character for 'music' could also be used to convey *lè*, or 'pleasure'. Whereas class five embraces some 90 per cent of all Chinese characters, class six is found in only one out of two thousand.

Xu Shèn himself used Li Su's Small Seal Script as the basis of his writing, but this failed to become China's everyday script. In later centuries, the Small Seal changed into the *lì shū*, or 'clerical script', which was widely used for official business. It was actually the *lì shū* that served as the prototype for all subsequent forms of Chinese writing.

The number of Chinese characters has grown tremendously over the millennia. Shang Dynasty inscriptions can tally a bit over 2,500 characters. Xu's dictionary from *c.* AD 120 contains 9,353 characters. By the 1100s, there were about 23,000 characters in use. The Qing Dynasty's *Kāng Xī Character Dictionary* of 1716, still the standard authority for Classical Chinese literature, lists more than 47,000 characters. And the most recent Chinese dictionary (1986–90) of single characters lists some 60,000. It has been claimed that all the Chinese characters that have ever existed – disregarding those of varying scripts – might amount to as many as 80,000.[12] This is because Chinese writing is 'open-ended': each new word in the language automatically requires a new grapheme in the system. And Chinese has had over three thousand years to collect new words. (In contrast, a 'closed' alphabetic system, like the one underlying the Latin script, can phonetically reproduce every new word with a very small inventory of letters.)

All the same, the number of active characters – in contrast to passive characters – amounts to only about one-tenth of all in current existence. And only about a third of active characters are recognizable to everyone. This is because the active command of individual Chinese readers appears to lie, on average, between 2,000 and 2,500 characters. So most characters listed in a Chinese dictionary are rarely, if ever, used.

The physical manner of writing Chinese also requires special mention, as this, too, differs from what we know about writing elsewhere in the world. For well over two thousand years, the Chinese have followed a fixed convention of writing each character, despite its complexity, in the same size square, sometimes called *fāngkuàizì*, or 'tetragrams'.[13] Until recently, all Chinese texts were written in columns that read from top to bottom and from right to left, with no word separation or punctuation (illus. 129); only in the 1900s did Chinese punctuation become common, though still not standardized. Now many published

129 The world's earliest preserved printed book: the five-m-long and 30-cm-wide Buddhist *Diamond Sutra* in Chinese translation, AD 868.

texts also appear in horizontal lines reading from left to right after the fashion of modern Latin-derived scripts.

The earliest Chinese writing was done with brush and ink on bark, bamboo strips, wood and other materials, as well as incised in ivory, ox scapulæ and turtle plastrons, or drawn in soft wax for bronze castings. Silk as a writing material became common at the time of the Eastern Han (AD 25–220) for compositions, official documents and correspondence. However, silk was expensive, so its use was limited. By the first century AD or so, old silk was being pulped and the gelatinous result spread thinly over frame containers to dry, yielding a serviceable writing substance. This process was probably the one first described by the eunuch Cai Lun at the Han emperor Wu Di's court in AD 105, only one of many experiments taking place in China at the time in order to create an inexpensive writing material.[14] It heralded the appearance of what was eventually to become the world's most useful and commonplace writing material: paper. Cai Lun's invention, allegedly far cheaper than silk, was made of old rags, fishing nets and tree bark, as contemporaries commented. Modern botanists who have examined China's oldest surviving paper, from the second century AD, have determined it to be a composite of rags and raw fibres (laurel, mulberry and Chinese grass). Until the 700s, paper manufacturing remained a state

蕩料入簾

monopoly and its technique a closely guarded secret (illus. 130), knowledge of it having diffused only as far as Turkestan.

When writing Chinese characters, the writer must follow the prescribed number of strokes (between one and 25) for each, in a given order and with a specified starting point for each stroke. There are eight basic strokes (though calligraphers note as many as 64). All characters contain one or more of these. The stroke numbering, ordering and orienting are not done merely for æsthetics – they also help to organize each character within a group of similarly learnt characters for later mental retrieval. Such mnemonic devices are necessary in a writing system that involves complicated semantic-phonetic characters reproducing each morpheme-syllable of the language.

Calligraphy, the art of beautiful writing, has always been

131 The Chinese calligrapher's gnome *Jīn shēng li shui*, or 'Gold can be found in Lishui', written, from left to right, in the traditional scripts: Small Seal, Scribal, Regular, Running and Cursive.

important to the Chinese. (Most Western curricula, in comparison, dropped 'penmanship' in the last quarter of the 1900s.) A Chinese person understands calligraphy to *be* writing, not its refinement or commercial exploitation. In past centuries, calligraphy was equal in importance to music, painting and poetry. Indeed, great calligraphers often held higher eminence in Chinese society than the country's best painters or poets.

Calligraphers need an assortment of brushes, paper, a paperweight, an inkstone, an inkstick and a small bowl of water. Brushes consist of the hairs of marten, goat or hare: those of autumnal wild marten offer prompt pressure responses that yield the loveliest character lines, it is alleged. Expert scribes could tell which animal's hair was used according to the vivacity of the strokes. With Chinese writing, one still perceives a miniature work of art in the individual character, each an expression of the calligrapher's education, skill and artistry (illus. 131). Whereas Western alphabets are almost entirely functional, Chinese logograms by their very nature are functional and artistic at the same time. Writers of Arabic can perhaps best identify with this – though their consonantal alphabet lacks the same breadth of artistic potential – in a way that is impossible for a writer of a Greek- or Latin-derived alphabetic script to fully appreciate.

Nevertheless, Chinese writing remains imprecise, as neither the phonetic nor the signific component of a compound *zì* provides an exact indication of sense or sound but only an approximation. As Victor Mair has observed, 'Readers [of Chinese] must guess or memorize the appropriate sound of the phonetic for each character in which it occurs; they must also associate the graph with a word that they already know. Only then can they arrive at the meaning of the sinogram [character] in question.'[15] Some phonetic components have as many as a dozen different pronunciations, each determined by the character in which it is found. There are also many possible pronunciations for one character (that is, multiple meanings), and many characters for one pronunciation. This multivalence was not always a feature of Chinese writing. Often, what one finds today is the result of convergent phonology over the centuries – the Chinese language itself changed, producing superficially identical features that were once historically distinct.

Chinese writing may be morpheme-syllable writing, but there are still many polysyllabic words, even in the artificial Classical or literary written language. Here, sound prevails over sense, despite logography. (In modern Mandarin Chinese, for example, the average length of a word is two syllables in contrast to the predominant monosyllabic nature of Old Chinese.) So are two characters needed to write one word, as one would expect in such a case? On the contrary. The characters remain monosyllabic but are pronounced polysyllabically, as seen in the single-characters *qiānwa* 'kilowatt', *túshūguan* 'library', and *wèntí* 'question'.

Classical Chinese works well with this system, but not the vernacular Chinese languages and regional variants (the Chinese dialects). There are no proper conventions here for conveying anything but Literary Chinese. Mair again: 'Still today, and even for Pekingese (which is the current foundation for Mandarin, the lingua franca), authors complain that it is impossible to write out all their favourite expressions in characters.'[16] This is because many of the most frequently used morphemes in the eight major Chinese languages are not represented in the standard set of 60,000 characters. To write languages like Cantonese or Taiwanese, one has two recourses: invent ad hoc characters, or use the Latin script. (Since the late 1800s, the latter has been an increasingly preferred alternative.) At present, there is a great chasm between written and spoken Chinese. Though Chinese writing, in both system and script, has remained remarkably stable over the past two thousand years, the spoken Chinese languages, as living entities, have changed dramatically. What is written today does not often reflect what is spoken – just as we find in English with such words as *light* and *enough* – by reason of impermanent language conveyed through a permanent orthography.

Reform of Chinese writing, to counter such divergence, is nothing new. We have already heard of the thwarted attempt nearly two thousand years ago to convert Chinese into a syllabic writing system. Since the 1100s, Chinese scholars have also been aware of phonetic writing.[17] However, two main factors have prohibited a system switch: cultural conservatism (which attends all writing systems), and personal attachment to Chinese characters (perceived 'ethnic identity'). Initial moves towards romanization occurred around the end of the Ming Dynasty (1368–1662) with the arrival of Jesuit priests in China: various schemes were proposed as missionaries used Latin-derived scripts to convey Christian texts in previously unwritten regional varieties of Chinese.

Near the end of the 1800s, mounting protests against the Manchu government and its policies led to a concentrated drive to reform all Chinese culture. Many phonetic proposals for Chinese writing were put forth to make China 'wealthy and strong', as was then proclaimed. The fall of the Manchu regime in 1911 saw the new Republican government replace Classical Chinese with Mandarin as China's official written language. A National Phonetic Alphabet (NPA) was disseminated in 1913 which aided in the diffusion of the Mandarin tongue; the NPA is still used in Taiwan as a sound-affixing technique to Chinese characters.

The founding of the Communist People's Republic of China

in 1949 brought two major thrusts to a writing reform: more romanization, and drastic simplification of the Chinese characters. Romanization of Chinese has long been a particularly contentious issue, as it is commonly perceived as a foreign intrusion. Though the Wade-Giles system has been the most common method of romanizing Chinese in the West, the People's Republic pushed the Pinyin system (from Chinese *pīnyīn*, or 'spell-sound'). This is because one of Mao Zedong's principal social plans, announced already in the 1930s, comprised the indigenous romanization of China's writing system. Mao felt that China was suffering too acutely from illiteracy: its traditional writing system was simply too difficult for many to learn in an adequate amount of time. (It is estimated that Chinese and Japanese pupils need an additional three years or more of schooling to achieve the same level of reading competence as their Western counterparts.) However, implementation of Pinyin was halted by scholars – as had happened nearly two thousand years earlier with the proposed syllabary.

So Mao offered a compromise solution: the simplification of Chinese characters. Simplification was a practice that had been observed for many centuries. However, under Mao, who eventually introduced the Simplified Script throughout all of China in 1955 (though most Chinese still continued to write in Regular cursives), it was taken to unprecedented lengths – eliminating nearly all alloglyphs (redundant characters) and drastically reducing stroke numbers in most of what remained. In many cases, traditional characters have been reduced to unidentifiable derivatives. Most mainland Chinese can no longer read the older, more complicated forms of Literary Chinese. And Taiwanese Chinese find it difficult to read the mainland's Simplified Script (illus. 132).

In 1958, over the continued objections of scholars, Mao proceeded to implement Pinyin, the Latin script used today as the official system for writing Chinese sounds and transcribing Chinese characters. The system also became the official way to spell all Chinese names overseas – which explains why, at the end of the 1900s, Peking became Beijing. However, during the Cultural Revolution of the late 1960s, Pinyin was held to be foreign contamination, and Red Guards destroyed any display of

132 (Above) from a mainland Chinese newspaper printed horizontally in the new Simplified Script, reading from left to right; (below) from a Taiwanese newspaper printed in traditional fashion – vertical columns of standard Chinese characters that read from top to bottom and from right to left.

the script. For many years, the Chinese remained confused as to which of the three forms of writing they were to use.

At the beginning of the 2000s, the confusion remains. The Simplified Script is still new and difficult to learn, while the traditional Standard Script appears archaic and impractical in the modern world. Pinyin is now the official script for elementary education (along with the Simplified Script), road signs, maps, fashionable stores and restaurants, brand names, Chinese Braille, telegraphy and, perhaps more significantly, computer input, as well as other uses. The Chinese people's confusion over their writing cannot be allowed to continue too long. 'A whole generation, both of people and of time, has been uselessly sacrificed in a timid, bumbling, and predictably unsuccessful attempt to achieve mass literacy through the simplication of characters.'[18]

Seemingly by default, then, China has officially adopted a policy of digraphia, whereby the Simplified Script and Pinyin are used complementarily. Pinyin is now generally regarded as the standard form of romanization for Mandarin. Whether this will lead to its eventual use as a full-fledged writing system and script in China is still unknown. Schoolchildren seem to be learning Pinyin much more quickly than the Simplified Script. Some scholars predict that if this practice continues, it may lead to Pinyin one day replacing the traditional characters altogether, but for a small literate élite engaged in classical studies.

Two new pressures have been imposed on Chinese writing that now force a decision: electronic word-processing, and foreign words and names. Perhaps surprisingly, the first is less consequential than the second, as one can now successfully process Chinese characters without recourse to Pinyin. Foreign words and names pose the real threat. China has always resisted outside influences, having created a social structure that is at once monolithic and uncompromising, as reflected in its writing system: Chinese writing is virtually closed to non-Chinese elements. Should a writer of Chinese wish to write a foreign word or name (which is achieved in rebus fashion, phonetically), then she or he must usually write as many characters as an entire Chinese sentence. This is impractical, and cannot continue. For foreign words and names are now, as a result of the new global society, flooding the Chinese lexicons.

To someone who knows the Chinese and their writing system intimately, it does not seem likely that phonographic writing, such as Pinyin, could ever successfully replace Chinese logographic writing altogether, at least not as the nation's normal writing system and script. Chinese logography has developed many mechanisms for eliminating ambiguities which a phonography could seldom resolve with the same convenience. And Chinese society will perhaps forever embrace its traditional *hànzi* as the most readily visual expression of Chinese cultural identity. However, as more important factors than systemic efficiency or ethnic identity determine the history of writing, the future of Chinese writing lies open.

VIETNAMESE WRITING

Vietnamese (or Annamese) belongs to the Mon-Khmer group of the Austro-Asiatic family of languages. For more than a thousand years – from 111 BC to AD 939 – Vietnam was ruled by China, and so Literary Chinese, first introduced there in AD 186, was likewise Vietnam's written language. Two traditions existed side by side: written Chinese and oral Vietnamese, the latter preserving its ancient literature unabated. Only centuries after Chinese domination ended did two distinct but related traditions of writing Vietnamese develop using Chinese characters.[19] Both Vietnam's *chū nôm*, or 'southern script', first attested in AD 1343, and the *chū Hán*, or 'Han (Chinese) script', took advantage of the fact that the Old Vietnamese language closely resembled ancient Chinese. Borrowing Chinese writing to convey Old Vietnamese thus presented few problems.

The *chū nôm* was derived directly from Literary Chinese. However, the *chū Hán* modified the Chinese script in order to create a more indigenous statement; this modified script is foremost preserved in inscriptions postdating the 1300s.[20] Both the *chū nôm* and *chū Hán* adapted Chinese characters in the same three ways (repeating what Koreans and Japanese had done centuries earlier; see below). First, a Chinese *wén* (unit character) or *zì* (compound character) would convey the same sound in

Vietnamese. Second, a Chinese *wén* or *zì* would be awarded a different Vietnamese meaning. And third, a new *zì* would be created in Vietnamese using standard Chinese methods.

In the 1600s, the Jesuit scholar Alexandre de Rhodes (1591–1660) codified a Latin-derived alphabet for conveying the Vietnamese language. This romanization was then introduced to Vietnam by Portuguese missionaries who used it in their grammars, dictionaries and Christian publications in the Vietnamese language. The alphabetic script was ignored by Vietnamese scholars, however, who regarded it as a foreign intrusion. They clung primarily to the *chū nôm* as an emblem of Vietnamese identity and independence.

France's violent annexation of Vietnam in 1883, with its subsequent 'Europeanization', also involved writing. In 1910, by official decree, France replaced the two indigenous Vietnamese scripts with the missionaries' Western alphabet. Today's *quoc-ngu*, or 'national language', as this Western alphabetic script has come to be called, is still Vietnam's official script. It makes use of diacritics to indicate vowel quality and/or to mark one of the six tones of the Hanoi dialect of Vietnamese, the nation's standard dialect. For the moment, a return to traditional *chū nôm* writing seems unlikely.

KOREAN WRITING

In the 1400s AD, King Seycong of Korea declared that his country's Chinese-based way of writing was 'too complicated, imperfect, and inconvenient a system for the Koreans to use freely in expressing their own ideas and thinking, because too many *hanja* [Chinese characters] are involved in it. Koreans are in great need of their own letters with which they can write the Korean language.'[21] Seycong's proposed replacement of Chinese-based writing, Korea's unique Hankul, eventually came to represent the most efficient system ever devised in the history of writing. (This discussion follows the Yale transliteration of Korean.)

Han Emperor Wu Di, the same ruler for whom paper had been invented, had conquered most of Korea in AD 108 and then implemented a policy of Chinese settlement. Chinese culture, religion, language and writing soon engulfed the country. Although China quickly lost northern Korea, Chinese culture remained firmly rooted in south-western Korea, where it blossomed. The earliest evidence of writing the Korean language using *hanja*, or Chinese characters, is a stone inscription from AD 414.[22] Chinese-language annals of the seventh century conveyed Korean proper names and terms without Chinese equivalents. Korean scribes employed two methods to write these: a *hanja* was used only for its Chinese sound, or a *hanja* was used for its meaning but pronounced in Old Korean. The scribes then began writing in Old Korean syntax – the significant sequencing of phrases and sentences – creating the official chancellery script, or *itwu* ('clerk readings'), which conveyed everyday official tasks, by the end of the seventh century.

In type and syntax, the Old Korean language could not have been further from Literary Chinese. Old Korean was an agglutinating language (Chinese an isolating language), whereby each word could also consist of polysyllabic root morphemes that needed a wide range of suffixal morphemes to show grammar. (This had been Akkadian's problem, too, when it had borrowed Sumerian writing; see Chapter 2.) In addition, Old Korean's syntax placed the verb at the end of statements, with 'postpositions' (not prepositions) after the word being governed. Despite these differences, Chinese writing, the only writing the Koreans knew, came to convey the Old Korean language. It was an unfortunate turn.

Itwu used a limited set of *hanja* to express Korean grammatical morphemes; lexical ones (non-grammatical words) continued to be written using the full inventory of *hanja*. (In this way, *itwu* was very similar to Japan's system.) This of course produced unwanted complexity and ambiguity, since the grammatical parts were indistinguishable from the lexical parts. In addition, the number of *hanja* used as individual syllables soon grew unwieldy. In time, the Koreans also wrote *hanja* using the *hyangchal* method (the latter greatly resembles Old Japanese *manyōgana*, which it probably inspired; see below). Here, Chinese lexical stems (sense) were read in the Old Korean language, while suffixes and grammatical particles (sound) were read in Sino-Korean. Still, Korean writing was too imprecise and ambiguous to convey the Old Korean language with the ease and efficiency with which Chinese writing could convey Literary Chinese.

In the 1200s and 1300s, many of the grammatical characters were simplified in order to set them apart graphically from *hanja* so that the reader could easily recognize them. This new set of grammatical characters was called *kwukyel*. It used abbreviated *hanja* in a system much like Japan's *kana*, and it, too, annotated Chinese texts.

The Koreans always realized that Chinese writing poorly conveyed their polysyllabic, agglutinative language. They also continued to resist Chinese domination and to express the Korean franchise, which was difficult so long as Koreans wrote in Chinese characters. Already in AD 690, the court of King Sinmum was writing Korean syllabically, inspired perhaps by Buddhist Devanagari texts. However, the 36 syllabograms were difficult to distinguish from Chinese characters; over time, an increase of syllabogram numbers complicated the system. By the High Middle Ages, new social pressures in Korea were forcing a reassessment of the country's writing needs. It was at this time, too, in the 1200s, that history's first serious exploitation of the Chinese invention of printing with movable type occurred in Korea.[23] In 1403, Korean printers were already printing with movable metal type (a full generation before Gutenberg in Germany). Such technological progress apparently caused Korean scholars to appreciate the unnecessary complexity their indigenous writing system and scripts posed – besides their obvious incompatability with the Korean language, they were too cumbersome for the new technology. They also hindered the exploitation of printing's perceived potential. 'Self-organized criticality' had evidently been reached. An effective writing revolution was the result, producing 'one of the most scientifically designed and efficient scripts in the world'.[24]

King Seycong, who ruled Korea from 1419 to 1450, is traditionally credited with the creation of the country's radically new writing system and script. However, the King's true role within his Bureau of Standard Sounds – whether inventor, manager or figurehead – still remains unclear. The new system and script were completed around January 1444, then promulgated two years later in Seycong's edict *The Standard Sounds for the Instruction of the People*. Irritated by the perceived desecration of traditional writing, Korean scholars dubbed the new script *onmun*, or 'sound-writing', a denigrating name that stuck until the name Hankul was coined in the early 1900s.

The inspiration, or inspirations, for the new system and script are obscure. Scholars sometimes point to the Mongols, who were using two alphabetic scripts at this time, Phags-pa and adapted Uighur. Others have suggested immediate access to a simple Latin-derived alphabet, implying a European influence. There is little doubt that Seycong and his scholars were acquainted with Indic's *abudiga* principle (consonant + vowel as diacritic), probably through Buddhist scriptures; it is also possible that a Western alphabet was known to them. Hankul's alpha-syllabic system is very similar to the *abudiga*, and some letter-shapes superficially resemble Mongolian Phags-pa.[25] (In turn, it is possible that Hankul writing later influenced the Manchurian scholars who adopted the Mongolian system for Manchurian.)[26] However, the system itself clearly did not originate with Phags-pa or any other segmental system. For Hankul is the world's only *featural* writing system – that is, one capable of reproducing the basic distinguishing features of its host language. There is no precedent for this. (Hankul's script, on the other hand, not its system, appears to be a drastic reduction and simplification of inherited Chinese *hanja*.) Hankul is the result, then, not of protracted and discrete adaptations of a borrowed system, but of deliberate, linguistically founded invention.[27] However, its capacity to achieve featural linguistic integrity places it in a separate dimension altogether from such Western-inspired 'inventions' as the Cherokee syllabary or Easter Island script.

At first glance, Hankul does indeed seem to be an 'alphabetic syllabary', as one scholar has called it (illus. 133).[28] But it is far more than this. It is alphabetic in that individual letters convey consonants and vowels, sharing equal status (a complete alphabet). However, these letters are then written together to form syllabic 'blocks', in pseudo-Chinese fashion. One of the most remarkable aspects of Hankul is that the shape of each letter

		ㅏ	ㅑ	ㅓ	ㅕ	ㅗ	ㅛ	ㅜ	ㅠ	―	ㅣ
		a	ya	eo	yeo	o	yo	u	yu	eu	i
ㄱ	g(k)	가	갸	거	겨	고	교	구	규	그	기
ㄴ	n	나	냐	너	녀	노	뇨	누	뉴	느	니
ㄷ	d	다	댜	더	뎌	도	됴	두	듀	드	디
ㄹ	r(l)	라	랴	러	려	로	료	루	류	르	리
ㅁ	m	마	먀	머	며	모	묘	무	뮤	므	미
ㅂ	b	바	뱌	버	벼	보	뵤	부	뷰	브	비
ㅅ	s	사	샤	서	셔	소	쇼	수	슈	스	시
ㅇ	※	아	야	어	여	오	요	우	유	으	이
ㅈ	j	자	쟈	저	져	조	죠	주	쥬	즈	지
ㅊ	ch	차	챠	처	쳐	초	쵸	추	츄	츠	치
ㅋ	k	카	캬	커	켜	코	쿄	쿠	큐	크	키
ㅌ	t	타	탸	터	텨	토	툐	투	튜	트	티
ㅍ	p	파	퍄	퍼	펴	포	표	푸	퓨	프	피
ㅎ	h	하	햐	허	혀	호	효	후	휴	흐	히

133 How Korea's Hankul script combines consonants (left column) and vowels (top row) in each 'syllabic letter'.

copies the way in which the sound is formed in the mouth: the /k/, for example, depicts a tongue touching the palate. There were 28 basic letters in original Hankul, 24 of which are still in use today. Diacritics are used systematically to provide those phonemes not represented by letters.

As King Seycong wrote in his edict of 1446: 'The [Hankul] is able to make a clear distinction between surd and sonant, and to record music and song. It is good for any practical use, and even the sound of the wind, the chirp of birds, the crowing of cocks, and the barking of dogs can be exactly described with it.'[29] This is almost true. Hankul's consonants are organized according to five different places of articulation: bilabial (lips), dental (teeth), alveolar (roof of mouth), velar (soft palate) and glottal (throat). Its three vowel shapes, however, were 'metaphysically' organized into Heaven (round dot), Earth (horizontal line) and Man (vertical line) – ostensibly to legitimize the system philosophically to Korean scholars who demanded a Chinese-fashion conceptualization to dignify the new system. Hankul thus maintained a clear graphic as well as conceptual distinction between consonants and vowels.

One writes Hankul not alphabetically but syllabically, beginning each syllabogram with a consonantal letter. If the syllable has no consonant, then the O-sign substitutes. (The O-sign is normally the semi-consonant /j/ or *y*-; at the end of a syllabogram, it conveys /ng/.) A vowel must then either act as a suffix or appear below the first element to complete the syllabogram, which is graphically a block. This use of a 'filler' is primarily æsthetic, preserving the graphic integrity of the 'syllable block' to achieve a regular outer appearance reminiscent of traditional Chinese-derived writing. Though its components are readily distinguishable, each Hankul syllabogram assumes primary status as a written unit, as each letter does in alphabetic writing. Syllable blocks similar to those of Indic *abudiga* are thus formed, composed of consonant + vowel; however, in Hankul the consonant and vowel of each block share equal status, as in a complete alphabet. This 'block writing' presumes the traditional dignity of Chinese writing while providing a system capable of adequately conveying Korean – at last.

Hankul is best designated as a featural system, as British linguist Geoffrey Sampson has noted, chiefly because of additive techniques.[30] If one doubles or adds strokes to any of the five consonants /k/, /n/, /s/, /m/ and /ng/, one is able to convey aspiration (an accompanying breath sound), affrication (forced friction of the breath, like /h/) and other linguistic features of Korean. Similarly, one need only combine the three vowel shapes (round dot, horizontal line, vertical line) in various ways to convey all the vowels and diphthongs in Korean. For a student of the world's writing systems, the chief 'beauty' of Hankul lies in the fact that the consonants are actually graphic depictions of the manner of articulating them, whereas the vowels are subsumed in three graphically marked metaphysical concepts.

Despite its obvious advantages, Hankul met fierce resistance from scholars and priests, the guardians of ancient Korean tradition. Though *hyangchal* writing was already defunct by the 1400s, the two other traditional scripts continued to dominate Korean writing for many centuries to come. Subsequent changes occurred in Hankul: old squarish and geometrical forms disappeared through the influence of brush writing, as did letters reproducing sounds no longer in the language. *Onmun* was perceived during these centuries as the domain of women and children and others of low social status. If Hankul was ever used by the learned, Chinese loan words were nonetheless still written in *hanja* and pronounced in Sino-Korean (not Korean).

Thus Hankul was not the replacement of Chinese writing in Korea that Seycong had intended. It became merely a suppletive system and script, written to aid in pronunciation, to provide grammatical words and particles, and to clarify Chinese ambiguities. Chinese *hanja* remained the prestige writing, the mark of an educated person of elevated status. There were very few Korean readings of the Chinese characters, too, unlike Japan's thousands of native *kun* readings of borrowed Chinese characters. Even today in South Korea, the level of one's erudition is measured by one's knowledge of the traditional *hanja*.

Seycong's *onmun* was known by several different names over this period: 'correct sounds for the instruction of the people', 'vulgar script', 'national writing' and others. The name Hankul – 'Han writing' – was finally coined by the linguist Cwu Si-kyeng (1876–1914) during his celebrated campaign to promote Korean language and literature at the start of the 1900s. The name Hankul was then actively promoted in order to polish up its centuries-old 'common' image.

The fact is that, Chinese being preferred, Korean had not often been used as a written language until the 1880s (illus. 134). In the 1910s and '20s, the diffusion of popular media and a Western form of education encouraged the development of a Sino-Korean 'mixed script' in both the Chinese and Korean languages. That is, borrowed words were still written using *hanja*, but Korean words and grammatical endings were now written in Hankul.[31] Only since the end of the Second World War has Korean been a standard written language used by the general population. And once Japanese domination ended in 1945, the influence of *hanja* decreased dramatically. Unlike Japanese writing, modern Korean writing no longer uses Chinese characters to convey Korean vocabulary; Hankul alone

마하반야바라밀다심경 관자재보살 행심반야바라밀다시 조견오온개공 도일체고액 사리자 색불이공 공불이색 색즉시공 공즉시색 수상행식 역부여시 사리자 시제법공상 불생불멸 불구부정 부증불감 시고 공중무색 무수상행식 무안이비설신의 무색성향미촉법 무안계 내지 무의식계 무무명 역무무명진 내지 무노사 역무노사진 무고집멸도 무지 역무득 이무소득고 보리살타 의반야바라밀다고 심무가애 무가애고 무유공포 원리전도몽상 구경열반 삼세제불 의반야바라밀다고 득아뇩다라삼먁삼보리 고지 반야바라밀다 시대신주 시대명주 시무상주 시무등등주 능제일체고 진실불허 고설반야바라밀다주 즉설주왈 아제아제 바라아제 바라승아제 모지 사바하

134 The *Heart Sutra* in Korean translation.

is used for this purpose.

In 1949, Communist North Korea abolished the public use of *hanja*, though limited school instruction has continued to the present day. North Koreans still have to write only in *cosenkul*, or 'Korean writing', the renamed Hankul. South Korea has been much less stringent. Almost all daily newspapers there still use some *hanja*. As in Japan, secondary-school graduates are expected to have a command of about eighteen hundred *hanja*. And some governmental ministries use them to a greater extent than others.

The five hundred years of Hankul writing have seen a constant struggle between the phonemicists (promoting sound) and morpho-phonemicists (word); the former have wanted to write Korean as spoken, while the latter have striven to maintain traditional verb and noun bases as graphic monuments, disregarding the language's automatic sound changes. History has seen Hankul writing move from sound to word, so that in the 2000s, at least in its nouns, it is predominately morpho-phonemic – that is, it chiefly reproduces the words and morphemes of spoken Korean rather than the actual sounds themselves. This has also allowed a unified orthography to develop (like the standard spelling rules of English, which disregard dialects) that, since 1945, has been in use in both Koreas. There were a number of attempted reforms of Hankul in the 1900s, including 'side-by-side' writing and wholesale replacement with romanization. However, since the late 1950s the Hankul system has remained essentially untouched and institutionalized.

At the beginning of the 2000s, a mixed writing of *hanja*, Hankul and European loan words and names in Latin script characterizes South Korean writing, with a clear trend towards losing the Chinese component altogether. North Korea already uses Hankul almost exclusively. The inevitable re-unification of the two Koreas will certainly change writing there in some way. Whatever form of writing triumphs, one must agree with Geoffrey Sampson's evaluation of Hankul as 'one of the great intellectual achievements of humankind'.[32]

JAPANESE WRITING

The Japanese language is presently conveyed through perhaps the most complicated writing that has ever existed: two separate systems (one foreign logographic, one indigenous syllabic) written in three scripts (one Chinese and two Japanese) at the same time. Most writing systems in the world represent a mixture of some sort, whereby one dominant system, such as our Latin alphabet, allows infrequent intrusion of some external component, such as ideograms (like 8, +, ?, %, >, † and many others). However, Japanese is in a class by itself. Japanese's borrowed Chinese characters also have both Chinese and Japanese readings, with all the complexities of the six different types of Chinese characters described above. Essentially, Japanese writing represents the distillation of a complicated re-analysis, over many centuries, of Chinese writing in order to convey both Japanese speech and Chinese loan words at several different and distinct levels of social interaction. The complexity of Japanese writing mirrors the complexity of Japanese society itself.

Basic to all Japanese writing, indeed its source, is the mor-

pheme-syllable writing of *kanji*, or 'Han script', Japan's borrowed Chinese characters.[33] Many centuries after borrowing
Chinese writing, the Japanese developed their own *kana* syllabic
writing system, which uses two separate syllabaries for different
needs: *hiragana* and *katakana*. Over the past century, *rōmaji*, or
the Latin alphabet, has been used increasingly for non-Japanese
words. Finally, there are also *kigō*, or 'symbols', which are customarily interspersed in Japanese texts using all of the above
writing systems and scripts at the same time.

It is unknown whether there was writing in Japan before the
introduction of Chinese writing. It appears that a knot-record
system, like the one known in Japan's southern Ryūkyū Islands,
may also have been used in Japan itself.[34] After the Han invasion
of Korea in AD 108, Chinese writing (both system and script)
became known to a very limited circle of Japanese practitioners.
Many Han cultural introductions influenced Japanese society at
that time, including inscribed metal mirrors. In AD 370, Japan
invaded Korea, which it held for some two hundred years.
During this time, Japan's Emperor Ōjin is reputed to have
brought two Korean scholars to the Japanese court to tutor the
Crown Prince in, among other things, Chinese writing and literature.

Buddhism became Japan's official religion in the middle of
the sixth century, introducing Chinese writing to other spheres
and centres; Japanese scholars regularly made pilgrimages to
China for their studies. In AD 645, Japan established a Con-
fucian-based central administration which thrived for over five
hundred years. It was during this time that Chinese writing was
institutionalized and adapted to convey Old Japanese, founding
the historical Japanese civilization (illus. 135).

Like Old Korean, Old Japanese was also a polysyllabic,
agglutinating language – entirely different from the Literary
Chinese being conveyed in *kanji*. The first Japanese writing was
kanbun, or 'Han writing'. This was an attempt to write in
Japanese syntax using Chinese characters alone. There were
two ways of reading *kanbun*: in Literary Chinese, or in Japanese
translation of Literary Chinese (using aid signs between
columns). *Kanbun* was almost entirely a written, not a spoken,
language. Its position in Japanese culture was similar to Latin in

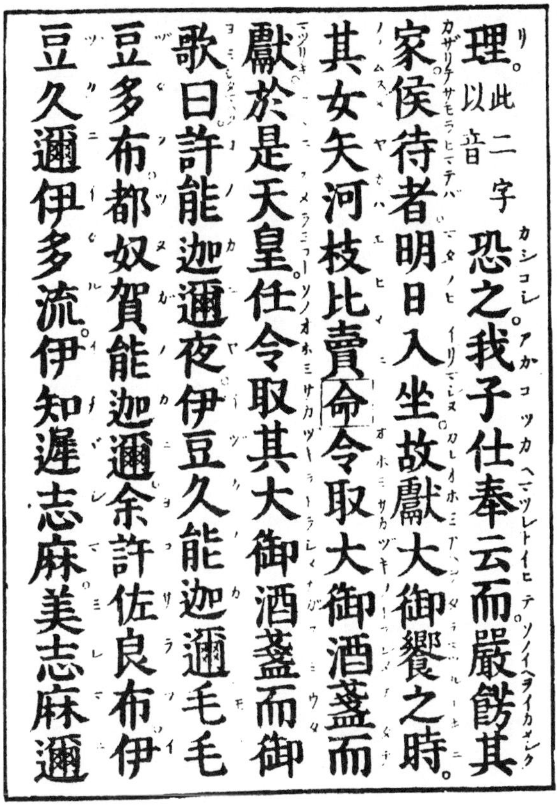

理
以音

其
家侯待者明日入坐故獻大御饗之時
其女矢河枝比賣命令取大御酒盞而
獻於是天皇仕令取其大御酒盞而御
歌曰許能迦邇夜伊豆久能迦邇毛毛
豆多布都奴賀能迦邇余許佐良布伊
豆久邇伊多流伊知遲志麻美志麻通

。此二字恐之我子仕奉云而嚴餝其

135 Japan's first native literature, the *Kōjiki*, completed in AD 712, relates the country's ancient history in Chinese *kanji*, here in a woodblock print of 1803 providing pronunciation aids in the *katakana* syllabic script.

the West: most scholars could read it, but few ever spoke it. *Kanbun* was not Japanese, but a literary vehicle between Chinese and Japanese.

When the Japanese borrowed a Chinese character, they borrowed not only its sense but also its *on*, or 'sound' – though this belonged to a foreign language. After centuries of borrowing, the predominance of Chinese *on* in Japanese writing was compensated for by reading each character with an indigenous Japanese value, too – this was the *kun*, or 'gloss'. Each Japanese *kanji* (borrowed Chinese character) can now possess several *on* and *kun* readings, although this is not a fixed rule: like a great number of characters, the *sai* character (for 'talent' and 'suffix for counting age') has only this one *on* sound, for example. However, there is never a character with only one native Japanese *kun* reading. The *on* readings will actually be supplemented with one or more *kun* readings only if the Japanese language possesses a word close in meaning to the Chinese *on*.

Complexity is further increased by the practice of writing *on-kun* (Sino-Japanese) compounds as well as *kun-on* (Japanese-Sino) compounds, each component of which might then have several possible readings. And the Japanese have invented several hundreds of *kanji* not found in Chinese which have both *on* and *kun* readings. Though single *on* words do adorn the Japanese language (all of them Chinese borrowings), most *on* are compounded with one or more *on* characters to form words of two or more syllables. In this way, the three *on*-read *kanji* for 'sound', 'voice' and 'field of study' form Japanese *onseigaku* or 'phonetics', for example.

As in China, writing in Japan was done with brush and ink in downwards-running vertical columns ordered from right to left. (As of the seventh century, the Japanese were manufacturing and using paper as a writing material, too.) But from the earliest days of writing Japanese in *kanbun*, it was realized that the foreign writing system, as it was, could not convey what scribes needed it to convey. For many centuries, Japanese scribes expected the reader to mentally 'fill in' those word endings and grammatical particles that the script failed to include. It was a laborious and equivocal way to read Japanese, in several ways history's most awkward instance of borrowing. A drastic solution was required.

Already in the early centuries of borrowing, to be able to reduce ambiguities and begin more adequately to convey Japanese speech – not merely Chinese meanings and sounds – the Japanese undertook various methods of adaptation, using the same strategies one finds among the Koreans and Vietnamese. The Japanese used a *kanji*'s Chinese meaning but pronounced it in Japanese – this was the *kun*, or 'gloss', reading used in *kanbun*. They also had certain *kanji* represent purely phonetic values independent of sense, forming *wabun*, or

'Japanese writing'. Already about thirteen hundred years ago, then, Japanese writing had less to do with actual 'Chinese' writing than with Japanese perception.

Scribes soon began mixing *kanbun* and *wabun* – that is, combining meaning and sound. By the eighth century, this had introduced the bi-systemic principle that underlies Japanese writing today: not one but two writing systems in mixed usage.

Wabun sound-writing made use of the so-called *manyōgana*, a syllabary used at the beginning of the Heian Period (AD 794–1192) that was probably inspired by Korean *hyangchal* writing. This syllabary was written small between Chinese characters or columns in order to explain readings of, or provide a commentary on, Buddhist sutras. But the *manyōgana* was clumsy, as there were normally ten times more Chinese characters being used than actual syllables in the Japanese language: in the eighth century, Japanese scribes were writing over 970 different Chinese characters to convey only about 88 Japanese syllable types.

Out of this early redundancy, however, *kanji* simplifications – Japan's *kana* syllabary – soon emerged. (The word *kana* might derive from the first two elements of a Korean syllabary that began 'ka-na-ta-ra', making *kana* similar to 'alphabet' from *alpha* and *bēta*.)[35] The *kana* was a wholly different type of writing system – syllabic – that was stuck onto, interspersed with and parasitic to the inherited Chinese logographic writing. It had two forms, the *hiragana* and the *katakana*. Both were identical syllabaries, differing only in outward appearance and use (same system, different scripts).

The cursive form of the *manyōgana* sound characters became the *hiragana* script in the eighth and ninth centuries. This was also known as the *onna-de*, or 'women's hand', as it was practised primarily by the female élite. (Japan's greatest literary work of the Middle Ages, *The Tale of Genji* by Lady Murasaki Shikibu, was originally composed and distributed entirely in *hiragana*.) Its sister *katakana*, or 'part *kana*', script also emerged in the ninth century directly from the *manyōgana*, and not always from the corresponding syllables from which the *hiragana* signs had derived (thus explaining their external contrast). By the end of the 1100s, the *kana-majiri* system of writing – that is, a mixed

Chinese-*kanji* and Japanese-*kana* writing – was in use. This method has continued in Japan, with occasional changes and adjustments, up to the present.

Throughout Japan's Middle Ages, *kanji* remained the country's prestige script. State documents were written in *katakana*. Women wrote in *hiragana* and *katakana* in both literary production and private correspondence. *Kanji* long endured as Japan's premier script, like *hanja* in Korea, though great courtly prestige still attended, within its limited domain, the female élite's *hiragana* literature. By the 1700s, however, women were also allowed to use *kanji*. Today, no socio-gender boundaries attach to any of Japan's writing systems or scripts.

By the end of the 1800s, the many allophonic members – different signs with the same sound – of the earlier *kana* inventory had been eliminated, reducing it to 96 syllabograms, or 48 in each of the two *kana* scripts. So one Japanese syllable now had only one syllabogram representing it in each script. And by the second half of the 1900s, two signs in the *w*-series (*i* and *e* doublets) had come into disuse, too. This left 92 *hiragana* and *katakana* syllabograms (46 in each), plus the *-n* that frequently ends Japanese syllables, making 94 syllabic (two *-n*) signs in total. These are still commonly arranged, reading from top to bottom and right to left, in the *Gōjū-on-zu* ('Fifty-Sound Chart', including some archaic syllabograms) according to a model borrowed from southern India's Tamil script (illus. 136). Most Japanese lexicons are 'alphabetically' arranged according to this chart.

Each of Japan's two *kana* scripts is characterized by an outer shape that allows instant recognition – *hiragana* generally being curved, *katakana* straight-lined. This crucial distinction is exploited in Japanese graphic art, with *katakana* preferred for store signs and advertising but *hiragana* for calligraphy and other more 'flowing' expressions (illus. 137).

The respective roles of *kanji* and *kana* in everyday Japanese writing have become 'standardized' only in the last century or so. *Kanji* characters are written to convey the primary lexical categories – non-Western nouns (Chinese and Japanese), verb stems, adjective stems and a few adverbs. Until the second half of the 1800s, *katakana* syllabograms provided the necessary grammatical

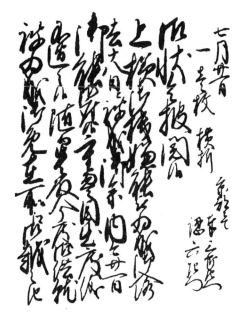

	ワわ wa	ラら ra	ヤや ya	マま ma	ハは ha	ナな na	タた ta	サさ sa	カか ka	アあ a
	ヰゐ i	リり ri	イい i	ミみ mi	ヒひ hi	ニに ni	チち chi	シし shi	キき ki	イい i
	ウう u	ルる ru	ユゆ yu	ムむ mu	フふ fu	ヌぬ nu	ツつ tsu	スす su	クく ku	ウう u
	ヱゑ e	レれ re	エえ e	メめ me	ヘへ he	ネね ne	テて te	セせ se	ケけ ke	エえ e
んン n	ヲを wo	ロろ ro	ヨよ yo	モも mo	ホほ ho	ノの no	トと to	ソそ so	コこ ko	オお o

136 Japan's 'Fifty-Sound Chart', reading from top to bottom and from right to left. The highlighted boxes enclose redundant vowels.

137 The model for official Japanese correspondence two hundred years ago: the highly esteemed 'grass style'.

morphemes and function words; since the official fixing of *kana* forms in 1900, *hiragana* syllabograms have conveyed these. But *hiragana* still does this without consistency. One will find full, half or even 'zero' use of *hiragana* in any Japanese sentence – that is, often only *kanji* characters appear, forcing the reader to mentally 'fill in' the grammar, just as in the early Middle Ages. The *katakana* syllabograms, on the other hand, now convey foreign names and loanwords, exclamations, mimetic words, onomatopoeic words and specialized terminology.

There has been a great increase in *katakana* use since the end of the Second World War, awarding the script a prominence it had lost when *hiragana* usurped its grammatical function. Due to foreign-language 'contamination', *katakana* now abounds in neon signage and other street, store, TV, Internet and magazine advertising. It also conveys particular emphasis, indicates euphemistic usage, signals irony and so on. Young people use it more frequently now in their mixed scripts, thus achieving a 'looser' conversational tone.[36] *Katakana* syllabograms have become the 'italic script' of Japanese writing.

Japan's *hiragana* and *katakana* syllabaries, which also make use of a small repertoire of diacritics – such as ", which can change a *k* into a *g*, and °, which can turn an *h* into a *p* – are each fully capable of conveying everything in modern Japanese speech. Indeed, in most books for children and adolescents, nearly all the *kanji* appear with miniature *hiragana* signs next to them. These are called *furigana*, or 'added *kana*', and, though meant to sound out a perhaps unfamiliar *kanji*, the practice merely serves to display how superfluous the *kanji* characters have actually become (illus. 138).

Two questions arise in this regard. First, why does Japan need two syllabaries? The explanation normally given is that *hiragana* is for informal writing and *katakana* for official documents and other formal contexts. But this is a historical observation, not a contemporary justification. Japan indeed fragmented the purpose of writing, sequestering, as in ancient Egypt (hieratic versus demotic), contexts in which only one of two related scripts was tolerated. Today, separate domains for either script still obtain. This is convention, not need.

Second, why cling to complicated mixed systems and scripts?

耳なし芳一のはなし

いまから七百年あまりまえのことです。下関海峽の壇の浦で、ながいあいだ天下をあらそっていた源氏と平家のあいだに、さいごの決戦がおこなわれました。平家は、この壇の浦で、われわれが今日、安徳天皇とおよびしている、あのご幼帝、それに平家の一門の女や子どもたちといっしょに、まったくほろびてしまったのです。

その後七百年のあいだ、壇の浦の海とあのへんいったいの海岸とは、ながらく平家の亡霊にたた

138 Reading from top to bottom and from right to left, the opening chapter of this modern book for Japanese adolescents furnishes nearly every *kanji* character with a miniature *furigana* for pronunciation.

This question betrays an alphabetic bias. A non-Japanese might feel that Japan is 'confronted' with three choices: keep the present system, adopt *kana* writing only, or use Western *rōmaji*, the Latin alphabet. It has been demonstrated, for example, that Japanese blind people can read *kana* Braille, which uses no *kanji*, far more easily than Japanese sighted people read the standard Japanese mixed writing systems. Logically, one should assume that abandoning *kanji* altogether (as Korea seems poised to do with its *hanja*) for *kana* would surely be of advantage to Japanese society as a whole, in terms of literacy, length of education, the economy and social progress in general. The Japanese might even adopt *rōmaji*, thus being able to enjoy its eminent adaptability. Indeed, the non-Japanese might add, in 1885 Japan's 'Society for the Roman Script' tried to eliminate both *kanji* and *kana* altogether. In reply, a Japanese might point out that there has not been a similarly strong demand since then, nor one to write only in *kana*. In fact, Japan is 'confronted' by nothing: Japanese writing is firmly entrenched in Japanese society.

In the realm of efficiency, Japanese people appreciate that Japan's present writing systems best accommodate the inherent problem of homophony (different words that sound the same). For intelligibility, logographic writing appears to be far more important for the Japanese than for the Chinese.[37] Educated Japanese language has developed along with thousands of *kanji* borrowings. These can only be distinguished by differences in their graphic – not their spoken – expression. (Imagine the confusion if we simplified English *know* to *no* merely because *k* and *w* are held to be 'superfluous'; Japanese writing provides the strongest proof that a written word's *graphic image* is also semantic conveyance.) This is because Japan has reduced most of the original Chinese words to homophones, through either original Japanese phonology or historical change: twenty-odd different Chinese characters (with their different pronunciations) have all been reduced to Japanese *kan*, for example. Japanese written only in *kana* or *rōmaji* would lead to ambiguity, the opposite of writing's purpose. There would be no 'simplification' at all.

In the social domain, *kanji* characters are part of ancient Japanese tradition – what it means to be Japanese. Many Japanese resent the notion of abandoning this system merely for the sake of (questionable) 'ease and efficiency'. But the social case is even stronger than this. Each writing system holds a built-in inertia. Writing systems and scripts are not simple tools but cornerstones of a society.

Japanese primary pupils, once they have mastered both *kana* syllabaries – first the 47 *hiragana*, then the 47 *katakana* – are expected to learn in eight years of schooling 960 *kanji* characters, beginning with native Japanese *kun* readings of these. In order to graduate from secondary school, Japanese pupils then have to command an additional thousand *kanji* (plus the borrowed Chinese *on* readings of those 960 *kanji* learnt in grammar school). So an educated Japanese is presently expected by his society to command nearly two thousand *kanji* for all normal purposes. (A particularly literate Japanese will command five thousand or more.) General *kanji* in newspapers and magazines total about 3,200 – many being place and family names using obscure *kanji* that are often glossed with *furigana* as a reading aid. Knowledge of two thousand *kanji* for ordinary reading is relatively new, however, the result of stringent educational reforms introduced during the American Occupation. Before the Second World War, illiteracy was common, due in no small part to the difficulties of learning Japanese writing. Though illiteracy is now much lower, it still exists, and for the same reason.

The 1980s saw a flood of foreign words, mostly English, appearing in *rōmaji* in contexts where *katakana* would previously have been used. The increase of *rōmaji* is now also apparent in Japanese texts on the Internet. Japanese writing's 'sponge-like' quality signals adaptability, hence viability.

Japan still follows the traditional Chinese custom of writing in vertical columns reading from top to bottom and from right to left. Like modern Chinese writing, however, many Japanese texts now also appear horizontally in Western alphabetic fashion, reading from left to right. There is still no word separation, but this is not as important as it is for alphabetic writing. Complete comprehension is achieved through segmentation cues (the mixture of writing systems and scripts) and modern Western punctuation.

As in China, calligraphy has always been one of Japan's greatest art forms, here representing a mixture of all three scripts. Some works appear in only one of these, as a special graphic statement. In Japanese calligraphy, literature and graphic art become one (illus. 139). A romanized script could not begin to imitate this artistry. Contrary to Western notions of calligraphy, whereby legibility precedes æsthetics, in both China and Japan æsthetics precedes legibility. (This obtains to such a degree that a cultured person in these societies might even be insulted if told her or his handwriting were 'clearly legible'.) Expertise in calligraphy is the mark of the erudite East Asian, in both production and reading ability. This, too, reverses Western concepts about the primary purpose of writing – as does so much attaching to East Asian writing.

The Japanese situation may exhibit history's most extreme case of writing's influence on a language. Japan had no common border with China, and very few Chinese visitors ever ventured so far; there was never a successful Chinese invasion of Japan. Yet more than half of today's Japanese vocabulary consists of Sino-Japanese loanwords (Chinese words in Japanese phonol-

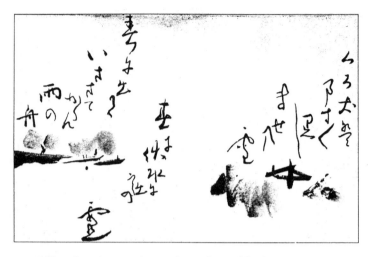

139 Calligraphy, painting and poetry fuse in this work by Ikeno Taiga (1723–1776) depicting a black dog in the snow (right) and a boat on a riverbank (left).

ogy). This means that China's massive influence on the Japanese language came almost entirely through the medium of writing, something that has occurred with no other language in the history of humankind.

Because of their complexity, the Japanese writing systems and scripts have perhaps also been history's most maligned writing. This is especially true of experts of the history of writing whose value judgement often prioritizes writing's 'ease and efficiency'.[38] As we have seen, there are several reasons why *gaijin*, or 'non-Japanese', should indeed question the rationale behind maintaining such perceived complexity. No-one can argue that Japanese is, in truth, the most difficult writing to learn in the world, and the claim that it is history's most complex writing is fully justified. (I started learning Japanese language and writing in 1956, when I moved to Okinawa, and still, after 45 years, feel very much the neophyte.)

However, Japanese writing is not only perfectly learnable, but manifestly successful. It has been for many centuries – and continues to be – the vehicle of a highly literate and prosperous people with an extremely rich written tradition. Boasting one of the world's highest literacy rates (higher than the US's or France's with their much 'simpler' alphabetic writing), Japan can also claim the world's largest per capita consumption of published material. Some scientists have even claimed that the added cerebral effort needed to command Japanese writing helps those who eventually do accomplish this task to excel in domains not immediately related to writing. It is well known that because of its writing system, Japan forces its young to endure many more years of education – placing demands on its young people and at great cost to the state – than are necessary in other countries. Yet this may also explain, if only in part, Japan's manifest success. One thing is clear: in no way has Japan's writing hindered the intellectual growth of its users. It is perhaps not entirely coincidental that the world's seemingly most complex writing is to be found in the world's technologically most advanced country.[39]

Japanese writing, with such complexity and multivalence of reading, is certainly not the 'graphic rendering of human speech' that one usually understands writing to be. The possibility of multiple readings with one sign – even of additional readings of these with compounds – displays the multi-dimensionality of writing in general, involving levels of perception transcending speech alone. This can partly be found in other writing systems, too, though never to the systemic extent observed in Japanese.

The two principal lessons of Japanese writing must surely be that writing systems and scripts can be anything their users not only need but also desire, and that writing's complexity in no way hinders ultimate accomplishment.

'The axiom of Western linguistics according to which a language is primarily a system of spoken forms, and writing is a subsidiary medium serving to render spoken language visible, is very difficult for an East Asian to accept,' Geoffrey Sampson has written.[40] This is because – particularly for a Chinese or a Japanese, whose language contains an extraordinary number of homophones – spoken language can be so ambiguous, imperfect and only fully transparent through the medium of writing. Written language, so East Asian writing teaches us, is not subordinate to spoken language.

There is a further insight to be gained from studying East Asian writing. The survival and success of Chinese writing contradicts the notion that writing systems 'evolve' and that complete alphabetic writing is the apogee of such 'evolution'. Writing can take plural forms, serving its users eminently in any of these. Chinese speakers have known of alphabetic writing for well over two thousand years. This knowledge has never caused them to change 'for the better'.

For many centuries, Classical Chinese language and literature comprised the canon of higher education throughout East Asia. Initially, Chinese writing was borrowed for content alone – principally Classical Chinese literature and Buddhist scriptures in Chinese translation. So Chinese language and script were borrowed as an inseparable unit. Only later was the borrowing used to convey local languages. As always, this necessitated adaptations according to the degree to which the borrowing language differed from Chinese. Vietnamese happened to be a language very similar to Chinese, and so few adaptations were necessary. Korean and Japanese, however, differed dramatically. In time, this process gave rise to entirely new systems which have helped to increase our knowledge about the intrinsic capabilities of writing systems.

The East Asian evidence further indicates that the course of writing's history is essentially determined not by efficiency or adequacy of conveyance but by socio-political factors. Though Chinese writing eminently suits the Chinese language, it is now clearly yielding to the foreign system of alphabetic writing, though this will probably never replace the inherited system entirely. The Vietnamese long used Chinese as their literary language before adapting it to the Vietnamese language, but then abandoned their patrimony under French domination for alphabetic writing, which foreign system endures to this day, despite the country's political independence. Koreans also borrowed Chinese language and writing, but then supplemented them in the 1400s with an indigenous creation which is only now replacing the Chinese heritage. Japan, too, borrowed both Chinese language and writing, which, because it suited Japanese as poorly as it did Korean, was expanded early on into two writing systems using three scripts. As we have seen, this unique hybrid is steadfastly maintained as a principal expression of Japan's cultural identity.

Chinese writing and its derivatives display a great ability to carry semantic weight on a character-by-character basis. This is quite unlike alphabetic writing, which is connective, with communication occuring in the letter-by-letter sequencing of discrete sounds. The visual effect of East Asian writing is thus much stronger than in alphabetic or other systems (though some claim that alphabetic 'whole-word' reading does achieve the same, or a similar, visual effect). The visual distinction is important. For it appears that, among a highly literate population, language production, reception and retention skills are neurologically linked to language's written form. While conversing, Chinese and Japanese write characters in the palm of their hand not to distinguish between ambiguous homophones but as part of fundamental language conveyance and retention – a unique 'middle ground' between spoken and written language. 'The differences between morpheme-based writing systems [such as Chinese] and sound-based writing systems [such as English],' writes linguist Florian Coulmas, 'are not just superficial differences of coding, but relate to neuropsychological differences concerning the storage and processing of written language units.'[41] In Chinese and Japanese, in particular, the graphic image of the word is apparently stored in the mind as part of the lexical retrieval process, perhaps to a degree far excelling that of alphabetic 'whole-word' retrieval processes in the West.

It appears, then, that different cerebral processing occurs with East Asians reading morpheme-syllable writing. Writing's cerebral activity is not a constant function of the brain, but depends on the type of writing one is using. In Japanese, for example, the fact that cerebral damage can cause someone to lose *kanji* (the Chinese characters) but still retain *kana* (the Japanese syllabograms) – as well as the reverse – also shows that major neurological differences distinguish the one writing system from the other. This indicates that Japanese *kanji* and *kana* are neurologically dissociated from one another, suggesting significant processing differences for the world's writing systems in general. There is no evidence of any such disruption, however, between the two types of *kana*, the *hiragana* and *katakana*. Though two separate scripts, they seem to be encoded as one in the brain. One can probably generalize from this that, throughout the world, different but related scripts (Latin, Greek, runes, oghams and so forth) are similarly processed in the human brain, while different writing systems (logographic, syllabic, alphabetic) are not.

Chinese writing has had 'a more lasting effect on the cultural identity of East Asia than any other culture trait'.[42] This may obtain in more general, perhaps even universal, ways that are only now revealing themselves. It represents an East Asian 'regenesis' of a higher order: the birth of our understanding of how the human brain itself processes the wonder of writing.

SIX

The Americas

In 1986, a two-m-tall basalt stela, or slab monument, was discovered in the Acula River near the village of La Mojarra in southeastern Mexico, a region not especially known for cultural attainment. The stela's discoverers were therefore astonished to find on it, in 21 vertical columns, a long inscription of 520 'glyphs' (short for 'hieroglyphs') facing and topping a kingly figure (illus. 140). The text, deciphered in 1993,[1] included in an Epi-Olmec script the dates AD 143 and 156.

This was the Americas' earliest dated inscription.

Until the stela's discovery and decipherment, scholars had believed that in Mesoamerica, only the Mayan people had possessed a fully developed writing system – this belief had found endorsement in the late 1980s. Predating by about 150 years the earliest Mayan inscription that included a date, the 'La Mojarra Stela', as it came to be called, not only proved that the Epi-Olmec people, too, possessed complete writing, but that their mixed logosyllabic (word-syllable) system stood in some genetic relationship to later Mayan inscriptions. Most archæologists now accept the Epi-Olmec texts to be the Americas' earliest readable inscriptions. The stela's discovery has also led many to believe that writing has an older and more complex history in the region. Indeed, the cumulative evidence appears to suggest the existence of several sophisticated local writing traditions centuries before the Mayan civilization.[2] The Mayans' elaborate writing would have developed from these traditions, whose existence and nature scholars are only now beginning to study in earnest.

Until the 1980s, archæologists and historians of writing alike still generally held that both Mayan and Aztec writing 'remained at the threshold of writing proper … In both systems

140 The Epi-Olmec La Mojarra Stela from Veracruz, Mexico, 2nd century AD.

we find a marked contrast between graphic complexity and sophistication and low systematic development ... Most scholars agree that neither of them are fully developed phonetic systems.'[3] However, as a result of the successful decipherment of Mayan writing in the 1980s (after the Russian Yuri Knorozov's discovery of the phonetic 'key' in the 1950s), soon followed by that of the Epi-Olmec La Mojarra Stela, it was appreciated that as many as fifteen distinct writing traditions may once have flourished in pre-Columbian Mesoamerica, several of these preserved in only one surviving inscription. Those texts of sufficient length to allow meaningful analysis appear to demonstrate that, at least in the main Mesoamerican scripts, a single logosyllabic system dominated writing, with extremes of logography and phonography between, and within, traditions.

Though the pedigree of Mesoamerican scripts remains unclear (illus. 141), five main traditions have been identified for the region which, as a culture area, comprises central and southern Mexico, Guatemala, Belize, El Salvador and a large area of Honduras. Earliest is the Zapotec tradition of logosyllabic writ-

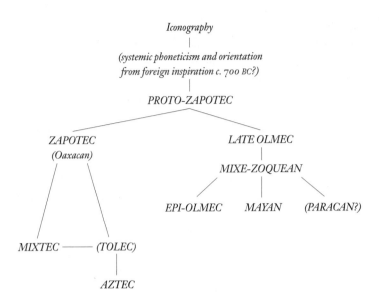

An abridged hypothetical family tree of Mesoamerican scripts.

ing, which probably generated the later Mixtec and Aztec traditions. Perhaps sharing a Proto-Zapotec source with Zapotec, a possible Late Olmec tradition evidently inspired, through a Mixe-Zoquean intermediary, the two main traditions of the Epi-Olmec and the Maya. It is possible that Mixe-Zoquean also inspired the Paracan people of Peru in the first few centuries BC to elaborate a special type of purely phonographic writing, which later Andean societies borrowed and adapted.

Zapotec, Epi-Olmec and Mayan texts all predate AD 900, whereas Mixtec and Aztec texts were written from AD 1100 until the first century of Spanish colonization. The first three traditions are known almost entirely from carved stone monuments; Mixtec and Aztec inscriptions, however, occur primarily in painted books of cloth, bark paper or animal hide. All known Mesoamerican inscriptions comprise only what has survived – that is, they are not representative of what once was. Formerly held merely to be an elaborate type of iconography, Mesoamerican monumental inscriptions are now recognized as historical records detailing royal births, marriages, deaths, battles waged, captives seized and rulers' all-important blood-letting sacrifices. Central to each message is the exact date of a particular occurrence. Indeed, dating is intrinsic to Mesoamerican writing, again implying a single tradition. Number glyphs were associated with the calendar, one of the most complex and socially pervasive calendars ever devised anywhere.

Mesoamerican scripts appear to comprehend a single mixed logosyllabic writing system. This mixed system, which occasionally includes pictography, displays varying, and sometimes extreme, degrees of logography and phonography. No Mesoamerican tradition ever attained to orthographic standardization. All complete writing in the region – that is, writing excluding pictography – more commonly favoured mixed logographic writing, whereby glyphs stood for known objects, ideas or sounds (from the names for known objects). There were also distinct syllabaries of purely phonetic glyphs written, like phonetic classifiers, in free association with other glyphs.

The logical inference of such a highly developed, single, shared writing tradition is either of a much longer development of writing in Mesoamerica than hitherto assumed – one that might predate the first millennium BC – or of a cultural importation that had already developed over a protracted period elsewhere.[4]

ORIGINS

The recent successful decipherments of the Epi-Olmec and Mayan traditions have led scholars to believe that they can better understand how Mesoamerican writing might have originated.[5] The prevailing theory is still that it emerged independently of any other system in the world. Indeed, most histories of writing appeal to 'the three known cases of independent script invention', customarily listing Sumerian, Chinese and Mayan.[6] However, as argued elsewhere (see Chapter 5), it has never been proved that Chinese writing emerged independently; some evidence suggests otherwise. And Mayan writing is now appreciated to be only one of several derivatives of a single tradition of writing in Mesoamerica.

Complete writing never emerges 'automatically' with the

development of complex societies. Complex societies may be specifically the ones who choose to use writing. But the emergent system and its orientation almost always reproduce a similar phenomenon elsewhere: the writing system that is closest in time and space. Common sense would perhaps argue for complete writing's simple diffusion throughout history, from one original source. Diffusion might also explain the sudden use of systemic phoneticism by those responsible for the iconography of the Americas around 700 BC.

The very earliest Mesoamerican texts – simple pairs or triplets of glyphs in sequence – date from 700–400 BC, the era of pre-state cultures called the Middle Formative period. These texts are found in southern Mexico, from the Valley of Oaxaca across the Isthmus of Tehuantepec to the Olmec region of southern Veracruz and Tabasco. Some believe that by about 500 BC there already existed two Mesoamerican traditions, Zapotec and South-eastern, both derived from a single precursor. If this is true, then writing must have been developing in Mesoamerica for a considerable length of time. The first appearance of symbols inscribed on jade and serpentine ceremonial axes, used in rituals throughout Mesoamerica, suggests a primitive iconography that eventually developed into a more intricate iconography. With this iconography, some believe, it was a 'natural step' to *invent* logography and phonography.

Many of the earliest Mesoamerican symbols appear on the artefacts of the Olmecs, a powerful people who first arose about 1200 BC in the Gulf Coast region around Veracruz. The Olmecs possessed a large iconographic repertoire, including portraits of rulers. Evidently in order to identify these leaders, symbolic motifs were used in headdress depictions as naming devices. If around 1000 BC it was true that leaders were portrayed seated before entrances to the underworld, by 500 BC the iconography on axes, pottery and other portable objects had reduced these images to parts of the body: a greeting or corn-casting ceremony, for example, could be conveyed by showing only the hand performing the action. The abbreviated icons then became abstract renderings of ideas, creating a primitive ideography. This sign system, still independent of speech as it was merely an abbreviated iconography, eventually assumed logographic status as more demands were placed on the system because of increased urbanization. Members of the social élite, it is further argued, needed to express themselves publicly, 'to record their deeds and dynasties as a way of legitimizing their role in society'.[7] Some claim that this public need engendered complete writing.

However, public exposition was surely the social result of writing, not its underlying cause. Mesoamericans might have possessed an elaborate iconography developed over many centuries, as did the Polynesians of pre-contact Easter Island. But connecting this iconography to systemic phoneticism – to complete writing – became possible only once the idea of complete writing, of graphic art representing speech (not just ideas), was either invented locally through some other dynamic or encountered by foreign visitors who already possessed complete writing. One must appreciate that the passage from iconography to systemic phoneticism is never the automatic outgrowth of an expanding society. Neither is it a small step of simple graphic standardization. It is a giant leap of discovery. This is because speech must be tied to graphic art in such a way that an entire abstract *system* – one that replaces the semantic value of an icon or symbol with its phonetic value within a repertoire of limited, similar values, cutting the link to the system-external referent (see Chapter 1) – is created that is both easily comprehensible and teachable.

Others scholars believe that the step to graphic speech in Mesoamerica occurred through the invention of the 260-day ritual calendar. This compelling argument must be taken seriously, though the proposed date for the invention – the era of the Epi-Olmecs – actually postdated by several centuries the first appearance of complete writing in Mesoamerica. The Epi-Olmec calendar used bars and dots to represent numerals, the days being conveyed by icons of animals, plants and other easily recognizable objects. A calendar entry might then read '3 Deer' or '10 Jaguar', for example. The special juxtaposition of numbers and icons might have led to complete writing, it is argued, once phonetic elements were added to avoid ambiguity.

Of course, origins cannot be discussed without invoking analogues. The one that immediately springs to mind in this instance, for several compelling reasons, is first-millennium-BC Chinese writing. There are so many features of early Chinese writing that find their counterparts in early Mesoamerican writing – most of them identifiable only after the successful decipherments of the Epi-Olmec and Mayan scripts – that it is difficult to believe they can be unrelated to one another:

- The organizing principle of both Chinese and Mesoamerican writing is the vertical column.

- This vertical column reads from top to bottom.

- Both systems include compounded 'glyphic blocks' containing two or more signs.

- These glyphic blocks hold, in most but not all cases, logosyllabic value.

- With compounded logograms, both systems use phonetics to assist in identification or pronunciation.

- The semantic determinatives of Mayan writing (the 'day' glyph cartouche and the *ahaw* scarf for the title 'lord'), signalling the class of phenomena to which the phonetically given words belong, correspond to Chinese writing's semantic classifiers.

Out of the hundreds of writing systems and scripts in the world, only Chinese (and its derivatives) and Mesoamerican writing include each of these principles and features. It would perhaps strain common sense to ascribe this to coincidence.

There are larger historical issues intimating that writing in the Americas might have been borrowed from elsewhere. For one thing, there was no immediate need for writing there. When it was encountered, it therefore did not serve the basic purposes of book-keeping and tallying, as these functions were already fulfilled by traditional means (knot records, for example). However, as with borrowed writing everywhere else in the world, the importation was immediately associated with rulers and deities, to record the previously unrecordable. If indeed borrowed, Mesoamerican writing would most easily have come from China than from elsewhere. It may be relevant that, for hundreds of years, Spanish galleons found a natural passage from East Asia to the Americas to lie in steering far northwards to the latitudes of Japan past the belt of east-to-west trade winds. Here, the westerlies would drive vessels east in the Kuroshio current. Once at the North Pacific current, ships would drive to California, then coast southwards to Mexico, to Acapulco just north of Oaxaca, where transfer to Veracruz on the Gulf of Mexico was effected.

This all remains speculation. The similarities between first-millennium-BC Chinese writing and first-millennium-BC Meso-american writing might indeed be too remarkable to ascribe to coincidence. But similarities do not comprise proof. Just as one cannot accept as fact that 'it was the Zapotec, and not the Maya or Olmec, who invented writing in Mesoamerica,'[8] one cannot affirm as a 'given' that a Proto-Zapotec people borrowed the idea, system and orientation of writing from arriving literate Chinese about 700 BC. The Chinese explanation is probably the more economical of the two. But economy of explanation is a guide, not a paradigm.

Pending the discovery of more conclusive evidence, one should perhaps adopt the position that 'Mesoamericans either borrowed writing from the Chinese or independently elaborated writing themselves,' acknowledging that there are insufficient data to prove which of the two explanations is the correct one.

ZAPOTEC

Evidence for complete writing in Mesoamerica first occurs among the Zapotec people, who occupied a wide region of southern Mexico stretching from the Valley of Oaxaca to the Isthmus of Tehuantepec. By around 600 BC, at the Monte Albán mountain redoubt and in neighbouring centres in the Valley of Oaxaca, local leaders were erecting stone monuments heralding victories and flaunting tortured and sacrificed captives. Most importantly, the monuments proclaimed a conquered rival's name, that of his people and the date on which he was con-quered (and/or sacrificed).[9]

Zapotec stelæ 12 and 13 at San José Mogote are currently

regarded as the earliest known examples of linguistically salient writing in Mesoamerica, dating from *c.* 600 BC. The glyphs' arrangement and abstract shapes resemble the logosyllabic scripts of the later Epi-Olmec and Mayan peoples. As Zapotec writing continued until the end of the Colonial period in the 1500s AD, it experienced many changes. These reflected not only the linguistic changes that occur naturally over time but also Zapotec society's own dynamic story – its growing power and subjugation of rival states, its dynastic expansion, its ever more complex royal genealogy. In later centuries, Zapotec scribes wrote colourful codices on paper made from indigenous plants; during the Colonial period, they also used paper imported from Spain. Included among their corpus of literature were account books (probably recording tribute), genealogical books and also territorial maps of Zapotec domains.[10] Most inscriptions appear to record 'the number of captives taken by a particular warrior, on a particular day, and at a particular city'.[11] In the main, Zapotec monuments are name-tagged sculptures that seem to include a verb, a name glyph and a place glyph.

While the inscriptions from Monte Albán I and II (*c.* 600 BC–AD 100) display glyphs of regular width closely stacked in columns, after *c.* AD 100 Zapotec texts show less regularity in the glyphs' shapes, which had grown further apart; some scholars deduce a Central Mexican influence from this.[12] Zapotec writing has not yet been deciphered. There are few inscribed monuments, and these bear only brief inscriptions. Many glyphs occur only once. Between a hundred and three hundred glyphs or glyphic elements have been classified.[13] Current understanding suggests that the script comprehends the mixed system – pictography, logography, ideography and phonography – evident in all Mesoamerican writing, again with no standard percentage of usage of each component.

The Zapotec script appears to have made little use of phoneticism. (This was also characteristic of the Chinese writing of *c.* 700 BC; in most writing systems, phoneticism increases with more frequent usage.) One scholar has argued that since the Zapotec language was monosyllabic (like Chinese), it was not conducive to phoneticism in the first place, but could rely primarily on logography to convey a message.[14]

By around 500 BC, two Mesoamerican writing traditions –
Zapotec and South-eastern – had apparently emerged from a
hypothetical Proto-Zapotec source system. South-eastern was
written by the inheritors of the great Olmec culture (1200–300
BC) attested from various sites along the Gulf of Mexico. These
were the same people who left a vertical column of three symbols on Monument 13, called 'The Ambassador', at the ruins of
La Venta, indicating that the Late Olmec, at least, might have
possessed complete writing.[15] The South-eastern tradition, first
represented by Late Olmec and then perhaps by a derivative
Mixe-Zoquean, later branched into the complex traditions of
the Epi-Olmec and Classic Mayan peoples.

The distinctive script of the Epi-Olmec, written between
about 150 BC and AD 450 in the heartland of the former Olmec
civilization,[16] may have developed out of an earlier Olmec-
derived tradition. The language of Epi-Olmec is very early
Zoquean, a branch of the Mixe-Zoquean family. (As Proto-
Zoquean was spoken around AD 600, Epi-Olmec texts are actually pre-Proto-Zoquean.) Epi-Olmec writing is known
primarily from two inscriptions found in the Mexican state of
Veracruz: the La Mojarra Stela (see p. 212), from AD 156, and
the Tuxtla Statuette, from AD 163. Epi-Olmec's sophistication
implies a protracted, revered and frequently used tradition of
writing, whose main legacy remains to be discovered in the
rainforests of Veracruz.

The more significant of the two inscriptions is that on the La
Mojarra Stela, with its more than five hundred glyphs depicting
an Epi-Olmec warrior-king and heralding a rather long
description of his ascendence to kingship that includes years of
warfare and ritual performance. Like so much of Mesoamerican
writing, the La Mojarra Stela is yet another monument of
propangandistic self-aggrandizement. The pattern of repetition of certain glyphs demonstrates that here, too, the writing
comprises a mixed logographic and phonographic system. The
stela's simple, abstract glyphs appear to be phonetic, its more
complex glyphs logographic. Other monuments, of older
provenance, in both Veracruz and Chiapas – Stela C at Tres

Zapotes is provisionally dated to 32 BC – belong to the same tradition and use a similar columnar format, but with eroded or destroyed inscriptions. In general, Epi-Olmec texts appear to be more 'prosaic, discursive, and explicit than Mayan texts'.[17]

As the Mixe-Zoquean languages offer a suitable foundation for the development of those spelling conventions identified on the La Mojarra Stela, it has been reasoned that this was the tradition that later inspired Classical Mayan. A close relationship does indeed exist between Epi-Olmec and Mayan writing. Some glyphs seem to be shared but hold different sound values, suggesting a traditional logography which was re-interpreted according to local linguistic needs. For example, the sign of a shiny stone is *tza'* in Epi-Olmec and *tūn* in Mayan. Then again, some Epi-Olmec glyphs might hold the same sound values as identical glyphs in Mayan writing. The Epi-Olmec and Mayan traditions might actually be much more closely linked than is currently demonstrable. The high degree of phoneticism – 'helping glyphs' that show how a main glyph is to be pronounced, like Chinese phonetics – might also explain later Classical Mayan phoneticism.

MAYAN

Well into the 1980s, the spectacular ruins of the great Mayan civilization – ranging from eastern Chiapas and Tabasco to western Honduras – remained mute, and histories of writing were still declaring that the hundreds of Mayan monumental inscriptions comprised little more than pictorial decorations. Now, perhaps as much as 85 per cent of the Mayan hieroglyphic corpus, recognized to be complete writing, can be read. This renders the ancient Mayan realm 'the only truly historical civilization in the New World, with records going back to the third century after Christ'.[18] Though still not fully deciphered, Mayan writing is the best understood of all pre-Columbian Mesoamerican scripts. Its characteristic features, found in monumental reliefs, on wood and painted pottery, and in paper codices, can be thought of as the quintessence of the American tradition (illus. 142).

142 Mayan hieroglyphic writing in wood relief, from the metropolis of Tikal, Guatemala, *c.* AD 700.

The recent decipherment of the Mayan script by many brilliant scholars from several nations has allowed a better understanding of the other American traditions. In many ways, a discussion of Mayan's internal structure and functioning can stand as illustrative of these other traditions as well.

Between 600 BC and AD 50, Lowland Mayans appear to have inherited their writing system from an earlier culture.[19] The site of Cerros in northern Belize, dated to 50 BC, provides the earliest examples, from recognized archæological contexts, of Mayan glyphs that possess identified values. Already at this early date, the three important glyphs *ahaw* ('lord'), *k'in* ('sun') and *yax* ('first') were being used in the same fashion as in later Classical Mayan inscriptions. Because of this, the beginnings of the Classical Mayan tradition are now recognized to lie in the period between 200 BC and AD 50. The earliest readable Mayan text, on a jade dating from about 50 BC, is already organized in double columns reading from left to right and from top to bottom. It also uses 'glyphic blocks' that include both main glyphs (logograms) and affixes (phonetic identifiers). This earliest readable text occurs, in other words, in already fully developed form.

This tradition of writing accompanied and empowered the Classical Mayan civilization, a term used to characterize the high point of Mayan culture that flourished from *c.* AD 250 to 900.[20] Classical Mayan writing differs significantly from Zapotec and Epi-Olmec. Its inventory of glyphs – both main glyphs and affixes – is different, particularly in frequency and distribution. According to Mesoamerican expert Joyce Marcus, 'These differences indicate different phonetic and grammatical structures and different degrees of phoneticism.'[21] One explanation for this is that each tradition closely reflected its respective phonology – that is, its system of significant sounds in the language. Both Epi-Olmec and Mayan appear to have developed a much greater facility to exploit phonetic components than the earlier traditions. This suggests that both inherited from a postulated Mixe-Zoquean source script a propensity towards phoneticism that led them away from the preferred logography of the Zapotec branch of Mesoamerican writing. Indeed, the volume of phoneticism in both Epi-Olmec and Mayan writing quite surprised the scholars deciphering both scripts in the 1980s and '90s.

Mayan writing – and, by inference, other Mesoamerican traditions – makes use of four types of signs.[22] First, the *logograph* denotes the sound and meaning of a whole word, like the glyph *balam* for 'jaguar'. The *rebus* conveys the sound of one word by using another word sharing that sound; this sign type is in fact rare in Mayan, its only clear use being in *lak* for 'plate', also used to convey 'next'. The *phonetic complement* conveys a desired pronunciation if more than one pronunication is possible. Finally, the *semantic determinative* denotes which of several potential meanings to read; the two most frequent semantic determinatives are the 'day' glyph cartouche (for the date) and the *ahaw* scarf (for the title 'lord').

Each pair of columns in a Mayan inscription is read in its full length, whereupon the reader proceeds to the next pair of columns; single-columned or horizontal lintels and small portable inscriptions comprise exceptions. Within a given 'glyphic block' (a single sign), the reader begins reading also from left to right and from top to bottom. Single-unit glyphs – that is, signs without affixes of any kind – generally constitute logographs denoting whole words. Multi-unit glyphs might also be whole words, but those comprehending affixes or further grammatical elements. These latter might be person markers and articles, or derivational or inflectional affixes – in other words, elements 'stuck on' to show Mayan grammar. This system of logographic roots being affixed by phonetic-syllabic signs to express grammatical endings of course prefigured the system that later Korean and Japanese writing used in order to express grammatical endings on borrowed Chinese logographic roots. In Mayan writing, the reader first reads the affix(es) appearing above or in front of the larger main sign of the compound glyph or character, from left to right (if applicable). Then s/he reads the main sign itself, followed by any affix(es) below or behind it.

In this way, the Mayan writing tradition, like the Epi-Olmec before it, is a phonetic one whose glyphs denote entire words and whose component signs convey syllabic sounds of the Mayan language, generally in the form CV, or consonant + vowel. Over 150 Mayan signs have been identified as having a phonetic-syllabic function, all (except pure vowels) of the CV variety. Mayan writing also comprises glyphs that are pictograms, depicting an object meant to be spoken aloud.

There is generous allowance in the Mayan script for artistic license.[23] One glyph can possess dual functions, both logographic (representing a morpheme or the entire name of an object) and syllabic (representing the first syllable of the name of the depicted object, to be pronounced separately). So most

Mayan words can be written in several different ways, combining logography and phonography in variant spellings (illus. 143). (We write many English words several different ways, too, with varying upper case, lower case, font, italic, cursive, even a variant spelling; however, we normally remain alphabetic, except for numerals (ideographs), and rarely mix systems.) This systemic alternation or complementation introduced greater complexity, and thus ambiguity, to the Mayan tradition.

Some eight hundred glyphs swell the Mayan inventory. Many of these are archaic logograms – mostly royal names written only once.[24] At any given point in time, a Mayan scribe perhaps used two to three hundred glyphs. Many of these were probably allographic (glyphs of different shape holding the same value) or homophonic (multiple glyphs sharing the same sound). Many Mayan glyphs are also polyvalent – that is, each can convey a number of different sounds or meanings. (English digraph *ch*, for example, is phonetically polyvalent: *chest, cholera, chef* and *loch*.) What is more, Mayan scribes would sometimes

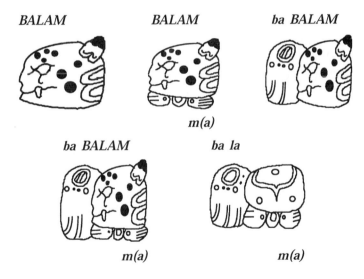

143 Five possible spellings of Mayan *balam* ('jaguar'), with initial logography yielding to increasing phonography: the top left glyph is wholly logographic, while the bottom right glyph – a compound of three phonetic signs – is wholly phonographic.

interchange signs within glyphic blocks, or combine two contiguous glyphs into one, for no apparent reason. All these possibilities greatly increase Mayan writing's ambiguity.

The Mayan tradition fully realized spoken language and was able to convey each nuance of sound, grammar, syntax and literary convention that was required of it.[25] As with almost all the world's writing systems and scripts, it was also defective. For one thing, the glottal stop so important in all Mayan languages was never awarded a separate sign like other consonants. It was only indicated by reduplicating the vowel after which it appeared: *m(o)-o-o* was written to convey *mo'* ('macaw'), for example.[26] And though the Yucatec Mayan language contains two phonemic tones as distinct from one another as English *bin* is from *pin*, there is no evidence of tonal distinction in Yucatec writing.

Again, as with the writing of the Chinese, Japanese, Sumerians and other peoples, though Mayan scribes had at their disposal a complete phonography, they did not use it on its own to simplify their mixed system, as someone accustomed to an alphabetic tradition might 'expect'. Throughout the world, logographic writing is usually maintained by its practitioners, for reasons sometimes transcending ease and efficiency. Such inherited systems hold great prestige or are attended by social taboos. Perhaps more significantly, logographic is often semantically superior to phonographic writing in message conveyance, as graphic objectification can be quicker to process cerebrally than phonetic abstraction (alphabetism). It appears that Mayan scribes felt no compulsion to discard their logographic component. In fact, among later peoples of Mesoamerica (see below), logography was distinctively preferred over phonography.

As one finds everywhere in Mesoamerica, the contents of Mayan public inscriptions remained limited, dealing nearly exclusively with births, heir-designations, accessions, deaths, wars and other details concerning dynastic rulers. Mayan monumental texts are unusually redundant, repeating the same events in slightly altered versions or with varying emphasis on different aspects. Nearly all surviving inscriptions from the Classical Mayan era involve the public sphere, chronicling in stone the history, and thus legitimizing the authority, of a local ruler. Sometimes, as at the great centres of Tikal and Palenque, public writings reveal supernatural sanction for those rulers who commissioned them, a common motif also of ancient Egyptian monumental inscriptions. This perceived dynastic aggrandizement as writing's primary function may be false, however: only public inscriptions in stone have survived, while forever lost are the erstwhile thousands of bark-paper books containing histories and genealogies (as in the Mixtec codices); records of tribute, trade and commerce; prescriptions for rituals; and so on. Most clearly indicative of the existence of great Mayan libraries is the high status of the scribe in that society.[27]

Mayan scribes, the *ah dzib*, belonged to the royal caste. Their duties were apparently regarded as among the most important of social roles. Little is known of their daily tasks or professional hierarchy, but one might compare them to those of ancient Egypt's scribes, who seem to have fulfilled similar responsibilities. Most of the Mayan scribe's business was probably done on bark-paper and deer-hide codices, each time using a fresh surface of lime sizing. Outlines were first drawn with red paint and then areas were filled in with various colours. Reds were iron compounds; other colours were most likely also of mineral origin. Black paint made of charcoal or soot was used afterwards to outline finished figures. Mayan scribes manifestly 'played with the script',[28] alternating back and forth between the semantic dimension (logography) and the phonetic one (phonography), as well as exploiting intermediary stages along the way. It was the lack of a standard orthography that imbued all Mayan writing with its playful dynamics. The Mayan scribal tradition was continued in later centuries first by Mixtec, then by Aztec, scribes, who appear to have enjoyed similar status in their respective cultures. The role of the traditional Meso-american scribe, and its accompanying respect, endured well into the Colonial era.

For several centuries, Mayan writing served many millions in the Lowlands. Could these millions read the monuments and other inscriptions? There are two opposing views. Some scholars assume a low rate of literacy, pointing out that the single word *write* finds wide diffusion among Mayan languages, whereas there are many different words for 'read', all these being heterogeneous and post-Conquest.[29] Other scholars believe that

144 Painted glyph on a Mayan beverage pot, *c.* AD 500: *cacau*, or 'chocolate'.

it was not all that difficult to learn to read Mayan writing, and that the average Mayan man or woman, regarding a colourfully painted stela in a public plaza, was perfectly capable of reading at least the date, events and names of the main protagonists – especially if there was an accompanying picture.[30]

If literacy was indeed common in ancient Mayaland, writing would have had an immediate and profound effect on the population and language – and on public opinion. Not only stelæ, but doorjambs and lintels of temples and palaces, steps leading up to these, rulers' tombs and other monuments in public assembly areas, similarly inscribed and painted in bright colours, proclaimed the glorious lives and genealogies of powerful Mayan personalities. This was hardly 'factual history' in the modern sense, but more of a propagandistic tool to uphold leadership, proclaim pre-eminence and justify tribute.[31] Like the Late Olmec a thousand years earlier, it appears, the Mayan élite used public writing principally to legitimize their claim to power. However, simple ceramics were decorated with glyphs, too, identifying such everyday things as chocolate containers (illus. 144), funerary vessels and so on.

Towards the end of the Classical Mayan era, thousands of bark-paper or deer-hide codices probably graced Mayan libraries, filled with histories, genealogies, astronomical tables, ritual prescriptions and other types of texts. In the wake of the wholesale destruction of Mayan literature following Spanish intrusion in the 1500s, only four codices miraculously escaped the bonfires, all of them post-Classical productions comprising ritual and astronomical tables. These are the *Codex Troano-Cortés* in two parts, in Madrid; the *Codex Dresdensis* in Dresden; and the *Codex Peresianus* in Paris. Thus, the accumulated knowledge of this once great New World civilization has disappeared almost without a trace. 'Even the burning of the library of Alexandria,' lamented American Mayan expert Michael Coe, 'did not obliterate a civilization's heritage as completely as this.'[32]

OTHER WRITING

Several cultures in first-millennium-AD Mesoamerica apparently used a highly pictographic 'writing system' that displayed some logography. From AD 400 to 700 in the Mixteca Baja region of Oaxaca, the Ñuiñe culture used a script preserved in brief inscriptions mostly on urns and stones, one similar to that of the Monte Albán inscriptions (see above). One scholar has listed 142 motifs, with over two hundred distinct components.[33] The accomplished artists of the Teotihuacan culture, which flourished between *c.* 200 BC and AD 650, appear at least to have distinguished between pictography and iconography, as some 120 signs of their 'script' seem to have notational significance of some kind.[34] One scholar actually regards the Teotihuacan signs as the source for the conventionalized glyphs later evidenced throughout Central Mexico.[35]

However, by the 1500s the Mixtec, Aztec and Zapotec peoples were displaying in their hundreds of colourfully painted codices containing myths and histories a highly depleted writing system that combined maximal pictography with minimal logography, reducing the phonetic component almost to insignificance. Today, these codices are more 'interpreted' than read, as the necessary context for word-for-word reading is unknown.[36] It seems ironic that the greatest source of written texts for the later Mixtec and Aztec cultures of AD 900–1521 constitutes specifically those brightly painted bark-paper or deer-hide codices that figure so tragically in the Mayan story. Many of these post-Mayan documents are in fact copies of earlier hieroglyphic or pictorial manuscripts, and the Mixtec, Aztec and even Zapotec peoples continued producing them well into the Colonial period.[37]

The Mixtec people, who occupied the area of southern Puebla and northern Oaxaca, adopted the earlier Zapotec script typically to record 'the number of captives taken by a particular warrior, on a particular day, and at a particular city'.[38] For the most part, Mixtec scribes wrote (and rewrote) genealogical and dynastic 'histories' – that is, the propaganda that each local élite wanted others to know. In essence, Mixtec texts comprise name-tags on pictorial sculptures or on paper or hide codices, including at most a verb, name glyph and place glyph. For this reason, both Mixtec and Aztec writing have been called 'labelling' or 'caption' scripts.

Most Mixtec codices appear in boustrophedon, though some are arranged in a dual-zone page. Mixtec scribes only rarely used the vertical column as an organizing principle. It was not really needed, as the text merely provided captions intended to reduce ambiguity by helping to distinguish between multiple rulers in one scene or to identify which towns had been conquered.[39] Some have claimed that this is not complete writing. However, the use of logography to convey personal names, place names, actions and other details justifies including Mixtec writing among the world's complete writing systems. The use of the rebus principle, for example, is extensive among the Mixtec (while rare among the Mayans); for example, the place name Chiyocanu ('great/bent foundation') is given by picturing a small man bending a platform foundation.

It appears that both the Mixtec and Aztec traditions were divergent developments that perhaps experienced some borrowing.[40] Evidently, Mixtec inherited features from Zapotec, its predecessor in the same region. The influence of the Toltec culture (1000–1200) shows in Mixtec calendrics and perhaps also in Mixtec writing, though it has yet to be confirmed that the Toltec possessed complete writing.

Until recently, Aztec writing of the Basin of Mexico was thought to be a picture-word system in which only the initial steps toward phonetization had been accomplished, leaving it 'at the threshold of writing proper'.[41] Now it is appreciated that, like the Mixtec, the Aztec people used a mixed system that included pictography, phonography and logography, as well as ideographic components.[42] Post-Conquest Aztec writing may indeed have contained the highest percentage of pictography among the Mesoamerican systems (illus. 145). However, Aztec codices antedating the Conquest are rare, and it is possible that these earlier works contained a greater percentage of logography and phonography than that displayed in later works.

Even post-Conquest Aztec texts include a significant amount of phonography. This phonography appears in three different ways:

* through pictography: a curved (*coltic*) mountaintop denotes the place name Colhuacán;

* through homophonous ideography: a swimmer with uplifted arms is 'merriment', which is Nahuatl *ahauializpan*, employed to convey the place name Ahuilizapan;

* through pictography plus phonetic: an arm (*acolli*), with water (*atl*) to reinforce the initial /a/, conveys the place name Acolhuacán.

In a well-known sequence from the historical-mythological *Codex Boturini* (illus. 146), for example, four named tribes are shown arriving at a named sacred locale to bid farewell to kinsmen of eight named tribes. All names in the *Codex* are phonetically written. On the far right, to give one example, the 'net' is Nahuatl *matla-tl*, which denotes the Matlazinco tribe.

The origins of Aztec writing are not yet fully understood. Some scholars believe that the Aztecs borrowed components from their predecessors in the Basin of Mexico. The Toltec, suspected as a possible source, are known to have borrowed in turn from the earlier Teotihuacan culture; however, they also are

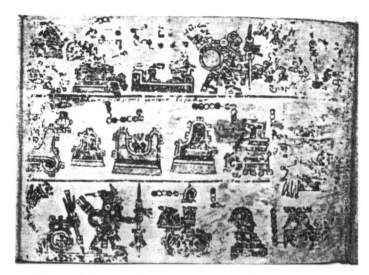

145 Pictography in the pre-Columbian Aztecan *Codex Colombino*, after AD 1048. This manuscript, in traditional Mixtec style, treats the life and history of a ruler from AD 1028 to 1048.

146 Sequence of images from the Aztec *Codex Boturini*.

known to have used only a calendric and iconographic system, not complete writing. Other scholars have suggested that the Aztecs borrowed writing from neighbouring Highlanders, such as the Mixtec (whose writing system shows many similarities) or the descendants of the Xochicalcans of western Morelos. The question of Aztec writing's origins has yet to be answered satisfactorily.

Mesoamericans were perhaps not the only ones to possess writing in the New World. There is growing evidence that a succession of scripts, based on a single phonographic writing system probably inspired by an early Mixe-Zoquean script, may have empowered various ancient cultures of the Peruvian Andes over a period of more than fifteen hundred years.

That the 'bean signs' of the Andes' early Paracan culture (*c.* 600–350 BC) might actually represent a form of writing was first suggested by Peruvian archæologist Rafael Larco Hoyle in the early 1940s.[43] Over twenty years later, the Peruvian epigrapher Victoria de la Jara identified 303 distinctive 'bean signs' in Paracan textiles and other artwork, a number close to that of identified Mayan glyphs in use at any one time. These occurred in vertical columns of distinctively positioned signs, shaped and patterned like beans, within particular 'blocks' that repeated themselves, often in distinctive patterns and with differently coloured borders (illus. 147). If this was writing, it was a pure phonography, as no pictographic or logographic component is evident. If it was a pure phonography, it consisted of a Paracan syllabary including pure vowels as well as more complex syllabic structures.

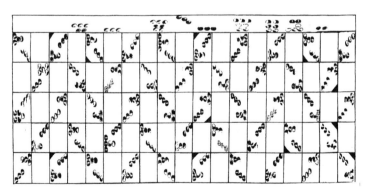

147 Possible inscription in vertical columns on a Paracan funerary *manto*, or ceremonial linen, from Peru, *c.* 400 BC. Each block holds a different series of 'bean signs'.

148 Possible phonography in the significant distribution of repeating signs in vertical columns on an Inca tunic sash, *c.* AD 1500.

This early borrowing, if it did occur, apparently became productive in Peru, inspiring a succession of similar phonographic scripts using only patterns, generally in vertical columns. The Nazca culture (*c.* 350 BC–AD 500) displayed similar signs in woven textiles, hitherto considered to be decoration. The Moche culture (*c.* AD 1–600) also used beans marked with dots or parallel lines (or a combination of both) when sending messages; leather pouches filled with such beans have been discovered in Moche graves, indicating a significant cultural value.[44] The same marked beans also feature in scenes on Moche pottery, in specifically those contexts in which writing occurs in Mesoamerica.

The Inca empire (1438–1532) appears to have borrowed the colourful designs of the Moche B culture, for some reason changing the latter's curved signs into rectangular ones. The geometrical Inca patterns called *tocapus* can be found on traditional wooden cups as well as on certain textiles (illus. 148), whereby their striking arrangement in vertical columns is reminiscent of Mesoamerican writing's orientation. The repetition of distinctive designs at odd intervals indicates a significant use for a specific purpose.

It is indeed possible that these designs comprehend a writing system containing a phonographic message in a complex syllabary, yet to be successfully deciphered. Eminent French epigrapher Marcel Cohen, confronted by the Peruvian data, was forced to conclude: 'From the number of signs and by reason of the alignments on certain documents, it does seem that one finds oneself before a true ideo-phonographic writing system as in ancient Egypt and Mesopotamia.'[45]

Complete writing appeared last in the Americas, in the first millennium BC. The mixed writing system of logosyllabic 'glyphic blocks', arranged in vertical columns, that underlies all American scripts is analogous to the early Chinese writing system and its orientation. After attaining to greatest phoneticism among Epi-Olmec and Mayan peoples, Mesoamerican writing became more pictorial in the later derivative scripts of the Mixtec, Aztec and other cultures, who nonetheless preserved, if only in 'captions', the original mixed system. In the first few centuries BC, the Paracan culture of Peru may have borrowed a Mixe-Zoquean script which it then adapted as a pure phonography, using variable 'bean signs' in similar columns of glyphic blocks. Among subsequent Andean cultures, Paracan writing inspired a succession of ostensible scripts founded on the same phonographic principle.

From its earliest use in the Americas, writing appears to have been first and foremost a propagandistic tool of the hereditary élite, the expression of aggressive societies in which warring and status competition were endemic.[46] The very first monuments showing writing herald victorious rulers or their slain and sacrificed captives. These public statements were aimed both horizontally and vertically – that is, at competing rulers and at local subjects – as legitimizations of the élite's franchise. Rulers' names and their conquests: these are the two predominant themes in Mesoamerican monumental inscriptions from writing's first use until the arrival of Europeans over two thousand years later. Of course, other writing traditions existed, too: astronomical tables, ritual prescriptions, histories, genealogies and so on. But these perishables fell to time and the Spanish Conquest.

It is perhaps as significant as it is ironic that the earliest three of the five Mesoamerican scripts detailed above – the Zapotec, Epi-Olmec and Mayan – were better capable of conveying speech than the later scripts of the Mixtec and Aztec peoples. In the history of writing, it is almost always the reverse that obtains: logography generally leads in time to greater, or even complete, phoneticism. While phoneticism appears indeed to have been the logical result of writing's development in South America (if the Peruvian patterns do prove to be writing), in

Mesoamerica the practice of writing became restricted to uses that favoured more pictorial expression. Monumental inscribing had all but been abandoned by *c.* AD 900, supplanted almost entirely by coloured codices of paper or hide telling histories and genealogies in pictorial fashion and using complete writing only for simple 'captions'. This may be evidence as well of the borrowing of a fully developed foreign system which, over time, fragmented among less socially developed borrowers whose fewer demands did not warrant maintenance of such an elaborate system.

SEVEN

The Parchment Keyboard

'Cum legebat, oculi ducebantur per paginas ...' penned St Augustine with seeming incredulity in the early 400s AD:

> ... when he was reading, he drew his eyes along over the leaves, and his heart searched into the sense, but his voice and tongue were silent. Ofttimes when we were present ... we still saw him reading to himself, and never otherwise ... But with what intent soever he did it, that man certainly had a good meaning in it.[1]

Augustine's wonder at witnessing his teacher St Ambrose reading silently to himself came from the fact that, well into the first few centuries AD in Western Europe, people still read aloud. Literature was primarily a memory aid, recalling what one had already heard somewhere else. Literary texts were almost exclusively intoned as in chant, or at least murmured for meditation and better memorization. Silent reading was practically unknown. Passages in works by Lucian, Suetonius, Horace, Ovid and others attest that silent reading was invariably perceived in antiquity as something extraordinary.[2]

This changed during the Middle Ages. Silent mostly replaced loud reading, effectively marking the first of two mediæval thresholds – one into, the other out of, this uncommonly fertile epoch lasting from *c.* AD 500 to 1500. St Augustine's wonder at seeing his teacher reading a text quietly to himself symbolically signals a new notion of writing's role in society as an autonomous form of information conveyance. This notion evidently had not obtained earlier, or only rarely. In the Middle Ages, the written word appears to have become something apart from the representation of a thought. The written word became thought itself.

The notion that written language now stood on a par with spoken language became principle, and it was fundamental to all mediæval thought. It was as revolutionary to Western Europe as the later threshold that ushered in the modern world: printing, or graphic communication by means of multiplied impressions.

The emancipation of the written word had immediately to do with its sudden proliferation. Antiquity's preferred writing material, papyrus, had been expensive. Since few people could afford to buy written texts, not many read longer works of literature. In the second century AD, however, parchment became available in larger quantities. This much cheaper writing material encouraged the increased production of written texts.³ In fact, parchment had been around for centuries. In 190 BC, Eumenes II (197–158 BC) of Pergamum in Asia Minor (today's western Turkey), wishing to establish a library to rival that of Alexandria in Egypt, encouraged his experts to perfect a technique of thinly stretching and drying the skin of sheep and goats. Parchment, the final product of this process, was named after its place of invention, Pergamum. Though parchment fragments from the second century BC have survived, it did not begin to compete seriously with papyrus until the second century AD.

Parchment eventually replaced papyrus as Western Europe's preferred writing material; the Middle Ages has even been hailed as the 'Age of Parchment'. Only towards the High Middle Ages, particularly in Islamic countries, did it begin to yield to paper. After the 1300s and 1400s, the use of parchment dwindled everywhere before paper's obvious advantages, except for charters and other documents. (Parchment is still used today for special occasions.)

Parchment was never used in India, South-East Asia or East Asia. The idea of writing sacred texts on the skin of butchered animals offended Hindus and Buddhists. And the Chinese never used it because they already had paper by the second century AD. But in Europe as of the fourth century AD, parchment's ubiquity meant that individual sheets of writing – no longer rolled-up papyrus scrolls – could be collated and bound to create something altogether new that facilitated written literature's use and conservation like nothing before: the codex, or book.

Mediæval Europe's enfranchisement of the written word, and

its greater proliferation there, transformed Western society ... and eventually the world.

When the Roman Emperor Constantine I (AD 306–337) transferred his capital from 'pagan' Rome to Christian Byzantium, renaming the latter Constantinople in AD 330, all of Greek culture – including written Greek – experienced a renaissance. The subsequent Byzantine Empire preserved and disseminated the teachings of ancient Greece; it also led the Western world in science and the humanities for many centuries. Furthermore, it directly influenced Arab scholars and scientists, whose own teachings and translations of Greek works were then carried to Muslim Spain and other centres of learning. Such transmissions introduced ancient Greek philosophy and science to Western Europe. As ancient Greece had inspired Rome, Byzantine Greece inspired the mediæval world, chiefly through the vehicle of the continuously developing Greek alphabetic script.

As described in Chapter 4, two classes of Greek writing have always existed side by side: the book 'hand' (style of writing by hand), which almost exclusively conveyed literature, and the cursive hand of everyday business. In early Greek papyri and vellum (the finer calfskin version of parchment) manuscripts, uncial was the ordinary hand.[4] Uncial used 'majuscules', or large, upper-case letters composed of curves instead of the angular capitals of monumental texts. (Curves were more easily written on papyri and parchment than capitals.) Uncial writing in early Greek manuscripts, of great eloquence and strength, flourished once vellum replaced papyrus altogether. The uncials led to smaller, flowing cursive forms that eventually tended towards 'minuscules', or small, lower-case letters. This process took centuries, however.

For Constantinople's first three hundred years, the hand of the earlier Roman era continued to prevail until a distinctive 'Byzantine' hand emerged (illus. 149). After AD 600, circular letters became more oval and compressed, narrower in proportion to their height. The Greek hand began sloping to the right, and

[Uncials: mathematical treatise, 7th century]

[Minuscules: Oxford *Euclid*, AD 888]

[Archaic church uncials: *Evangeli Tarium*, AD 980]

[Formal book hand: *Sermons of St Theodore Studites*, 1136]

[Elegant book hand: Homer's *Odyssey*, 1479]

[Post-mediæval book hand: *Manual of Jurisprudence*, 1541]

149 Greek mediæval and post-mediæval hands.

diacritics or accent marks began to be used systematically – not randomly, as had been the case for over eight hundred years – to convey a more precise reproduction of contemporary Greek speech. The early lightness of the Greek uncials became heavier and more strained. By the 900s, uncial writing in Greek was reserved for ecclesiastical works.

Greek minuscule writing had appeared in the ninth century, comprising the normal Greek cursive written with greater care. Minuscules eventually replaced all other forms of Greek writing. There are over a thousand dated Greek manuscripts in European libraries written before 1500, and almost all of them are in minuscules. Capitals often appeared side by side with their small cursive forms in the same text. By about AD 900, Greek minuscules had become exceedingly small, upright and exact, with breathings – the *h*'s – shown as rectangular marks.

Greek book publishers thrived in Constantinople. Their works were translated into Arabic and distributed throughout the Muslim world. While there was great uniformity of hand in these productions, there was great contextual variety. In contrast, Rome's once numerous publishers – located in that city as well as in other major Roman centres in Germany, France, Britain and North Africa – declined after the sixth century. There, Latin book production became the responsibility of monasteries' and abbeys' scriptoria. While there was great regional variety of hands, there was even greater contextual uniformity.

By the High Middle Ages, a formal style of Greek writing had emerged, with lengthened strokes, prominently featured marks conveying both contraction and accent, and much rounder breathings. By the 1400s, a wide variety of hands was allowed in Greek, some invoking the style of the 1200s, others introducing a modern cursive hand, compact and with flourishes. By 1600, a loose hand of modern type was emerging that influenced the first printers of the Greek language in their search for a legible typeface that would best convey the Classical texts in such demand by Humanist scholars (illus. 150). From this source there eventually developed the Greek typefaces familiar to students of the Classics.

Printing in Greece itself employed many different typefaces, especially in the 1800s, when general education was introduced and public literacy rose. Breathings and accents – whose invention is generally attributed to Aristophanes of Byzantium (d. *c*. 180 BC) – were maintained rigorously during this time, though the modern language had changed to such an extent that

ΕΛΤΟΙ Ρωμαίοις ἐπιχείρησ᾽ σεῶπαι, ἢ ἡ Ρώ-
μην εἶλον αὐθ᾽ τῶ Καπιτωλίν, ἢ ἐμπιωρήκασι. Κά-
μιλλος ἢ αὐτοὺς ἐνίκησι, ἢ ἐξήλασι, ἢ μ᾽ χρόνοις ἐ-
πελθόντας αὖθις ἐνίκησι, τὴν ἐ.θριάμβωσιν ἀπ᾽ αὐτῶν, ὁ ἐδόκει τα γεγονὼς ἔτη. ἢ τείτη δὲ Κελτῶν
ςρατιὰ ἐμβέβληκαι εἰς τὴν Ἰταλίαν τῦ καὶ αὐτὴ
οἱ Ρωμαῖοι διεφθάρκασιν, ὑφ᾽ ἡγεμόνι Τίτω Κοΐντω.
μ᾽ δὲ ταῦτα Βοίοι, Κελτικὸν ἔθνος ἡμεγιδίσατο ἐ-
πῆλθε Ρωμαίοις, ἢ αὐτοὺς Γάϊος Συλπίκιος δικτά-
τωρ μ᾽ ςρατιᾶς ἀπίντα, ὃς ὑς ἢ ςρατηγήματι τοιούτω χρήσασθαι λέγεται· ἐ-
κέλευσε γὰρ τοὺς ὑπὸ τῶ μετώ που τεταγμένοις ἐξακοντίσαντας ὁμοῦ συσκάσαι

[Appian's *Roman History* printed by Charles Estienne in Paris,
1551]

Ἄνδρα μοι ἔννεπε, μοῦσα, πολύτροπον, ὃς μάλα πολλὰ
πλάγχθη, ἐπεὶ Τροίης ἱερὸν πτολίεθρον ἔπερσεν·
πολλῶν δ᾽ ἀνθρώπων ἴδεν ἄστεα καὶ νόον [1] ἔγνω,
πολλὰ δ᾽ ὅ γ᾽ ἐν πόντῳ πάθεν ἄλγεα ὃν κατὰ θυμόν,
ἀρνύμενος ἥν τε ψυχὴν καὶ νόστον ἑταίρων.
ἀλλ᾽ οὐδ᾽ ὣς ἑτάρους ἐρρύσατο, ἱέμενός περ·
αὐτῶν γὰρ σφετέρῃσιν ἀτασθαλίῃσιν ὄλοντο,
νήπιοι, οἳ κατὰ βοῦς Ὑπερίονος Ἠελίοιο
ἤσθιον· αὐτὰρ ὁ τοῖσιν ἀφείλετο νόστιμον ἦμαρ.
τῶν ἁμόθεν γε, θεά, θύγατερ Διός, εἰπὲ καὶ ἡμῖν.

[Homer's *Odyssey*, printed in italics in London, 1919]

Ο άνθρωπος κοιμάται. Το σύμπλεγμα νεύρων και μυών ανα-
παύεται χαλαρωμένο στο κρεβάτι · εξωτερικά δεν υπάρχει κίνηση.
Εσωτερικά ο εγκέφαλος βομβεί λειτουργώντας σε άτακτα διαστή-
ματα. Μια δύναμη συντήρησης καταγράφει ακατάπαυστα την εσω-
τερική δραστηριότητα που μοιάζει με απέραντο σιδηροδρομικό
δίκτυο νεύρων.

[Modern novel, printed in Athens, 1990]

most such marks were acknowledged to be 'superfluous' (though still significant in the visual recognition of words). During the last quarter of the 1900s, Greek orthography finally abandoned its complex system of markings, leaving only the acute accent (´) to indicate stress on each Modern Greek word of more than one syllable.

THE LATIN MIDDLE AGES

It was the Romans who created the basic forms of our letters. Like the Greeks, Romans wrote only in capitals (majuscule writing) and cursive, with no upper-case/lower-case distinction. Basic Roman letter shapes were originally monoline, like Greek letters, with no variation of thick and thin. However, the Romans later introduced a light, oblique (slanting) stress to their capitals, copying the thick-thin variations caused by writing in ink with a broad nib on papyrus. Special literary works on papyrus, and later on parchment and vellum, were also written in these capitals. The Romans used more serifs than the Greeks, to enhance both legibility and æsthetic appeal. Though Roman capitals survived into the ninth century AD (for example, in the Utrecht Psalter) as an accidental imitation of a long-deceased script, capitals were essentially defunct for writing entire texts by the end of the fifth century. They only survived the Middle Ages – as both square and rustic capitals – because they were preferred for writing titles and initials.

Uncial writing, a modification of square capital writing, was a curving round hand avoiding angles that became Roman scribes' preferred book hand as of the fourth century AD (illus. 151). Uncial writing's earliest examples show it to be precise, as well as very easy to read. The oldest datable uncial script, from Hippo in North Africa, is from about AD 400. By the eighth century, however, uncial writing had greatly degenerated.[5] Uncials were used in Italy especially for biblical texts, particularly in Rome. Christian missionaries carried uncials to the far reaches of the Empire, though not, as is sometimes claimed, because Christians preferred them over the 'pagan' rustic and square capitals.[6]

ƲeΝeꞂꞀNTA𝖣eꓴꟿꓲNᴧꓴSΡꓲ

[Late Roman uncials: Fulda New Testament, *c.* AD 546]

cꞃeꞑꞃeꞇqꓰꟾꙇꙠꝑeꞃeꞃꞃꙋ

[Half uncials: Biblical commentary, before AD 569]

ʜ ꓴꟿ ᴧNᴧeN ᴧꞇꓴꝑᴧecᴧꝑᴧcꓲꞇ

[Mixed uncial and cursive hand: *Pandects*, or Roman civil law, 7th century]

dimur &-quꝛꞇꟾnquodꞑm̃ꝑꝛꞇꓴlꞑ

[Late Roman cursive book hand: *Homilies* of St Maximus, 7th century]

151 Early mediæval Latin hands.

During the fourth century, the vellum codex, a manuscript volume of individual sheets bound together, began to replace the papyrus scroll. With vellum or parchment, one could write on both sides of a sheet, thus doubling writing capacity. The first reference to the codex had appeared in six epigrams of the poet Martial (AD 40–103) written as labels for six codices holding the works of Homer, Virgil, Cicero, Livy, Ovid and Martial himself – the earliest known 'books' in the modern sense. After the fourth century, the parchment or vellum codex, or 'book' as it came to be called in English (a derivative of Germanic *bōkā*, or 'beech' after the earliest material of rune tablets), remained Europe's preferred literary form. As the French historian Henri-Jean Martin has asserted, 'The appearance of the codex – the work presented on pages written on both sides rather than on one side of a continuous scroll – was undoubtedly the most important revolution in the book in the Common Era.'[7]

New Roman Cursive arose from a reform of Old Roman Cursive that had been completed by the fourth century.[8] As we have seen (Chapter 4), Roman handwriting had developed many different styles, often called 'cursive' (which customarily means a flowing, connected hand) though in fact maintaining separate, disconnected letters, even in the most hastily drafted messages or graffiti (see illus. 112–14). Scribes simplified letters to such a degree that nearly all of them could be written by a solitary pen stroke.[9] Over time, a smaller script, a 'minuscule' that no longer used capitals or uncials, developed which allowed three different letter heights: ascending (like *b*), neutral (*n*) and descending (*p*). A scribe's choice of lettering often depended on the message to be transmitted, and to whom: '… the medium was an important part of the message.'[10] Various styles of lettering commanded by individual Latin scribes bore socially recognized political and cultural messages in themselves, each deemed appropriate for specific uses and texts. As society changed, so too did the frequency and distribution of particular hands and their domains of usage.

New Roman Cursive was widely used throughout the Empire and contributed to the development of the Latin regional scripts, or national hands of Europe. Cursive writing in Latin, as in Greek, had always been far more extensive than capital or uncial writing. Sometimes, it intruded into the domain of book hands, at first as marginal notes and comments, then as the script itself. The oblique or slanting uncial of the sixth century began to give way to cursive forms. A new mixed uncial developed in the seventh century, a cursive uncial mixed hand that maintained disconnected letters which took on new, lower-case shapes.

Half-uncial writing developed in Italy and southern France in the late fifth century and became a preferred book hand. Its letters formed the model for the creation of the Carolingian minuscule. Though the roundness of Roman uncials was preserved in half-uncial writing, only a few of the letters were truly uncials. Indeed, half uncials already comprised the national hands that would emerge centuries later.

Latin cursive continued to be written well into the Merovingian era, until *c.* AD 650, even as a literary hand for private and quick use. Late Latin cursive became the foundation for the scripts of Italy, Spain and the Frankish realm, creating the Beneventan, Visigothic and Merovingian hands (illus. 152). The cursive book hands, with uncial and half-uncial admixtures, were the starting point for many national branchings.

These firm, recognized regional scripts emerged just as Rome was beginning to fragment politically in the fifth century. From then until the eighth century, New Roman Cursive combined with the half-uncial script to produce a great variety of Western scripts, all of them written in lower case. The Lombards of northern Italy, under Frankish rule, followed first

[Beneventan cursive book hand: Albinus Flaccus' *De Trinitate*, AD 812]

[Visigothic cursive book hand: St Isidore's *Etymologies*, 9th century]

[Merovingian cursive charter hand: Charter of Childebert III, AD 695]

[Merovingian cursive book hand: Eugyppius from the 8th century]

152 Beneventan, Visigothic and Merovingian hands.

Merovingian, then Carolingian, hands, while the Beneventan hand of Italy's south, as a formal book hand, developed its own unique appearance, with heavy, oblique strokes to the short verticals' head and feet. Visigothic, the national hand of Spain, flourished from the eighth to the twelfth century; it was characterized by a 'clubbing' of tall, vertical strokes in early specimens and by squareness and thinness of letters in the 1000s and early 1100s. Merovingian writing comprised all the hands of the Frankish realm before Charlemagne, in many cases immediately identifiable by an often cramped, laterally compressed, slender and almost illegible appearance. A complex system of ligatures (marks connecting two letters), abbreviations and suspensions (marks indicating omitted letters) also greatly inhibited legibility. Later Merovingian hands, however, often from Italy and drawing heavily from half uncials, prefigured the later Carolingian minuscule and achieved a certain graceful legibility.

By the end of the eighth century, the most frequent Merovingian hands appear to have been legible only to their authors, however. So if the King of the Franks ever wished to implement the far-reaching educational goals he had announced, a revolution had to occur in Frankland's scriptoria.

Charlemagne realized this, and in 789 commanded the complete revision of ecclesiastical books in all scriptoria in the main monastic centres of Germany, France and northern Italy. The most influential of these was the abbey of St Martin's at Tours, whose abbot from 796 to 804 was the Englishman Alcuin of York. Alcuin personally oversaw the creation of what later came to be called Carolingian minuscule, the West's most significant writing reform of the past two thousand years (illus. 153). Carolingian minuscule is a fortuitous blending of Continental half uncials and Irish-English hands, the latter probably introduced to the Frankish realm by Alcuin himself, who also supervised the realm's educational reform. Alcuin and others evidently perceived a need for the clarity of a classically based script close to the conservative hands used at the time in Ireland and northern England. Carolingian minuscule developed from the Roman half-uncial script, purposely integrating new regional minuscule scripts. It was a very clean, simplified script that avoided ornateness and created an even, flowing appear-

copiosilacaseffluere! puer. sur

[*Sulpicius Severus*, early 9th century]

Aitparalytico · tibidico

[*Gospels* of the Emperor Lothar, mid-9th century]

ut legati apticisuggesserunt per gundharum ag

[*Annals of Fulda*, before 882]

pater ompsacinadis. honoruauc

[*Sacramentary of Corbie*, 10th century]

ctiam dominica que aduenerat nocte acdie

[*Lives of the Saints*, 11th century]

153 Frankish Carolingian minuscule hands from France and Germany.

ance. Ligatures, abbreviations and suspensions almost totally disappeared; some Carolingian manuscripts display none at all. The obvious scribal imperative was legibility.

Carolingian script prevailed throughout Western Europe. (Only Ireland has used its own Irish hand, even in typeface, up to the present day for all Irish-language texts.) The Frankish realm's writing and educational reforms first promoted an easily legible book hand in what later became France and Germany, then further afield as the new hand's popularity grew. Carolingian minuscule was used for books and documents in Italy from the ninth to the thirteenth century alongside other scripts, and for Latin texts in England from the mid-tenth to the end of the eleventh century.

In the history of Western writing, the creation of Carolingian minuscule remains a watershed – it became Europe's most important script and determined the course of writing in the West until the Renaissance, seven hundred years later.[11]

The Carolingian script's diffusion throughout Europe over the following centuries saw its lower-case minuscule everywhere replacing the half uncials and mixed cursives that had dominated Western writing. Capitals, or majuscules, were now reserved for initials (beginning letters of text) and other special uses. What had once been the Latin alphabet's model script now became marginalized, as ancient scripts everywhere tend to be. Much later, capitals assumed a highly refined role within conventionalized writing, subject to precise rules of usage.

Once a distinction obtained between majuscule and minuscule, it could be exploited to convey information (compare *Bill* and *bill*). For this reason, all Latin-derived modern scripts usually have between 40 and 65 letters which have to be learnt (not the traditional '26 letters of the alphabet'): upper case or capitals, and lower case or small letters. These 40 to 65 are the lower-order *functional letters* conveying between 20 and 30 higher-order *systemic letters*.

During the Carolingian reform, Frankish scribes, probably at St Martin's at Tours, also effected important alphabetic modifications. The letter *u* was invented to distinguish the vowel /u/ from the consonantal use of *v*, and *j* was innovated to distinguish the consonantal function of the letter *i*. However, these changes were not systematically implemented for many centuries. After Charlemagne, nearly all changes involved the addition of new letters, or the attachment of diacritics to old ones, when conveying national languages containing sounds that cannot be conveyed by means of the standard letters of the Latin alphabet.

By the tenth century, Carolingian minuscule had become the standard hand in most of Western Europe, with many regional variants and remnant local forms for special purposes (see illus. 153). Because Latin's continued use of *v* for both /u/ and /v/ confused Germanic speakers' /w/ with /v/, a century later German scribes began distinguishing the /w/ by writing the Latin *v* double as *vv*, which is why we have the 'double *u*' today. In time, this *vv* was no longer perceived and written as a digraph but as an autonomous grapheme (in contrast to *ch*, *ph*, *th*, *ng* and other digraphs). (The full differentiation of *u*, *v* and *w* was not complete in England before the 1800s; even today, some English dialects still merge the /v/ and /w/ though the written language maintains strict separation.)

By the 1100s, the graphic unity of the Carolingian script had begun to fragment, and regional hands emerged, each expressing a characteristic form – not separate scripts within one writing system, as in India, but the same script with only minor differences (illus. 154). Again, complicated ligatures, abbreviations and suspensions appeared, mainly to conserve precious parchment. The twelfth century also saw the creation of large books and strong, bold, new letters, while the thirteenth century witnessed a sudden reduction in letter size, lateral compression, a new angularity and slanting strokes refined into hairlines (a great demand for Bibles in the second half of the 1200s had thousands being penned in this tiny, compressed script). As a result of the Crusades, scribes began using Arabic (1, 2, 3, 4) instead of Roman numerals (i, ii, iii, iv), thus conserving even more space; Arabic numerals are now used worldwide.

In the 1300s, burghers began to seize local political control and demand education for their children. Locally underwritten public schools opened. For the year 1338, for example, the Florentine chronicler Giovanni Villani recorded that 'The boys and girls who learn to read are about 10,000 [in Florence]; the children who were learning calculation and mathematics in six schools were from 1,000 to 1,200; those who were learning grammar and logic in four [advanced] schools were from 550 to 600.'[12] The powerful mercantile class that was emerging rapidly was founded on books and learning. This was a new trend, and one that transformed all of Western Europe.

With quantity came loss of quality. The scribes of the 1300s and 1400s no longer observed the high standards of their predecessors, their letters being less exact, less elegant. Theirs were the hands that soon became the typefaces of the first printers (see below). The 1400s also saw the ultimate dissolution of minuscule book hands, as almost every non-printed work after this time appeared either in charter hand (used for documents) or in everyday cursive handwriting.

habentem in se et dignitatem qua

[Italy: *Homilies*, 12th century]

C onſentit aſtruit tr iouis impio

[Italy: *Horace*, 1391]

en annerghie fut Jadis vne

[France: *Miracles de Nostre Dame, c.* 1450]

neq̃ regerentur a caſibuſ magiſq̃ regerent caſuſ.

[Italy: *Sallust*, 1466]

154 Italian and French hands of the High and late Middle Ages.

In fact, two competing hands had developed out of the protracted fragmentation of the Carolingian script: Gothic and Humanist (illus. 155).

From *c.* 1050 to 1500, Gothic defined the cursive script of Europe.[13] Also called 'Black Letter', it developed out of Carolingian minuscule in many variations, displaying a progression to ever-increasing angularity of individual letters and ever-greater compression of letters within individual words. Gothic was written with a broad nib, held at a sharp angle to the horizontal. It avoided curves whenever possible – even to the point of turning the Gothic *o* into a narrow hexagon. The earliest model for printer's type, Gothic became the exclusive vehicle for Western Europe's Germanic languages.

The Humanist scribes of Italy, on the other hand, attempted to revive the classic hand of ancient Rome. In practice, however, they held closer to Carolingian minuscule.[14] This Humanist, or Roman, hand became the instrument of the Renaissance – a

Sicut unguentum in capite quod des-
cendit in barbam barbam aaron.

negocia transferunt. Quod si hominibus bonay
rerum tanta cura esset: quanto studio aliena ac
nihil profutura multoqp etiam periculosa petut.

155 The two competing hands of the mid-1400s: Gothic (above) and Humanist (below).

narrow nib describing round, wide, spaced letters. It conveyed
sunny, open Italy and the new secular learning based on
Classical Antiquity. As with Alcuin of York six hundred years
earlier, Italian Humanist scholars purposely simplified ornateness to enhance legibility and to introduce classical elegance
into their books. This movement proceeded in conscious oppo-
sition to Gothic.[15] Based on twelfth-century Italian hands, the
first Humanist Minuscule was developed in Florence in 1402–3.
It was written small, with lengthened ascenders (like *l* and *h*) and
descenders (*p* and *g*). A Humanist Cursive emerged a decade
later as a book hand, characterized by a forward slant – today we
know it as italic.[16] Humanist or Roman writing, which originally was called Antiqua as a declaration of fidelity to ancient
prototypes, became the model for Roman letters as used by the
earliest Italian printers. Over five hundred years later, it is the
world's preferred typeface. The script you are reading is a direct
descendant.

Italy's Humanist Cursive became the sixteenth-century's
hand *par excellence*.[17] France, French-speaking Switzerland and
Spain quickly adopted it, and in England the Gothic Cursive
Secretary Hand commonly used in business had finally yielded
to Humanist Cursive by the end of the 1600s. German speakers
never accepted Humanist Cursive, regarding Gothic as the
expression of Germanic identity. In the 1500s, they modified
Gothic Cursive into a special variant called *Kurrentschrift*, which
was taught in schools as the standard German hand until 1941
(see below).

In the early Middle Ages, Europe's abbeys and monasteries only became centres for study and copying as a result of sustained exchange and supply and inspiration from outside.[18] Already in the fifth century AD, Irish Christians were importing books from Continental Europe and hosting foreign pupils. In this way, Irish ogham writing yielded more and more to the Latin prerogative – all education was in the Latin language of the Church, written in the Latin alphabet. Even Irish itself came to be written in Latin letters.

The term *Insular* has come to designate the scripts of the British Isles written up to the middle of the ninth century; this is often subdivided into Irish and 'Anglo-Saxon'. In fact, Insular writing was essentially Irish, and was only later taken to northern England by Irish monks. This is because a separate Irish Christian tradition had developed, with its own characteristic hand, once the Roman occupation forces had left the British Isles. Writing had developed differently here: the national hands of Continental Europe emerged from Roman Cursive, but Irish and English handwriting emerged from the earlier Roman half uncials. This is because Irish scribes were first influenced by the earliest Roman missionaries, who still wrote principally in the half uncials of the fifth and sixth centuries AD, long before Roman Cursive's appropriation on the Continent. Ireland's relative isolation led to a separate, conservative development. Ireland's, in fact, is one of the most conservative hands known to palæography (the study of older writing and inscriptions).

Early Irish handwriting using the Latin alphabet occurs in two styles: round and pointed (illus. 156). Round is half uncial and closely resembles writing in French and Italian manuscripts of the fifth and sixth centuries. It rapidly developed on Irish soil into one of Europe's most ornamental hands, as exemplified in Ireland's celebrated seventh-century Book of Kells (illus. 157). Pointed hand is merely a lateral compression of the round hand, a minuscule that draws out into 'points' or hairlines. It developed after the round hand had been elaborated, probably first appearing in the seventh century. (Some pages of the Book of ñœidiuntneq:siquis ǫmor

[Round hand: *Gospels of MacRegol, c.* AD 800]

nēq: Conꝟꞇ.unꝯ́ mihounrn ⸱ pꝛ́
uñ Goꝛꝑnꞏr ꝑ.ꞏpꞇ̇ẛl꞊.ı rmꞇ uoꝗ

[Pointed hand: *Book of Armagh,* before 844]

℈Gmꞇꝵqā ⁊ nꞟmꝛonꞟm pæcꝺꞇꞃī ɩomꞃ gꝵ
ꝺer mꜹꝛꞁꝵꝗbꝫ ab ıꝟꞇꝓoꝵꞃꞇꝼ. ꝗoꝓꝥꝺꝯ

[Pointed hand: *Gospels of Maelbrighte,* 1138]

156 Early Irish handwriting.

Kells appear in pointed hand.) In the early Middle Ages, Irish missionaries took their writing to Luxeuil in France, St Gallen in Switzerland, Würzburg in Germany, and Bobio in Italy, where it was further copied. However, Irish writing soon yielded to Continental cursives in all these places.

By the eighth century, Irish scribes had refined everyday cursive writing in minuscule to allow its use for the production of quality vellum books. This process also included consistent word separation and punctuation.[19] By the 1000s and 1100s, Irish pointed hand had assumed its characteristic angular shapes.

England had long had two ways of writing before the Irish missionaries arrived: the Romans' Latin alphabet, for writing Latin, and the Germanic runes, for writing the several German tongues resident in the British Isles. Following Irish intrusion, two different schools of writing emerged: Irish in the north, which eventually produced the English national hand, and Roman Rustic Capitals, a legacy of the Roman missionaries who had been centred at Canterbury (this script ceased to be used early on). In the tenth century, increased trade with the Continent introduced the minuscule, which then replaced the

feac· Se ipsum hohp
úum faccere strex israh
cendac hunc decruce
mus ei · Cohfidit ih chīo
bera eum siuult dpic

157 Ireland's Book of Kells, late 7th century.

beaa quilugunt
quōniam ipsi
cousolabunuar
beaa qui esuriunt
asrauut iufaaam

158 England's Lindisfarne Gospels, *c.* 698. Written above each line, in 10th-century Anglo-Saxon Cursive, is the earliest Gospel translation in English.

English national hand.

England's main writing influence in the early Middle Ages had come from Ireland. Beginning in the seventh century, northern English scribes were copying and further developing the Insular half uncials of the Irish, as best exemplified in the famous Lindisfarne Gospels of *c.* 698 (illus. 158). The monastery of Lindisfarne, on Holy Island off the north-east coast of *carmmumaliqñoðioicqrat*

[Bede's *Ecclesiastical History*, mid-8th century]

ILIUTCOON ILTqLacne quœ duos

[*Canterbury Gospels*, late 8th century]

|11.'1c'tjone.u. flegn quoq: slopuopiypmn me·

[Charter of King Cynewulf of Mercia, 812]

Siautân quoð obrrt. aliqpur piabol framinœriomr ðie. rtpiðula cla

[Charter of Æthelstan, 931]

hominum. uc uioêao siest intælle·

[Latin Psalter, *c.* 969]

159 Early English handwriting.

Northumberland, is generally regarded as the cradle of English handwriting. At first indistinguishable from the Irish hand, English handwriting developed into a school with its own characteristic features (illus. 159). The round and pointed hands of Irish Insular also distinguished the two styles of English writing, the round having developed from Roman half uncials, and the pointed from the round. The round was used for books and only rarely for charters; early on, it grew lighter in appearance. Pointed was used mainly for documents but also for books; an early elegance yielded to lateral compression and whimsical

⁊hiſ broðor eac eadmund æþeling· eal
ætrocce·ſpuſða eſgum· embebſun na
dufon· heopon heaþo linða· hamoﬁa la
peaﬀoeſ· ſpahim ge æþeleſeſ· ſﬁamen
campeoﬀ· wið laﬁﬁa gehſæne lanð eal

160 The *Anglo-Saxon Chronicle* in English, *c.* 1045.

variation, with the script becoming more rugged and coarse over time.

By the end of the tenth century, the Franks' Continental minuscule was influencing English writing – a 'return' of the Englishman Alcuin's own creation.[20] In places, Frankish minuscule replaced English pointed altogether, especially for Latin-language texts. Anglo-Saxon texts continued to be written in Pointed Minuscule, which was popular until the middle of the 1100s. Throughout the 1000s and 1100s, however, Pointed Minuscule increasingly lost compactness to become ever closer to the Frankish style of writing then in use throughout the Continent.

Writing English in the Latin alphabet was problematical (illus. 160). The first scribes used the Irish Insular hand employed exclusively to write only the Latin language. However, four sounds in Old English did not occur in Latin as written in the seventh century, so new letters had to be found to convey them:

- /w/ was written with the letter ᚹ of the Runic alphabet also indigenous to Anglo-Saxon England. This was the so-called 'wynn'. In Middle English, it was replaced by minuscule *uu* or *w*. It is rarely seen in manuscripts after 1300.

- /θ/ as in *thin* and /ð/ as in *this* were both written using the single Runic letter ᚦ, or 'thorn'. Eventually, the letter ð was created simply by drawing a line through Latin *d* – a sophisticated featural distinction. In time, this letter came to be called 'eth'. Scribes still failed to separate the two sounds, however, and so by Middle English a digraph – *th* – was being used for both instead. This we still use today, though graphic *th* conveys at least two separate phonemes (compare *thin* and *this*). Thorn þ survives as a cultural remnant in such artificial names as 'Ye Olde English Inn' in which Y is merely a late mediæval variant of þ.

◆ Anglo-Saxon *a* as in 'hat' reproduced a high sound unknown in Latin, halfway between Latin's *a* and *e*. So Anglo-Saxon scribes chose to write *a* and *e* together as the digraph *æ* to convey this sound, later called 'ash' after the Runic letter conveying the same sound. But again by Middle English, scribes were no longer using *æ*, probably because the sound had dropped somewhat and come closer to the standard Latin *a*, which was then used instead, as it is today.

After the Norman Conquest in 1066, English minuscule almost entirely disappeared – the conquerors had brought their own writing. Only some English-language texts continued to use the English hand. Eventually, this too was replaced with that from the Continent (illus. 161). By the 1100s, English scribes were writing a modified Saxon hand for English but normal minuscule for Latin. A cursive revival began at the end of the century, introducing calligraphic features into Gothic writing, as seen in the Secretary script used chiefly for informal documents (such as land transactions) and general correspondence. Characteristic of this script is a pointed, angular appearance with swelling ascenders (*f* and initial *s* in particular). In the 1200s, Latin minuscule, with some English letters, was used to write English. By the close of the century, such cursive scripts were also being used for books, especially those designated for use at Oxford and Cambridge universities. Soon, a variety of mixed scripts emerged that integrated features of cursive and book hands. In the 1300s and 1400s, many English scribes preferred to use charter hand for their books, elaborating a special 'English' hand quite distinctive from Continental book hands. This was the hand of England's first printing presses. After the 1400s, book hand disappeared altogether because of printing, leaving only charter hand and cursive handwriting.[21]

[*Anglo-Saxon Chronicle, c.* 1121]

[*Homilies*, early 13th century]

[The *Ayenbite of Inwyt*, 1340]

[Chaucer's 'Legend of Good Women', mid-15th century]

161 English hands of the High and late Middle Ages in English.

English handwriting bears little resemblance to the English printed script, something most of us take for granted. But it should be appreciated that most contemporary English hands constitute wholly different scripts – though all 'share' the Latin alphabet as a writing system. In addition, there is the calligraphy of cursive writing, the prescribed way to write English by hand versus the way most people actually write. At the beginning of the 2000s, hundreds of hands convey the English language. Of these, one can distinguish two basic groups: British (or Commonwealth) handwriting, also to be found in British-influenced educational systems, such as Israel's, and American handwriting, also prevalent in areas of American influence, such as Puerto Rico, Guam and American Samoa.

In English, too, the use of upper-case and lower-case letters means that each pupil learning to read and write has to learn not 26 letters (that is, different signs in the writing system), but 42, plus prescribed cursive forms, as well as a large number of significant abbreviations, ideograms and other marks: &, 8, +, =, @, £, $, % and many more. Some of the letters hardly change at all from upper-case to lower-case, such as *C/c*, *O/o* and *S/s*; others have a variety of forms, like *A/a/a* and *F/f/f*. All current Latin-derived alphabets share this characteristic.

How alphabetic scripts are borrowed, adapted, then expanded over millennia is reflected in the fact that nearly one-fifth of the English alphabet's 26 systemic (as opposed to 42 functional) letters – F, U, V, W and Y – all derive from a single Phoenician ancestor letter: the Y or *wāw*. This is because, over thousands of years, the *wāw*'s shape has been altered by successive borrowings – Greek, Etruscan, Latin and English – that have also included secondary internal borrowing. Such alterations were effected in order to accommodate new sounds that were unknown or unwritten both in the Phoenician source and in later stages of these borrowing languages. This process highlights the almost unparalleled adaptability of the Latin alphabet. And it is adaptability that ensures a system's survival and growth.

PUNCTUATION

Nearly all ancient scribes ran their words together, with no separation. (Crete's syllabically imprinted Phaistos Disk from *c.* 1600 BC – with verticle strokes separating 'fields' consisting of a word, phrase, even a short sentence – represents a rare exception.) Ancients apparently found lack of word separation no great impediment to reading, otherwise word separation would have been practised systematically at a much earlier date.

Early Greek and Latin scribes also left no space between individual words, though some marked these off in monumental inscriptions and literary papyri with small points. Only paragraphs were routinely separated as autonomous units of text, distinguished by the *parágraphos*, or dividing stroke. Aristotle (384–322 BC), for one, placed a short horizontal stroke under the start of a new line to indicate a break of sense or the end of a topic. As of the fifth century AD and throughout the entire Middle Ages, the first letter of the first full line of a new paragraph was routinely drawn into the margin and enlarged. We preserve this convention today with our rule of capitalizing the initial letter of a sentence. The indenting of new paragraphs dates from the 1600s.

Early mediæval scribes almost always ran their words together. Only once minuscule writing became the literary hand did scribes perceive a need to represent the word as an independent unit – perhaps because of more frequent silent reading in mediæval scriptoria. However, leaving a space between words in order to mark word boundaries did not become general practice in Western society until the ninth century. Since then, most of the world's alphabetic orthographies have chosen to 'group letters in clusters with some space intervening between the clusters'.[22] These clusters are then generally recognized to be 'words'. With some language families that now use the Latin alphabet – such as Polynesian, which expresses grammar through special particles – the definition of 'word' is often unclear and causes ambiguity when a conventionalized regional orthography is lacking: compare Hawaiian *iāia* 'her/him', of one 'word', with Rapanui (Easter Island) *i 'ā ia* 'her/him', of three 'words' for the same thing. Even in English writing, pauses do not consistently coincide with recognized word boundaries. Nonetheless, we generally acknowledge a 'word' from its semantic quality and autonomous function in given contexts.

Chinese and Japanese as a rule still do not observe word separation, and the modern borrowed practice of Western punctuation is kept to a minimum. Unhappily, venerable conventions can cross writing systems, sometimes with amusing results. An electric sandwich toaster purchased in the UK bore the warning sticker: 'Do not immerse in any liquid made in China.'[23] The earliest word separation in Western writing was not punctuation as we understand the term today: a system of marks designed to help make a text's sense clear. Punctuation, as one can easily see in the above anecdote, has come to bear a significant semantic load in Western alphabetic writing systems. Plato

(427–347 BC) apparently used a colon (:) to indicate the end of a section of text (only since about AD 1480 has the colon separated a general statement from an explanatory one or an example). Aristophanes of Byzantium (d. *c.* 180 BC), director of the Library of Alexandria in northern Egypt, is credited with having devised a system of point punctuation: the high point ˙ signalling a full stop (North American 'period'); the middle point · an ordinary pause; and the low or line point . a pause between the two, like today's semicolon. Aristophanes' system of punctuation was used extensively in Hellenistic times, and endured well into the first centuries AD. However, Roman scribes practised this Greek system only indiscriminately, confusing the points' meaning.

Aristophanes of Byzantium was also credited with originating long (¯) and short (ˇ) syllable marks and the hyphen (-), originally a curve or line drawn underneath letters to signal connection of some sort (as in compound words). Many other reading signs were employed in the oldest preserved Greek and Latin manuscripts – diæresis (the *ï* in *naïve* and *ö* in *coöperate*), quotation marks, single-letter identifiers, space fillers and so on. All attest to a widespread, active and fluent use of writing, very similar to how we write today.

In the early Middle Ages, Aristophanes' middle point (·) disappeared. Breathings (the *h*'s) and accents were not applied systematically to Greek texts before the seventh century. The comma, initially written as a high point, was introduced into Greek and Latin texts around AD 650; two centuries later, with minuscule writing, it became the baseline comma we know today. The modern full stop or period was introduced by Alcuin of York around 800 to signal the end of long passages of text; this was customarily written as ·7 or other point combinations. By this time, the semicolon (;) already possessed its present value. A bit later on, paragraph or chapter endings were marked with : or :- or ∴..

The question mark (?) first appeared around the eighth or ninth century in Latin manuscripts, but did not appear in English until 1587 with the publication of Sir Philip Sidney's *Arcadia*. This mark derived from the Latin *quaestio*, or 'enquiry', written at the end of a sentence containing a query. Having earlier been abbreviated to *Qo* – with the *Q* above the *o* – it was then written as ?, and eventually as ?.

In similar fashion, the exclamation mark (!) conveys Latin *iō!*, or 'hurrah!', with the *i* written above the long *o*: ǒ. It first appeared in English in 1553, in the *Catechism of Edward VI*.

The ampersand – the &-sign – derived from Latin *et*, meaning 'and', until recently also printed as ℰſ. It also first appeared in English print in the 1500s.

Finally, the apostrophe ('), also attributed to Aristophanes, was employed in ancient, mediæval and later manuscripts to indicate the omission of letters. Its use was extended in England in the early 1700s to include the English language's unique marking of possessives. After the Second World War, German also introduced this practice, though it never became prescribed usage as in English.

Most of these punctuation marks are now used in nearly all alphabetic systems. As of the 1900s, many of them had been borrowed into non-alphabetic writing systems as well. For example, the full stop or period, comma, apostrophe, quotation mark, question mark, exclamation mark, paragraph indentation and so on occur regularly in modern Chinese, Korean and Japanese writing (see illus. 138). In Japanese, even the ampersand is used for *to* ('and') between foreign words in *katakana* script.

First described in China in AD 105, the manufacture of paper was thereafter kept a closely guarded secret (see Chapter 5). Centuries passed before others successfully produced paper. Japan, for example, was making and using paper as of the seventh century, probably through Korean intermediaries. The West learned of paper-making through a considerably more circuitous and prolonged route.

In a Central Asian conflict of AD 751, Samarkand's Muslim governor captured many Chinese, some of whom were proficient in paper production. From that moment until the end of the ninth century, Samarkand paper – composed of linen rags rather than mulberry bark – constituted a valuable export.

However, the knowledge of its manufacture rapidly spread throughout the Muslim world: to Baghdad (793?), Damascus (ninth century), Cairo (*c.* 900) and Fez (*c.* 1100), as well as to Sicily (*c.* 1100).[24] Though Arabs were using paper regularly by the ninth century, they still preferred to use vellum for copies of the revered Koran until relatively recently. Muslim Spain was manufacturing paper by about 1150, and in the 1200s Arab merchants introduced its manufacture to India, where it almost wholly replaced traditional writing materials.

Thirteenth-century Spain referred to paper as *pagamino de paño*, or 'cloth parchment', since rags still comprised its chief ingredient.[25] After the Muslims fled Spain in 1492, paper-making became the domain of less skilled Christian craftsmen, and quality declined rapidly. At the same time, paper's use in Western Europe increased dramatically. Since 1338, Troyes in France had had a paperworks, as had Nuremberg in Germany since 1390. (As of 1690, Germantown, near Philadelphia, was producing North America's first paper.) Already in the second half of the 1300s, European paper was beginning to rival vellum as the preferred material for book production. Within a century, paper had replaced parchment and vellum almost entirely, chiefly because of the invention of the printing press.

People seldom appreciate paper's impact on Western civilization. Parchment and vellum could never have supported mass literacy, worldwide printing, modern offices, newspapers, government records, general education and so on. These are the consequences of paper and the printing press. Indeed, the printing press itself only made practical sense because of paper's availability. In the 1800s, an increased demand for paper as a result of general education finally saw wood replacing rags as its chief ingredient. An almost unlimited supply of paper was thus ensured for the world – but at the cost of quality and durability. (Compare the lovely paper of a volume from 1780 with the inferior paper of one from 1880.) By the 1900s, paper had become 'the most important, efficient and totally irreplaceable medium of modern information storage. Economically and intellectually our society had become a paper society.'[26]

Only now, with the advent of electronic information storage and the personal computer, is paper's pre-eminence being publicly challenged for the first time: entire libraries can fit on a few CD Roms, we are often told. This hardly signals paper's decline, at least at present. E-mail communication and Internet access have greatly increased the frequency of personal messages and personally printed information. Everyone with e-mail, access to the Net and a computer printer usually makes several print-outs a day. The new technology has created a demand for paper not witnessed since the educational reforms of the mid-1800s.

PRINTING

Scribes require much time to copy a book. Even today, to copy a Torah, the five Books of Moses, can take a Jewish scribe more than a year, his work governed by hundreds of laws. Hand-copying usually means very expensive books and very few readers. Few readers means low literacy, carrying considerable disadvantages for a society. Europeans became readers on a large scale only after the printing press appeared in the mid-1400s. How Europe arrived at printing is a fascinating story.

Printing is 'graphic communication by multiplied impressions'.[27] Impressing a text is much more rapid than copying each sign by hand. Impressing also fossilizes the original, avoiding those frequent errors and changes of hand copyists. In this way, the process ensures uncontamination and authenticity, converting the entire text into a seal of authority. Already by *c.* 2500 BC, Sumerian scribes were *rolling* complete texts onto soft clay using both single-column 'cylinder seals' and dual-column 'barrel seals', the latter tilting the columns in opposite directions for separate impressing.

Perhaps authenticity was also the intention of the inventor(s) of the process witnessed in ancient Crete's Phaistos Disk from *c.* 1600 BC, the world's earliest known example of printing with movable type (see illus. 47). Though the Disk's Ægean syllabic writing was probably inspired by the idea of the Levant's Byblos syllabary, its separate punches for each *in-di-vi-du-al* syllable of Minoan Greek were perhaps inspired by contemporary seals. Each seal – previously used only for names, places or consignments – thus became a punch of movable type to construct a complete message, syllable by syllable. Because of this, Minoan Greeks must be regarded as the original inventors of printing with movable type.[28] As remarkable as this invention is the fact that the ancient Mediterranean evidently had no use for it. Printing apparently enjoyed only a limited, local use, then simply disappeared.

China has a long history of various techniques that eventually led to block printing.[29] Block printing reproduces an entire face of text as the smallest printable unit, whereas printing with movable type, as with the Phaistos Disk, uses smaller interchangeable units – individual logograms, syllables or letters – to produce a face of text. In the first millennium BC, the Chinese cut stamping seals in relief and multiplied inscriptions using moulds. Once they had invented paper *c.* AD 100, they made impressions on this new material by means of rubbing and other techniques. Chinese scribes of the sixth century were already producing high-quality paper texts with complete fidelity of reproduction using stone, baked clay, wood and metal. This was not yet block printing, however, as the original text was always used. But in order to prevent damaging an original, scribes soon began to produce an exact copy on wooden blocks, first using negative (that is, backwards) characters, then cutting positive ones, like the original text, in relief. Using ink, they produced a black script on white paper. The earliest surviving complete and dated block-printed book is the Chinese *Diamond Sutra* from AD 868 (see illus. 129).

Until the 1800s, wood-block printing remained the chief printing method in China, Korea and Japan.[30] Its technique remained virtually unchanged through the centuries. A text was first written down on thin paper. This was then turned over and placed on a wooden block to dry. Once dry, the paper's surface was rubbed away and oil was spread over the block to bring out the characters left behind. An engraver then cut away the wood *around* the characters, leaving them in relief. Indian ink was then applied to these relief characters with a brush. Moist paper was laid over the block of relief characters and rubbed with a special bamboo-fibre tool. There was also block printing using metal plates, but this was more expensive and not as widely practised.

The rapid spread of printing in East Asia in the first millennium AD is attributable to the great demand for Buddhist texts.[31] Block printing actively fed this demand as literacy increased. In this way, much more literature was produced in East Asia than in Europe at the same time. European scribes continued copying slowly by hand as Chinese book publishers were printing out unprecedented numbers of texts. In 764, for example, Japan's Empress Shotoku commanded the printing of one million *dhāraṇī*, or Buddhist charms, to be distributed throughout her realm; the task took six years to complete (illus. 162). And in 839, the Japanese monk Ennin, for one, had seen on China's holy mountain Wu Tai Shan a thousand printed exemplars of a Buddhist *sutra*.

China also devised a technique for producing movable characters and printing with them. Bi Sheng, an alchemist-smith, is alleged to have created Chinese-character movable type in baked clay in AD 1045. Later, others created movable type in wood, metal and porcelain. However, wood-block printing was always the preferred technique in China because of the large number of characters in the writing system, which rendered movable type impracticable.

In Korea, wood-block printing, borrowed from China, also began at an early date. King Taejo (ruled AD 1392–8) published a series of wood-block booklets. King Tagong (ruled 1400–18) issued a royal decree for the casting of movable characters in bronze in 1403, financed by the palace treasury. Though a slow

162 The earliest preserved example of East Asian printing: Buddhist charms in Sanskrit printed in Chinese characters in Japan *c*. AD 770.

and laborious undertaking – thousands of characters had to be cast – the set of characters was serving the royal print shop as of 1409. This shop continued to publish books into the 1800s using punches of incised wooden cubes to form a 'matrix' (female die) in sand placed within a metal mould. Bronze, and sometimes lead, was then poured into the mould to cast metal characters of movable type. By the end of the 1400s, Korea's royal court housed its own type foundry.

Indeed, the recognition of the eminent advantages of printing with movable type, and the obvious difficulty of accomplishing this with Chinese, is generally regarded as the principal reason why King Seycong (ruled 1418–50) encouraged, and perhaps even oversaw, the invention and implementation of Korea's Hankul script of eighteen consonants and ten vowels. Modern Hankul now requires only 164 movable signs instead of several thousands of Chinese characters.

Japan learnt of movable type from Koreans and Portuguese in the 1500s. The Japanese practised typography for only about 50 years, creating outstanding productions. However, typography as a rule did not catch on in East Asia. The region's writing systems and social demands were vastly different from those in the West. Wood-block printing prevailed as typography nearly disappeared in the 1600s. Block printing worked best for East Asian logographic texts because their approximately six thousand most frequent characters were difficult to store and use as movable type. Europeans re-introduced typography to East Asia in the 1800s, whereupon it quickly replaced block printing almost entirely.

It is unclear how much Europe knew of East Asian printing techniques. However, the mechanical multiplication of written texts in fifteenth-century Europe could hardly have been an independent discovery.[32] Its retarded development in the West was perhaps attributable more to Western intransigence than to a lack of ingenuity. When the time was right, printing exploded in Europe, and to a degree unprecedented in East Asia – because of Europe's simpler alphabetic writing, which perfectly suited printing with movable type.

As distinct from East Asian printing, Western advances were almost entirely private and commercial, powered by profit and

163 The first dated woodblock print: the so-called 'Buxheimer St Christopher' from south-west Germany, 1423.

steered by market forces. Book collecting in Europe was a very lucrative trade in the 1400s because of private collectors, Church demands and secular education fuelled by a suddenly expanding international economy. In the early 1400s, many book publishers realized that hand copyists were too slow to fill their swelling orders – too much money was being lost simply because it took too long to copy one book. Publishers needed a faster and cheaper technique. Wood-block printing began in Europe in the early 1400s (illus. 163). However, this technique only fully developed in the same period as printing with movable type – that is, as of the mid-1400s. It was practised well into the 1500s before being abandoned as too time-consuming.

Though the 1400s saw the invention of printing by movable metal type in Europe, the hand-copying of books continued out of custom, religious devotion, poverty or political necessity; it continues even today. The first printers simply imitated the familiar book hands of the mediæval copyists.[33] Scribes hand-lettered large initials in the earliest printed books, while others dedicated themselves to designing wholly new typefaces that advanced the new technique. Soon, printing was exerting its own influence, and the letters of the printing press were freed at last from human hand and pen.

164 A compositor, printers and a bookseller shown in a woodcut from
Matthias Huss, *Dance of Death* (Lyon, 1499).

The history of printing from movable type describes three
general periods.[34] From 1450 to 1550 was the creative period of
printing (illus. 164). An era of consolidation and refinement
characterized the years between 1550 and 1800. And from 1800
to the present, technical advances brought about changes in the
methods of production and distribution that then changed the
habits of producers and readers.

This process began in Mainz, Germany.

Johann Gensfleisch zum Gutenberg, born into a Mainz
patrician family between 1394 and 1399, was a goldsmith who
began experimenting with printing work around 1440 while in
political exile in Strasbourg. Similar experiments were being
conducted at Bruges, Avignon and Bologna, as Gutenberg may
have been aware. Back in Mainz between 1444 and 1448, he was
sufficiently successful to exploit his multiple techniques com-
mercially by 1450. As a goldsmith, he was adept at engraving
letters on metalware. He was also accomplished in mass-pro-
ducing pilgrim badges, a process that included shallow metal
casting in a mould. The idea of a screw press was probably borrowed from the small domestic presses found throughout
Europe that extracted olive oil or flattened linen.

Altissimi presidio cuius nutu infantium lingue fi
unt diserte. Qui sp nii sepe puulis reuelat quod
sapientibus celat. Hic liber egregius. catholicon.
Dnice incarnacionis annis M ccc lx Alma in ur
be maguntina nacionis indite germanice. Quam
dei clemencia tam alto ingenii lumine. dono sp sp
tuitu. ceteris terrau nacionibus preferre. illustrare
sp dignatus est non calami. stili. aut penne suffra
gio. sp mira patronau formau sp concordia proper
cione et modulo. impressus atsp confectus est.
Hinc tibi sancte pater nato cu flamine sacro. Laus
et honor dno trino tribuatur et uno Ecclesie lau
de libro hoc catholice plaude. Qui laudare piam
semper non linque mariam DEO. GRACIAS

165 Colophon, or publisher's inscription, of the *Catholicon*, probably printed by
Gutenberg in Mainz in 1460.

To these existing techniques and devices Gutenberg added
two personal inventions: replica-casting, which created a
'matrix' of a letter in reverse, into which molten lead could be
poured to produce any number of copies of the same size and
height; and an ink that would adhere to metal types. As S. H.
Steinberg has observed,

> What is perhaps Gutenberg's greatest claim to fame is the
> fact that, after the early experimental stage of which we know
> nothing, he reached a state of technical efficiency not materi-
> ally surpassed until the beginning of the nineteenth century.
> Punch-cutting, matrix-fitting, type-casting, composing, and
> printing remained, in principle, for more than three cen-
> turies where they were in Gutenberg's time.[35]

Gutenberg's techniques and press were hardly distinguishable from Benjamin Franklin's.

Gutenberg's main publications were the 42-line (1452–6)
and 36-line (1460) Bibles and a 1460 edition of Johannes
Balbus's thirteenth-century compilation, the *Catholicon* (illus.
165), though the authenticity of the latter two is often ques-

tioned. The 42-line Bible, the first book printed using movable type, remains one of the greatest works in the history of printing. In it, Gutenberg adopted the style and format of contemporary German manuscripts in Gothic Quadrata hand (even standard scribal abbreviations and ligatures were copied in type). Scribes then hand-inserted the Bible's marginal initials and other letters, commonly in red to contrast with the black of the text. Gutenberg apparently abandoned printing after 1460, perhaps because of blindness. He died in 1468.

'It can be safely said,' historian Albertine Gaur has asserted,

> that the two decades Gutenberg spent on the perfection of typography signalled the start of the modern period and that all subsequent scientific, political, ecclesiastical, sociological, economic and philosophical advances would not have been possible without the use and the influence of the printing press.[36]

The business of book publishing also changed. Individual patrons were no longer necessary; only hard capital mattered. Europe's main commercial centres – not the royal courts, monasteries, abbeys or chapter houses – became the new printing and literary centres. The small coteries of intelligentsia who had surrounded individual scribal schools abdicated to an anonymous literate public. This in turn forced printers to standardize their texts to ensure widest comprehension, turning local dialects into national tongues; this standarization led to the 'written languages' of Europe, which became more influential and prescriptive. Printers strove for greater simplification of typeface, too, in order to achieve maximal legibility. Texts were also printed that held greater mass appeal, changing tastes forever. All of Western society was altered in this synergism of commercial, linguistic and cultural homogenization, a process that continues today in accelerated fashion.

Gutenberg's press and possibly also his types were used in Mainz by Johann Fust and his son-in-law Peter Schöffer to create the celebrated Mainz Psalter of 1457, reproducing a thick but majestic Gothic Quadrata typeface with large initials painted in two colours and small capitals entered by hand in red. (Some of Fust's Psalters were also printed on vellum, a rare process.) But the invasion of Mainz in 1462 brought printing there to an abrupt end, with printers fleeing to other European centres. The most important of these was Venice, where printers chose to use the Humanist minuscule for their typefaces, with capitals drawn from Roman Square Capitals that were fifteen hundred years old.[37] The first Roman type (today's most widespread typeface) was produced in 1470 by the Frenchman Nicolas Jenson, who had come to Venice perhaps by way of Mainz – certainly one of the airiest, most elegant and most legible of the early typefaces (illus. 166).

In 1473, Aldus Manutius set up a printing shop in Venice and improved on Jenson's methods. Francesco Griffo, who joined Manutius as a typeface designer, created capitals that were shorter than the ascenders (such as initial *s*'s), as was known from calligraphy, in order to achieve a more æsthetically balanced text page. Called 'white page' typography, this Venetian method established the printing model that is still followed in the 2000s. Griffo designed a Chancery Italic type as well, which first appeared in Virgil's *Opera* printed by Manutius in 1501. The use of italic script throughout this book condensed the text considerably, calling for fewer pages and thus saving production costs and improving portability. Several Italian scribes of the era designed italic typefaces for similar reasons, among them the famous Ludovico degli Arrighi. Italic type was used until the mid-1500s for printing entire books.

England's first printing with movable metal type occurred at the shop of William Caxton in London on 13 December 1476. (England alone in Europe owes the introduction of printing to a native.) Unlike other European printers of the era, Caxton was a gentleman, scholar and beneficiary of aristocratic and peer favour.[38] Born in Kent in 1420 or 1424, he had spent some 30 years in Bruges as a businessman and as the equivalent of England's Consul-General. Once free of his office (perhaps involuntarily), he dedicated himself to translating the French romance *Recueil des histoires de Troye* into English, and then set about learning the new craft of printing in order to publish the translation himself.

Caxton learnt the art of printing from a German printer in Cologne between 1471 and '72. Returning to Bruges, he set up

Hoc Conraduſopuſſuueynheym ordıne mıro
Arnoldusꝗ fimul pannarcſuna ede colendı

[Sweynheym and Pannartz, Rome, 1468]

fcrıptas·Magnam tıbı gratıã gaſparınus

[First book printed in France, by Freiburger, Gering and
Kranz, Paris, 1470]

F ormoſam reſonare doces amaryllida ſiluas.   TI.
O melibœe deus nobis hæc ocia fecit.

[Nicolas Jenson, Venice, 1475]

T roianas ut opes,et lamentabile regnum
E ruerint Danai,quǽque ipſe mıſerrıma uidi,

[Francesco Griffo's italic fount by Aldus Manutius, Venice, 1510]

Popolo d' Iſrael fuſıı ſchiauo in Egitto , & à conoſcere la grandeꝛ̃
& lo animo di Cıro, che i Perſi fuſsero oppreſsi da Medi,& ad illu

[Antonio Blado, Rome, 1532]

multo poſt carceris catenas fregit, ingentíque animi
virtute non ſemel cæſis Barbaris,vltus iniurias,patriã

[Robert Estienne, Paris, 1549]

A Lyoy.
De L'Imprimerie & Robert Granjoy.

[Robert Granjon, Lyon, 1557]

Admonitiones ad ſpiritualem vitam vtiles.

[Imprimerie Royale, Paris, 1640]

166 Significant early Roman typefaces.

> ¶If it plese ony man spirituel or temporel to bye ony
> pyes of two and thre comemoraciõs of salisburi vse
> enpryntid after the forme of this preset lettre whiche
> ben wel and truly correct, late hym come to westmo;
> nester in to the almonestrye at the reed pale and he sha)
> haue them good chepe .**.**
>
> ## Suplico stet cedula

167 William Caxton's advertising poster announcing 'commemorations of Salisbury use', London, *c*. 1477.

his own press in 1473, first publishing *Recuyell of the Histories of Troye* in 1474, then three further publications. In 1476, Caxton returned to England, where he established the country's first printing press in London, initially close to the Chapter House of Westminster Abbey but soon after at the Almonry, at the sign of the Red Pale (illus. 167). There, Caxton also became the first English – as opposed to Dutch, German or French – retailer of printed books in England. The first book ever printed in England, Earl Rivers's *Dictes or Sayengis of the Philosophres*, left Caxton's press on 18 November 1477.[39]

Until his death in 1491, Caxton's shop was patronized by, among others, King Edward IV, King Richard III and King Henry VII. In all, he published some 90 books in sixteen years – 74 of them in English, at a time when Latin was almost exclusively the language of scholarship. Around twenty of these were Caxton's own translations. Also included in his productions were the works of England's greatest authors: Chaucer, Gower, Lydgate and Malory.

On Caxton's death, his business went to his assistant Wynkyn de Worde from Wörth in the German Elsass (now Alsace in France). Until his own death in 1535, Wynkyn published approximately eight hundred individual titles. Some two-thirds of these were directed at the rapidly expanding grammar-school market. By 1500, Wynkyn had moved from Westminster into the City of London, where other printers of note – such as William Fawkes and Richard Pynson (illus. 168) – were already active. There, from 1500 to 1530, Wynkyn and Richard Pynson

He shal no gospel glose here ne teche
We leue al in the grete god quod he
He wolde sowe som difficultye
Or sprynten cokyl in oure clene corn
And therfore hoost I warne the Biforn
My ioly body shal a tale telle
And I shalle crynke you a ioly Belle
That it shal wakyn alle this company
But it shal nat Be of philosophy
Ne of phpsstias ne termes queynte of lawe
There is but lytel latyn in my mawe

        Here endith the squyers prologue
        And here Begynneth his Tale

a   T surrye in the londe of Tartary
There duelled a kyng that warzed russy
Throught whiche ther dyed many a doughty man

168 A page from the third printed edition of Chaucer's *Canterbury Tales*,
published by Richard Pynson (London, 1492).

were responsible for the publication of approximately two-thirds of all books for the English market.[40]

By then, two typefaces had attained prominence throughout Western Europe: Roman (or Antiqua) and Gothic (Fractur) (illus. 169). The coming centuries marked Roman's gradual replacement of Gothic – in the 1500s, most of the Romance languages; in the 1600s, England and America (with some

Esope sprach /warumb nit!zôge mir nûn die statt da hin du in buwen wilt· Der kûnig gieng bald

[Johann Zainer, Ulm, 1476–7]

CHer nach stet gescribē die gnade vnd ablaß: Auch das heiltū by den·vii·haubt kirchē: vnd allen kirchen zu Rom vnd vil wunder zeichen

[Stephan Planck, Rome, 1489]

Deus Jacob miserere mei Et

[Johann Schönsperger, Augsburg, 1512–13]

(Gemeinschafft) lich seied auff den tag vnsers Herrn Jhesu Christi. Denn Gott ist
Das ist/ Ir seid trew/durch welchen jr beruffen seid/zur a gemeinschafft seines Sons
miterben vnd mit- Jhesu Christi vnsers Herrn.
genossen aller gü-
ter Christi.   Ich ermane euch aber/lieben Brüder/durch den namen vnsers
Herrn Jhesu Christ/das jr alzumal einerley rede furet/vñ lasset nicht

[First complete Luther Bible, Hans Lufft, Wittenberg, 1534]

runder zum Heyligen Röm. Reich Teutscher Nation ge-
hörig/begriffen/mit sondern Freyheiten vnd Gnaden be-
gabet/Bey welchē hernach alle folgende Römische Keyser

[Sigmund Feyerabend, Frankfurt, 1566]

169 Significant early Gothic typefaces.

exceptions); in the 1800s, most of Northern Europe but for German speakers; and in the 1900s, the German-speaking countries.[41]

In the early days of printing, Gothic type was much more commonly used than the Humanist Roman founts of Italy. (A fount or font is a complete set of type of one style and one size.) France began accepting more Humanist founts already at an early date, and as France grew wealthier and more powerful, its founts came to influence those of other European countries. During the first half of the 1500s, France assumed pre-eminence in typography. Typefounder Claude Garamond created a new Roman typeface that was Venetian in appearance but more refined: the letters joined more harmoniously, and the three registers of CAPITALS, lower case and *italics* blended as an æsthetic unity. Roman and italic types were now re-defined as 'fellow halves of a single design'.[42] Italics were used, as today, only in distinctive words or phrases for differentiation and emphasis, supplementing Roman. (Other typefaces and alphabets do not have this italic distinction; to emphasize a word in a Hebrew text, for example, one simply sets space between the letters.) This was the father of the famous Garamond style still used throughout the world.[43]

There are three main families of Roman bookfaces: Old Face, Modern Face and Sans Serif.

Old Face remains close to the earliest Roman type of the 1400s (illus. 170). Some Old Faces are actually quite recent: one of the world's most popular is Stanley Morison's Times New Roman of 1931. Stressed lightly and obliquely (with a slant), Old Face's serifs are bracketed, with slanting at the upper end of verticals. Other currently popular Old Faces are Bembo (reproducing an original of 1495), Garamond (1621) and Imprint (1912).[44]

In the 1700s, one of Britain's more popular Old Faces was developed by William Caslon.[45] Many British typefaces were of Dutch origin and tended to be heavy and 'primitive' in appearance. Using an 'English design' that ultimately derived from Garamond and Griffo, Caslon personalized lower-case letters and gave his italics æsthetic flourishes, making use of pointed-pen calligraphy to distinguish between thick and thin strokes.

170 The first book published in British North America, printed in Old Face by Stephen Daye of Cambridge, Massachusetts, in 1640.

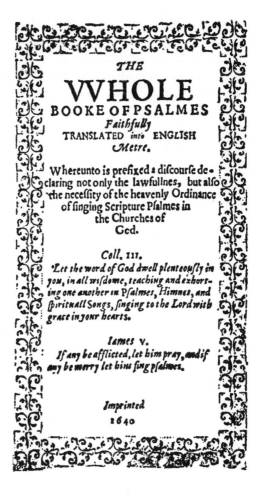

THE
WHOLE
BOOKE OF PSALMES
Faithfully
TRANSLATED *into* ENGLISH
Metre.

Whereunto is prefixed a difcourfe declaring not only the lawfullnes, but alfo
the neceffity of the heavenly Ordinance
of finging Scripture Pfalmes in
the Churches of
God.

Coll. III.
*Let the word of God dwell plenteoufly in
you, in all wifdome, teaching and exhort-
ing one another in Pfalmes, Himnes, and
fpirituall Songs, finging to the Lord with
grace in your hearts.*

Iames V.
*If any be afflicted, let him pray, and if
any be merry let him fing pfalmes.*

Imprinted
1640

Characteristic of Caslon's typeface is a large, thick ampersand. Caslon's Old Face was particularly popular in British North America, even after independence. Benjamin Franklin insisted that the first printings of the (originally handwritten) Declaration of Independence and United States Constitution be in Caslon's Roman type.

Modern Face is a product of eighteenth-century rationalization, though the earliest 'Modern', or *romain du roi*, was proposed already in 1692 by a royal committee encharged by Louis XIV of France to create new typefaces for the Royal Print. This task was only completed in 1745.[46] Rejecting Old Face, the committee abandoned penmanship's slanting, bracketed serifs in favour of mechanical printing's horizontal serifs with no brackets. It also exploited the latest technology to create stress contrasts between thick and thin lines. The thinnest parts lay on the vertical axis – O, for example, was thin only at top and bottom, its sides thick.

At first intended only for royal use, Modern Face grew in popularity in Europe from 1750 to about 1830. Britain long resisted it, as printers there favoured Old Face and 'Transitional' typefaces which retained slanting, bracketed serifs (such as Baskerville of 1757 and Bell of 1788). One British type-founder railed that popular taste had forced him to melt down thousands of pounds' worth of type 'superior to what replaced it!'[47] Throughout most of the 1800s, however, British printers favoured Modern Face. In the 1900s, it found a new direction, especially in America, with Monotype, still widely printed for technical literature. Today, those using Monotype are gradually changing to Times, which is assuming global status.

In non-English-speaking countries, Moderns such as Bodoni (originally designed around 1767), Didot (about 1784) and Walbaum (about 1805) are still popular. The first two of these are especially popular in France, where they remain closer to the original typefaces of the 1700s, lending a 'quaint archaism' to modern printed French works. Still, many Europeans favour Old Face for literary texts with æsthetic appeal and Modern Face for serious academic and scientific literature. In Britain, at least, Modern Face is perceived as 'Victorian' and is now little used, Times Roman being preferred.

Sans Serif types began as 'display faces' – for printing announcements, posters, circulars and so on – in the early 1800s (Caslon had already produced such typefaces in 1816), and before 1850 only in capitals.[48] Sans Serif letters of course have no serifs (French *sans* means 'without') and are usually monoline – that is, there is no thick-and-thin variation in the strokes. In the 1800s, commercial advertising significantly influenced the development of typography: patrons demanded large, bold letters to ensure their legibility at a distance. Out of this came three basic Sans Serif styles: Egyptians, with their serifs exaggerated as big, black slabs (familiar from the 'wanted' posters of the Wild West); Ornates and Fat Faces; and thick, black 'Gothics'.

Sans Serif types are especially popular for posters and signs, such as the London Transport System's notice-boards in Railway Type (1916). After the First World War, German and Swiss typographers started using Sans Serif types as bookfaces, influenced by the Bauhaus movement in architecture and design. Stripped of all ornamentation and openly competing with the traditional Gothic script, Sans Serif was soon regarded as the expression of 'twentieth-century man' and became extremely popular in the journals and newsletters of German-speaking countries (though most still printed in Gothic). In the 1970s, Britain started using Sans Serif in book texts, too. The most popular Sans Serif typefaces are Helvetia and Univers, both from 1957 and now often used as standard founts on personal computers.

Sans Serif types continued to develop throughout the 1900s. Designers purposely chose either to 'return to their roots' – reviving famous typefaces of the past – or to innovate independently.[49] Among the more famous faces in the first group are Bruce Roger's Centaur (reviving Nicolas Jenson), Slimbach's Garamond, Louis Hoell's Bodoni and Adrian Frutiger's Univers, all representing a united 'Gothic family' of Sans Serif typefaces. Among the innovators, there are Paul Renner's Futura, a geometric Sans Serif; Eric Gill's Gill Sans, a Roman Capital Sans Serif; Gill's Perpetua, a serif epigraphic typeface; Hermann Zapf's Melior, an elliptical typeface; and Zapf's Optima, a Sans Serif Roman typeface.[50]

However, due to its austerity Sans Serif is unlikely to dislodge Times Roman, an Old Face, from its ranking as the world's most popular typeface. Studies have shown that the reading of longer texts is quicker and easier with Times, and most readers prefer its elegance. Still, a large percentage of today's readers only read in Sans Serif – that is, road signs, shop signs, package labelling and TV commercials.

Marking an historic moment in the history of writing in Western Europe, Germany at last abandoned Gothic for Roman script on 3 January 1941. Before this, Adolf Hitler had praised Gothic as the traditional Nordic typeface. He then realized that, in order to reach a larger audience, the Nazi creed had to be read beyond German-speaking lands. For this reason, he had it officially declared, through his Propaganda Ministry, that 'the so-called Gothic type' was a Jewish invention ('*Schwabacher-Judenlettern*' after the town Schwabach near Nuremberg) and that Roman was now to be the 'normal script' of the German people. The German Reich at once replaced Gothic with Roman script – that is, with an adapted Latin alphabet, like Gothic, but in the Roman hand that also included the special German phonemes *ä, ö, ü* and *ß* (ss). 'Despite its non-sensical argumentation,' the historian S. H. Steinberg has written, this was 'the one good thing Hitler did for German civilization'.[51] After the Second World War, the Allied occupiers of Germany and Austria maintained this change as Roman was also their script (except for the Russians, of course). With the formation of a new German state and eventual autonomy, the Roman script remained. Now all of Western Europe except for Ireland officially uses Roman hand and typeface.

As with printing, the invention of the typewriter also changed writing's method, appearance and role in society – its keyboard underlies today's PC revolution. Until the middle of the 1800s, all type had been set by hand. The number of characters was unimportant, so long as they were easily accessible. Even the typology of writing was unimportant, whether one was printing in a logographic, a syllabic or an alphabetic system. The typewriter changed this completely.[52] With German and Austrian wooden forerunners, the first *practical* typewriter was invented by an American, Christopher Lathan Scholes, in 1867 and placed on sale by the Remington Company in 1873. With 44 keys, it could type all the capital letters, numbers and some punctuation. Soon after, the key shift was invented, with each lower-case letter on the same type-bar as its capital. From then on, all common typewriters could type between 88 and 92 characters, sufficient for all ordinary needs. Additional copies could also be created by inserting carbon paper, invented before 1880. The first author to submit a novel in typescript – not in hand-writing – was the American Mark Twain (1835–1910). (Hand-written submissions continued to be accepted by publishing houses until the end of the 1900s.) For the first time, non-printers, freed from pen and ink, could print like professionals, though they were limited to one typeface per machine.

Further inventions quickly followed.[53] In the 1880s, Ottmar Mergenthal invented the Linotype, the first successful type-casting machine. In 1881, James B. Hammond produced the Hammond typewriter, which incorporated a type shuttle that permitted the typing of an unlimited number of typefaces. Hammond's invention was superseded by VariTyper, a machine for producing print copy for offset reproduction imitating the capability of hot-metal typesetting. These machines were in use until about 1970, when electronic photo-typesetting usurped the market. At the same time, the photocopier appeared. By the 1980s, the personal computer had arrived, increasing the frequency of writing – but with the keyboard of the earliest typewriters.

Today, everyone with a personal computer has immediate access to the world's scripts and writing systems, including many of those of antiquity. Modern word processors, electronic typewriters and personal computers have overcome many of the inherent disadvantages of the basic typewriter by offering a wide range of typographical options, including founts, sizes, italics, boldface, justified setting and many special symbols. The home and office desks have become the printer's shop.[54]

Printing with movable type changed language itself. Until the age of printing, every scribe who was writing creatively – that is, not copying – wrote phonetically. He (only rarely she) tried to reproduce each word as he spoke it. (And copyists wrote according to local monastic or chancery guidelines.) With printing, new standards were set. Printers usually printed the language of the commercial centre where their books were sold. This was done in order to be understood by the largest number of potential clients – in other words, for greater profit.

Caxton, for this reason, chose to print in the London dialect. Printing in London helped to establish a unified English lan-guage, offering an artificial, standardized dialect of the Home Counties and London that was never abandoned.[55] Forms of vocabulary, grammar and syntax were fossilized in early London printing – often as the result of a conscious decision by the city's first printers – that have survived to the present day. One can even claim that the London 'house style' (a publisher's preferred language and conventions) created the modern English language, as London printers purposely changed uncommon or dialectal usage to conform to a perceived model which, in time, became Standard British English. Already in 1495, for example, Wynkyn de Worde had altered the text of a manuscript that had been written some 50 years earlier in order to make it conform to the London speech purposely adopted by his master Caxton. In this way, *twey* became *two*; *wend* became *go*; *clepe* became *call* and *name*; and so forth.

First in Germany, Italy, France, Britain and Spain and then throughout the world, the printed word has levelled dialects to create standard national written and spoken languages. For centuries, the printing press has centralized, levelled and prescribed. This was, of course, the death knell for hundreds of regional dialects, particularly in the 1800s and 1900s – first marginalized by printing, then extinguished by the advent of radio, films and television.

The refining of the Latin alphabet continued well into the era of print. In the 1500s, speakers of Romance languages (Italian, French, Spanish, Portuguese, Catalan and others) noted the confusion that resulted from writing Latin *v* and *i* as both vowels and consonants, despite the Carolingian reforms. In 1524, the Roman printer Giangiorgio Trissino recommended using the minuscule form of *V* – which was *u* – to create a separate vowel *U*, and using the *V* to create a lower-case consonantal *v*. (In this way, two separate letters were formed, with both upper case and lower case.) At the same time, Trissino recommended that variants *J* and *j* of the two Latin letters *I* and *i* be used as consonants in their own right to represent various sounds developed by the Romance languages since Latin's decline. Most European alphabets, including our own, adopted Trissino's innovations: today, we write *I* and *i* as vowels and *J* and *j* as consonants, and *U* and *u* as vowels and *V* and *v* as consonants.

The French added diacritical marks to their written language around 1770 to regulate the use of accents, cedilla (ç), diæresis (as in *naïve*) and so on. Because of such diacritics, the one letter *e* in French, for example, now fulfils no fewer than five differently marked functions: *e*, *é*, *è*, *ê* and *ë*.

'The history of printing,' wrote S. H. Steinberg, 'is an integral part of the general history of civilization.'[56] Printing changed society in a fundamental way. By making almost unlimited copies of identical texts available by mechanical (now electronic) means, it brought society from limited access to knowledge to almost unlimited access to knowledge. Printing actually enabled modern society. It would be no exaggeration to claim that printing has been as important to humankind as the controlled use of fire and the wheel.

More revelant to a history of writing, printing has also exalted the Latin alphabet. Indeed, it appears that printing's increased use in this alphabet over the past five and a half centuries has been the single greatest factor in the Latin alphabet's becoming Earth's leading writing system and script at the beginning of the 21st century.

LATIN-ALPHABET-INSPIRED CREATIONS

As we have seen, writing systems and scripts have inspired imitation throughout history. In the 1800s and 1900s in particular, Western expansion into previously isolated regions of the globe inspired numerous scripts that copied the Latin alphabet. Missionaries' and traders' writing was borrowed wholesale, with minor changes or added diacritics. Or it was adapted in some fundamental way, using only the letters' shapes, not their sounds. Or only the *idea* of graphic art representing human speech was comprehended and imitated. In this way, most hitherto unwritten African, American, Asian and Oceanic languages experienced writing for the first time.

Significantly, many Western-inspired creations avoiding the Latin alphabet followed the development – if they had time to develop – of *ideography* to *logography* to *phonography*, ultimately culminating in syllabic rebuses. The final script, usually achieved within two generations, represented a boundary simplification. Most smaller societies who came into contact with Westerners and their Latin alphabet in the 1800s and early 1900s and wished to emulate writing actually had no need for it. Once they had created their imitation, increased commerce with Westerners led to greater familiarity with the Latin alphabet. The imitation lacked the authority of native tradition and could never compete with the Latin alphabet itself and so was eventually abandoned for the latter.

Some inspirations were simple exchanges. For example, in 1928 Kemal Atatürk abandoned Turkey's Arabic consonantal alphabet, which had always been closely tied to Islam, for the Latin alphabet in order to break with the past and foster progress. Several diacritic-marked letters had to be created. The ğ became the 'soft' /g/, like a *y*. The ş was the 'sh' sound (Turkey purposely avoided German's trigraph *sch* for this). Turkey did borrow *ö* and *ü* from German for the identical sounds. Today, Turkey still uses this special form of the Latin alphabet.

Other tongues that had never been written before needed only half of the Latin alphabet, or less. Rotokas in the Solomon Islands uses only eleven letters; it has the smallest alphabet in the world. At the other end of the scale, Khmer of Kampuchea has 74 letters, the largest alphabet. The Latin alphabet is eminently adaptable for such borrowing. When writing Polynesian languages, for example, one need only mark vowel length with a macron (ˉ) and glottal stop (as in English *uh-uh*) with a '. The phoneme / ŋ / (as in English *sing*) of many Polynesian languages is usually resolved with digraph *ng*, as it is in English and German, or even with simple *g*: Pagopago (pronounced PAN-GOPANGO), for example, is the name of American Samoa's capital.

Maltese, an Arabic language, also uses the Latin alphabet; it is the only Arabic tongue to do so. And since 1958, the Chinese government has allowed, to varying degrees, Chinese to be written in the Pinyin system, which also uses the Latin alphabet (Chapter 5).

A political statement invariably underlies the selection of a national script. Somalia, for example, won independence in 1960 and at once perceived the need for a national script. Somalia is home to several languages: Somali and Arabic are the national tongues (Islam is the official religion), but Italian and English are popular. A governmental committee scrutinized eighteen scripts, and in 1961 two of these were selected for national use: the Osmanian script and an adapted Latin alphabet. (Osmanian was a twentieth-century creation by Osman Yusuf, who combined elements of Italian, Arabic and Ethiopic scripts, the latter especially influencing the new script's appearance.) In 1969, Somalia experienced a coup; four years later, the Osmanian script was abandoned in favour of the adapted Latin alphabet, which better accommodated the coup leaders' ideology.

North America knew several invented scripts. The British Methodist missionary John Evans, for example, created the Cree script of the Hudson Bay territory from 1840 to 1846; the Inuit of Baffin Island in north-east Canada still use a modified version of it today. The Alaskan script created by Inuit Uyako (1860–1924), with others, was far more sophisticated than the 'script' developed in 1920 by the Chukchi shepherd Tenevil, which remained a pictography.

The Cherokee script is of considerable historical and social significance. It was created between 1821 and 1824 by Sikwayi (Sequoya or George Guess), a half-Cherokee member of this northern Georgian and North Carolinian tribe of the Iroquois nation. By 1821, Sikwayi had learned of the Latin alphabet and had recognized the potential benefits of a similar system for his people. Initially creating a sign for each word in the Cherokee language, one year and several thousands of signs later he saw the impracticability of such a writing system and decided instead to break the words down into simple (and less numerous) units – the most significant syllables, consonants, vowels and clusters in the Cherokee language. Then, using an English spelling book, Sikwayi arbitrarily appointed letters of the alphabet to these significant units of sound; no English letter corresponds to its given Cherokee value. He also invented signs, some modified from the alphabet but most of them contrived. The resulting Cherokee script is a syllabary that also includes pure vowels and clusters.

Unlike India's expansion of the Aramaic consonantal alphabet and its sound values into an indigenous syllabary, the Cherokee script was an independent innovation: Sikwayi's creation was not substantially influenced by the Latin alphabet. The alphabetic principle and its sounds were not used at all – only the graphic shapes of some letters were cannibalized. Otherwise, Sikwayi borrowed only the idea of writing, linearity and the left-to-right direction (just as the Easter Islanders did with their *rongorongo* script, as we shall see).

Initially proposing two hundred signs, Sikwayi later simplified the inventory to a total of 85 (illus. 171). In 1827, a Boston printer designed a Cherokee typeface. Soon, a newspaper and other literature were appearing in the Cherokee script, and many Cherokee became literate in their own writing system. (It is claimed that about 90 per cent of all Cherokee were at one time literate in Cherokee writing.) Even after the tragic ethnic cleansing of the Cherokee tribe by the US government, and their expulsion to foreign Oklahoma territory in and after 1830, the

171 Sikwayi's Cherokee 'alphabet' – a syllabary that includes pure vowels and clusters.

Cherokee clung to their writing, which had become a symbol of pride and ethnic identity. Later, Cherokee writing fell into disuse, though it never wholly died out – religious publications and newspapers still appear in it. In fact, efforts are underway to revitalize Sikwayi's grand creation.

Africa, too, has known similarly inspired creations. The Vai script appears to be an early nineteenth-century phoneticization of an older picture script. Sierra Leone's Mende script is said to be the product of a Muslim tailor from the early 1900s. And the Bamum script of central Cameroon was developed by King Njoya and his counsellors between 1903 and 1918.[57] This latter is particularly illustrative. Having learned of missionaries' writing, King Njoya decided that his people needed something similar. In a dream, it is alleged, he saw how he should invent a picture for each object or action in Bamum. Upon waking, he asked his subjects for drawings and thought he would then simply choose which of these to use for writing. When this proved too impractical after five separate attempts, Njoya turned to rebus writing. This was eminently successful, as most Bamum words happen to be monosyllabic of the type CV(C), or consonant-vowel (with arbitrary final consonant). And, since many Bamum words share the same shape, differing only in phonemic tones, a very small inventory of (logo)syllabic signs was needed to allow an adequate, if incomplete, transmission of the language.

Another fascinating African inspiration is the N'ko alphabet for Mandekan.[58] (N'ko is 'I say' in all the dialects spoken across the West African Sahel and regions to the south.) This alphabet, the creation of Soulemayne Kante in Kankan, Guinea, soon after the Second World War, is read from right to left, with eighteen consonants and seven vowels. To mark nasalization, a dot is placed below the respective vowel. Various diacritics placed above a vowel or syllabic nasal indicate length, tone and special tonal distinctions.

In the early 1900s, two separate scripts were used to write the Woleaian language of the Caroline Islands (now Federated States of Micronesia) in the Pacific.[59] Picture-writing had already existed there in the mid-1800s.[60] However, in 1878 an English missionary brought to the island of Truk an alphabet

that was then taken, in 1905, to Woleai, where it was imper-
fectly understood and developed into a syllabary of nineteen
signs, all taken from letters of the Latin alphabet. Syllables are
of the type *Ci* (consonant plus the vowel /i/), except for the pure
vowels. Within a couple of years, however, a larger syllabary of
at least 78 signs was devised on Faraulep Island. This was done
to amend the Woleai script's inability to convey syllables holding vowels other than /i/. The signs of this second inventory
display a mixed origin: some are pictographic, some appear to
be Japanese *katakana* syllables, and others must be local inventions. It was an open-ended system, in that a writer could simply
create new signs when he perceived a need.

Apart from Celebe's Macassar-Buginese scripts and the
Philippines' Bisaya scripts – daughters of scripts introduced
from India – it was long believed that Oceania had remained
without complete writing until the 1900s. Evidently, there had
been no need for complete writing in the region, as oral literature and mnemonic devices fulfilled all of these societies'
requirements for information storage, including exceedingly
long genealogical recitations. However, on isolated Easter
Island in the south-eastern South Pacific, one of the world's
most intriguing Latin-alphabet-inspired inventions emerged,
apparently as the result of witnessing a Spanish deed of annexation in 1770.[61] Easter Island's *rongorongo* script evidently borrowed from the Spaniards only the idea of writing, linearity and
a left-to-right direction. All else – the script's system, signs,
sound values and social application – was the product of the
insular genius.

Using approximately 120 basic logograms – birds, fishes,
deities, plants, geometrics and so forth – that accept assorted
semasiograms (glyphs indicating ideas directly without language) and phonograms as attachments, the Easter Islanders of
the early 1800s wrote in a mixed system of main glyphs, fusions,
attachments and compoundings. Writing had not suddenly
become 'necessary' on primitive Easter Island. The *mana*, or
'socio-spiritual power', of the writing the Spaniards had displayed – as only the second outsiders ever to have visited the
island – was exploited to re-establish the waning authority of its
ruling class, the chief and his priests. Easter Island's *rongorongo* is

$$A_1 + B > C$$

manu ma'u   *ika*   *ra'ā*

manu mau   *ika*   *ra'ā*

bird all   **fish**   *sun*

(Te) **manu mau** *[phallus: ki 'ai ki roto ki] (te)* **ika***: (ka pū te)* **ra'ā**

'All the birds copulated with the fish: there issued forth the sun'

172 Reading Easter Island's *rongorongo* script.

writing in that it reproduces human speech through graphic art. However, it is not 'complete writing' as it cannot reproduce 'any and all thoughts' in its society's language – only a highly limited corpus of rhetorical statements. The system does not intend to convey even linguistic adequacy: it remains restricted to a set repertoire of genres displaying limited linguistic and structural parameters. Most of the 25 preserved *rongorongo* inscriptions, all incised on wood, appear to consist of sequences of simple formulaic procreations, such as 'All the birds copulated with the fish: there issued forth the sun' (illus. 172). The *rongorongo* convey primarily the divine 'begets and begats' of the Easter Islanders and their island world, preserving an ancient oral tradition through the medium of a foreign inspiration. *Rongorongo* activity ceased in the 1860s because of pandemics, house burnings, loss of taboo, failure to pass on the art and other reasons. Now all Easter Islanders write Chilean Spanish in the Latin alphabet; only a small number attempt to write the indigenous Polynesian Rapanui language, also using the Latin alphabet.

Western manuscripts first appeared in capitals or cursives. Once minuscules developed from half-uncial capitals, these then filled entire manuscripts. Sometimes, capitals were inserted into these to emphasize first letters or whole names. The indescriminate combining of capitals and minuscules continued from the ninth to the fifteenth century. In the 1500s, Italian typeface designers formalized an upper case of letters based on Roman monumental capitals, and a lower case of letters closely reproducing minuscule writing. This became very popular. It also explains why we really have 42 functional letters in today's English alphabet (more, if one includes italics). The difference between most of English's upper case and lower case – with only ten exceptions, like *C/c, K/k, O/o* – are extreme, constituting wholly different signs: *Aa, Bb, Dd* and so forth. Other alphabets, like Greek, borrowed this Humanist idea. Others did not: most Russian capitals, for example, are merely big lower-case letters.

Today, the Latin alphabet is Earth's most important writing system.[62] Conveying the majority of the world's languages, it remains in essence the same system as that on Roman monuments and papyri from over two thousand years ago, its upper-case letters identical to Roman capitals. (There is no little irony here. Most non-Western countries embrace the Latin alphabet for its perceived 'modernity', associating it with technology and future prosperity.) Perhaps most importantly for a history of writing, the general phonetic values of these letters – allowing for regional pronunciations – still convey the same general sounds they prompted from Roman readers. In comparison, Classical Chinese characters retain their ancient shape but, two thousand years on, are pronounced wholly differently. For this reason, the Latin alphabet is regarded as the world's oldest consistently used writing system that still maintains its original signs and sounds.[63] As its upper case is Roman and its lower case Carolingian, Charlemagne himself would have little difficulty slowly sounding out each printed word of this book.

However, typewriting and computer print-outs have all but destroyed penmanship. In British North America of the 1700s, one patterned one's handwriting, then the first measure of an educated gentlewoman or gentleman, after those European writing manuals favouring a Copperplate Style: looping flourishes, ligatures and ornate capitals. In the 1800s, a unique 'American hand' emerged – Spencerian Style (Commercial Cursive), a light Copperplate only occasionally using heavy strokes. Two simplifications of Spencerian dominated the classrooms of the US until the end of the 1900s, when penmanship was largely abandoned as an 'unnecessary skill'. Great Britain also followed simplified Copperplate models, in this case those of such practitioners as Vere Foster for the early part of the 1900s, until a variety of Printscript or Manuscript replaced these. However, Great Britain, too, has largely ceased to teach penmanship. Indeed, most handwriting in North America and throughout the Commonwealth today, because of the decision of educators, is sloppy, ugly and generally illegible. Instant æsthetics are sought in desktop founts at the click of a mouse.

In what pertains to the printed word, the 'parchment keyboard' perpetuates a system and script unlikely ever to be superseded. One of the adaptive advantages of the Latin alphabet is its compactness.[64] Its sheer simplicity lends it a flexibility and strength that appear to ensure survival and encourage further expansion. Over five hundred years ago, the advent of printing with movable type favoured alphabetic writing and changed the world. The personal computer founded the electronic society on an alphabetic plinth.

It is now scripting our future.

EIGHT

Scripting the Future

'Writing is the painting of the voice,' penned the French philosopher Voltaire in the mid-1700s, reflecting his era's anthropocentric valuation of writing's innate purpose and scope. Over 250 years – and one electronic revolution – later, many would concede that writing transcends even humanity. It has been a protracted weaning.

After millennia of 'incomplete writing' using token signs and other techniques and graphic images on soft clay and other materials, scribes developed the idea of 'complete writing'. The systemic phoneticism that defines complete writing apparently first appeared, in various forms, between 4000 and 3500 BC in Mesopotamia. Through 'stimulus diffusion' – the transmission of an idea or custom from one people to another – writing's function and technique inspired neighbours to create similar systems or scripts. Surprisingly, throughout history only three main writing *traditions* have obtained: Afro-Asiatic (Mesopotamia, Egypt and the Levant and its derivatives), East Asian and American (illus. 173). All may share one Sumerian source.

Three main writing *systems* have prevailed, too, with many transitional variants and combinations – that is, mixed systems and mixed scripts (even both together, as in Japanese):

- *logography*, or 'word-writing', whereby the graphemes or writing signs represent words;

- *syllabography*, or 'syllable-writing', whereby the graphemes convey *in-di-vi-du-al* syllables;

- *alphabet*, whereby signs called 'letters' stand for individual consonants (consonantal alphabets, like Arabic and Hebrew) or individual consonants and vowels (complete alphabets, like Greek and Latin).

Over time, most logographic systems have tended to become syllabic, their earlier semantic (sense) content gradually superseded by phonetic (sound) content. Alphabetic writing does not change in this way. Once ancient Egyptian scribes elaborated it and Cyprian Greeks 'perfected' it, alphabetic writing remained *systemically* the same, though displaying many different types of advancing scripts. Today, because of globalization and modern technology, alphabetic writing is beginning to challenge all other writing.

In the 1800s, one of the founders of modern anthropology perhaps too Darwinistically championed the notion that society's evolution from 'barbarism' to 'civilization' was enabled first and foremost by literacy, the ability to read written language.[1] Today, one would possibly be more inclined to view language as society's chief tool, with written language the haft: writing did not enable, but greatly facilitated, social development. One might also do well to avoid identifying evolutionary 'stages' in the use of writing. The three writing systems – logography, syllabography and the alphabet – are each maximized by a particular language, society and era. The three systems are not quality grades, nor are they stages in a model of 'writing evolution' (which does not exist). They are simply different forms that accommodate different linguistic and social needs as they arise.[2]

Contrary to popular opinion, economy and simplicity are not the driving forces behind a writing system's or a script's development: otherwise, Indic Brahmi, for example, would never have 'regressed' from a simple consonantal alphabet to a complex system of diacritic vowel marking, creating a large pseudo-syllabary of signs. Much more significant in writing's history than economy and simplicity are precision, greater phonetic salience, resistance to change, unambiguity, veneration and many more, often superficial, factors.

'All writing,' French historian Henri-Jean Martin has recently declaimed, 'is tied to the form of thought of the civilization that created it and to which its destiny is linked.'[3] This would be lovely if it were true. Instead, it appears that no autonomous 'form of thought' underlies any civilization; that all writing involves borrowing and adaptation, not 'creation'; and that 'destiny' actually pits the practicalities of phonetic expedi-

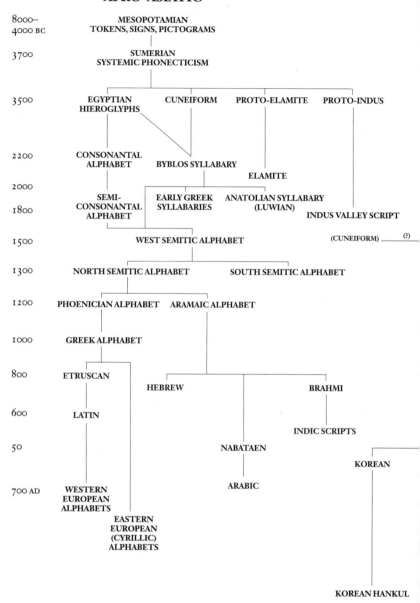

AFRO-ASIATIC

8000– 4000 BC	**MESOPOTAMIAN TOKENS, SIGNS, PICTOGRAMS**		
3700	**SUMERIAN SYSTEMIC PHONECTICISM**		
3500	**EGYPTIAN HIEROGLYPHS**	**CUNEIFORM**	**PROTO-ELAMITE** **PROTO-INDUS**
2200	**CONSONANTAL ALPHABET**	**BYBLOS SYLLABARY**	
			ELAMITE
2000			
1800	**SEMI-CONSONANTAL ALPHABET**	**EARLY GREEK SYLLABARIES**	**ANATOLIAN SYLLABARY (LUWIAN)** **INDUS VALLEY SCRIPT**
1500	**WEST SEMITIC ALPHABET**		**(CUNEIFORM)** (?)
1300	**NORTH SEMITIC ALPHABET**		**SOUTH SEMITIC ALPHABET**
1200	**PHOENICIAN ALPHABET** **ARAMAIC ALPHABET**		
1000	**GREEK ALPHABET**		
800	**ETRUSCAN**	**HEBREW**	**BRAHMI**
600	**LATIN**		**INDIC SCRIPTS**
50		**NABATAEN**	**KOREAN**
700 AD	**WESTERN EUROPEAN ALPHABETS**	**ARABIC**	
	EASTERN EUROPEAN (CYRILLIC) ALPHABETS		
			KOREAN HANKUL

173 The world's three main writing traditions: Afro-Asiatic, East Asian and American.

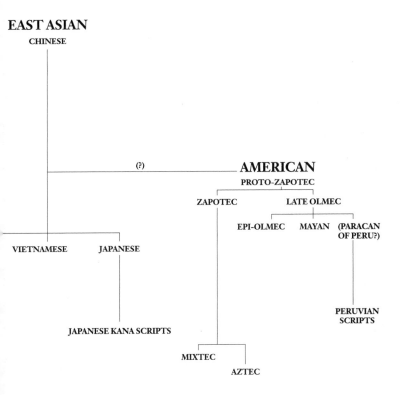

ence against the vagaries of social sufficiencies. In those societies in which literacy is limited to a select few, such as ancient Egypt or pre-missionary Easter Island, writing seems in fact to have little effect at all.[4] In societies in which literacy is widespread, however, writing's impact is profound. It preserves spoken language; it levels, standardizes, prescribes, enriches and generates many other language-oriented processes with far-reaching social implications.[5] Advanced human society as we know it in the First World cannot exist without writing. The acquisition of literacy has become, at least among humankind's privileged, second in importance only to the possession of language itself.

If one lesson is to be learned from a history of writing, it is that writing did not gradually 'evolve' from mute pictures. It began immediately as the graphic expression of actual speech and has remained so for millennia. This seems to be changing, however. Modern studies have revealed that reading sequences of characters or letters – not writing them – cerebrally links them directly to thought, bypassing speech altogether. And modern computers are now writing regularly to one another independently of human mediation. It is not these phenomena themselves so much as our new understanding of them that heralds significant future supplementations to writing's role, appearance and technique.

DIGLOSSIA

When a people's written language differs so greatly from their spoken language that two separate tongues obtain, this is *diglossia* (from Greek *di* 'two' and *glōssa* 'language'). The phenomenon has several causes. First, only the cultivated language becomes the object of written conveyance in a society acknowledging 'correct' and 'incorrect' forms of language.[6] Second, the vernacular continues to advance as a living language, but the written language changes much more slowly, or not at all – compare English's spelling of *laugh* with its pronunciation. This separation produces problems similar to those known from the calendar: periodic adjustments are necessary to avoid confusion.

There are further factors retarding a change in writing: tradition, æsthetics, veneration, social control, limited literacy and many more. The result of these processes, diglossia, has become a serious social problem in some modern cultures.

Diglossia directly involves not the writing system or script but the *language* they convey, which is no longer a spoken language. This does not mean dialects. All writing systems, phonetically deficient as they are, allow at least some dialect variation. Australians, for example, write *day* and say 'die' – for they know that 'correct' *die* is /doi/. Here, English's alphabet allows local internal regulation. Only when external rules intrude (i.e., American into Australian) does confusion result. Diglossia represents such a confusion, but of style and time.

Diglossia was first recognized a century ago by the Munich Classicist Karl Krumbacher.[7] While studying modern Greek's relation to Classical Greek, Krumbacher identified greatly divergent written and spoken varieties of the one language. Since then, diglossia has been identified in many of the world's major scripts with a long literary tradition.[8] The practice includes a broad spectrum of phenomena from English's petty archaisms to Welsh's 'linguistic schizophrenia'.

India's literary culture sees diglossia as 'one of [its] most salient features'.[9] Most of that country's languages that possess a written form display an unfordable Ganges separating the written 'high' variety from the spoken 'low' variety.[10] Each literate Indian is in fact bilingual, speaking both the language of the library and that of the marketplace. Already in the fifth century BC, Sanskrit had become a language of scholars, studied and maintained according to strict rules of grammar, while the Prakrit languages of the people continued to advance. By the third century BC, Sanskrit writing no longer had a relationship to the spoken language, and therefore one needed special tuition to learn and practise it. Over the following centuries, the same thing happened many more times with newly elaborated scripts, as scholars repeatedly fossilized 'correct' forms of speech that were altered by common usage. Now the meaning of 'to read and write correctly' in India is to read and write the perceived 'high' variety of language, while literacy in 'low' varieties of speech – the actual language of the people – is regarded as inferior and undesirable. As a direct result, over 50 per cent of India's population remain illiterate.

Classical Chinese, or *Wényán*, is as different from spoken Chinese as an Indic 'high' language is from an Indic 'low' one. Students must now learn Classical Chinese writing character by character in order to understand it.

Modern Standard Welsh, or *yr iaith safonol* ('the standard language'), is a literary language only, the Welsh of education and publication. Colloquial Welsh, or *yr iaith lafar* ('the spoken language'), is the everyday spoken language of the Welsh community. For example, the sentence 'I did not know you had seen him' would be Modern Standard Welsh *Ni wyddwn eich bod wedi ei weled*, but Colloquial Welsh *O'n i 'im wybod bo chi di weld e*. Many Welsh today have access only to Colloquial Welsh, being unable to speak, read or write Modern Standard Welsh at all – though they may sing hymns in it every Sunday. The situation is even more complicated by the fact that Modern Standard Welsh displays many varieties ranging from archaic biblical forms to bureaucratic official forms. And Colloquial Welsh exists in extreme regional forms. In addition, a standardization of Welsh called *Cymraeg Byw*, or 'Living Welsh', has been proposed in recent years as a non-regional national language bridging the gap between Modern Standard and Colloquial Welsh. This new form is being rapidly adopted by younger speakers, increasingly suppressing the use of local regional forms; it is also being used more in writing. However, today's prescribed Modern Standard Welsh remains the written language of nearly all Welsh-language instruction in Welsh schools.

In India, with its high illiteracy, the written languages that differ markedly from the vernaculars will evidently continue to prevail, retarding the country's growth. In Wales, on the other hand, the ultimate success of *Cymraeg Byw* might result in greater literacy in the Welsh language – alongside English literacy – and eventually eliminate diglossia there altogether.

Most languages display a wide gap between written and spoken style(s). The mark of an educated person is often how closely s/he speaks the written language. Those who speak most closely to the written style would generally be leading members of that society. It is writing alone that causes this phenomenon.[11] In many cases, an elimination of diglossia would be unthinkable. For example, in the 1300s Literary Sinhalese of Ceylon (Sri Lanka) emerged as a literary standard. This purely written language is still venerated by all Sinhalese, who perceive it to be more beautiful, cultured and 'correct' than today's spoken language. Indeed, Literary Sinhalese is greatly respected by all in Sri Lanka chiefly *because* the country is one of high illiteracy.

Sometimes, a society regards the discrepancy between written and spoken language as unnecessary historical baggage. It hinders a society's growth when it leads to confusing and ponderous writing that serves its users poorly and is laborious – that is, expensive in time and money – to pass along to one's children. When this belief becomes common cause, a spelling reform can occur.

ORTHOGRAPHY AND SPELLING REFORMS

All writing systems and their scripts, no matter how revered or innovative, are imperfect and conventional, being an approximation – not a reproduction – of speech.[12] Ambiguity, the doubt or uncertainty in meaning arising from indistinctness or obscurity, occurs often with syllabic and alphabetic systems. In English, as we have seen, the single letter *a*, depending on dialect, can represent as many as six different phonemes (smallest significant sounds). English in particular fails to reproduce its suprasegmentals – that is, pitch (*Yes?/Yes!*), length (British English *cot/cart*), stress (*désert/desért*), juncture (*Van Dyke/vanned Ike*) and tone (*eee!/duhhh*) – because it uses a deficient alphabet. Writers of English try to correct the problem with unsystematic punctuation, space between words, capital letters and other devices. However, a precise reproduction of English as spoken simply cannot be written with the standard English alphabet.

Ideally, an alphabetic script should perhaps represent all phonemic utterances. But only the linguist's special symbols can reproduce fairly exact pronunciations, and these are too ponderous for popular use. Standard alphabetic scripts in use throughout the world constitute only convenient approximations, then, with many ambiguities and enormous differences in pronunciation not only between different languages using essentially the same system and script (German and English) but also between different dialects of the same language (British English and American English). Though the demonstrable efficacy of simple alphabetic writing has assured its adoption by most of the world, morpheme-syllabic writing such as Chinese and Japanese still continues to be practised by a significant portion of humanity, who find it eminently preferable for their respective languages.

Is 'precise reproduction' of speech desirable in a writing system? Probably not. Greatest international comprehension of written English, for example, is assured through maintenance of phonological and other latitudes. In other words, the looser the system, the greater its general usefulness.

All the same, changes take place frequently in writing systems and scripts. There are two basic types: gradual and abrupt. The gradual happen 'of themselves', usually because someone simplifies something and others copy it. For example, until the 1960s schools throughout the English-speaking world insisted on the maintenance of diacritics, yet *rôle* is now *role*, *naïve* is *naive*, and *coöperate* is *co-operate* or *cooperate* – and few seem to have noticed the reform. New words are constantly being coined, too, by altering the spelling of existing ones: *lite* for 'of low alcoholic content' is a recent example, from *light*. Such minor orthographic adjustments and supplementations are natural, and are steered by common acceptance.

Abrupt reforms are steered by governments (usually successfully) or private societies or individuals (almost always unsuccessfully). These changes are unnatural and problematical. As general literacy is a prerequisite of the modern state, most modern societies hope to encourage greater literacy through simplified spelling, the most common form of abrupt reform.

English, for one, is often cited as a language requiring a spelling reform that would encourage greater literacy and reduce learning time. After more than two hundred years of carefully directed standardization, English orthography is still not completely standardized. One of the problems is the difference between Commonwealth and US English, chiefly attributable to the fact that standardization commenced in earnest only after British America's settlement. Though the chasm between these spelling systems is now closing, many systemic differences remain (Commonwealth *left* / US *right*): *litre/liter*, *colour/color*, *marvellous/marvelous*, *worshipping/worshiping*, *traveller/traveler* and so on. Dual spellings are allowed in both, but with differing preferences: *spelt/spelled*, *learnt/learned*, *gaol/jail*, *practise/practice* (verb), *encyclopædia/encyclopedia*. There are also individual word differences that are not systemic: *grey/gray*, *programme* (except computing)/*program*, *licence/license* (noun), *defence/defense* and many more. Even one letter can hold different sound values: *z* (ZED)/*z* (ZEE). *Spelt* and *learnt* are everywhere becoming the US's *spelled* and *learned* – the latter now indistinguishable from the adjective *learned* (rarely still written *learnèd*), meaning 'erudite'. Britain's *-ise* and *-sation* endings are now yielding to the US's *-ize* and *-zation* (as in this book), but not in Australia and New Zealand, where the *s*-forms command a greater domain than in the UK. (New Zealand is currently considering adopting US orthography.)

The orthographic differences between Commonwealth and US English are few in number when compared to their linguistic differences. Both orthographically and linguistically, however, the two varieties are converging into one shared International Standard English, an emergent tongue, rather than generating the entirely separate daughter systems that historical development would have produced in the past.

English orthography has greater problems than international variation, including being a system often perceived as 'awkward' and difficult to learn. Early on in its history, only 24 signs had to represent 40 phonemes, so 'doubling-up' has long featured in English spelling. After the Norman Conquest, the Norman-French scribes filling scriptoria and chanceries on English soil began re-spelling English words in Norman fashion. Printing later introduced linguistic norms; it even added extra letters to words (like the *e* in *write*) merely to stretch a printed line to the margin. Printing also fossilized spelling, while spoken English continued to change (*light* now preserving only in its spelling an ancient Indo-European sound otherwise lost in English). Latin and Greek spellings became fashionable, using many letters not even pronounced in English. And a wealth of foreign words entered the lexicon, particularly in the 1500s and 1600s, with other spellings incompatible with the English norm.

English spelling is thus a hybrid – the product of 'Anglo-Saxon', French and classical traditions, with many outside influences. One can suggest any number of classes of systemic spelling anomalies in the English language, some of which can fit into more than one class and all of which complicate the process of learning to read and write English. In many of the following (and the list could easily be expanded), visible language – the written word – can immediately place a phonetically ambiguous word in its proper semantic slot, actually improving on speech's adequacy. In other cases, the written word cannot adequately convey the necessary distinction(s) inherent in the spoken word.

> ◆ **Class 1:** same spelling, same pronunciation, different meaning
> *bear* 'mammal; to bring or support'
> *can* 'metal container; to be able'
> *row* 'linear arrangement; to propel using oars' [also Classes 2 and 3]
>
> ◆ **Class 2:** same spelling, different pronunciation, different meaning
> *read* 'to comprehend written material (present verb); to comprehend written material (past verb)'
> *row* 'linear arrangement; to quarrel noisily'
> *tear* 'eye secretion; to rip'
>
> ◆ **Class 3:** different spelling, same pronunciation, different meaning
> *roe/row/rho/Rowe*
> *so/sew/sow/soh*
> *way/whey/weigh*
>
> ◆ **Class 4:** same spelling (but for upper-case/lower-case distinction), same pronunciation, different meaning
> *Faith/faith*
> *Rugby/rugby*
> *Sue/sue*

- **Class 5:** same spelling (but for punctuation), same pronunciation, different meaning
chills/chill's
its/it's
were/we're

- **Class 6:** same spelling (but for punctuation), different pronunciation, different meaning
coop/co-op
coward/co-ward
learned/learnèd

- **Class 7:** same spelling, different pronunciation (irrespective of dialect), same meaning
data pronounced /dæta/, /deta/ or /data/

In addition, English orthography has a redundancy frequency of approximately 50 per cent – *wch mns tht abt hf of th ltrs n a rtn Eglsh sntnc r uncsry to achv fl cmprhnsn, mst of ths bng vwls.* (Written Arabic and Hebrew have long exploited the principle of consonantal alphabetism with eminent success.)

Despite its shortcomings (and long-windedness), English spelling is still fundamentally phonemic – that is, written using English's smallest significant sounds. However, the phonemes do not always lie in the individual letters, but frequently occur in patterns of letters. As with Chinese 'significs' (sense identifiers), English spelling maintains visual cues, usually through the so-called 'unnecessary letters', in root relationships between words – as in *sign* and *signature* – quite distinct from their pronunciation, allowing rapid visual identification of a word's meaning without recourse to speech. All the same, the spoken language continues to move away from the written, and so teachers of English are forever explaining to their pupils why *would of* and *'cause* have to be written 'would have' and 'because'.

The gradual changes in orthography that have accompanied written English's history have sufficed for most purposes. However, not everyone has thought this. Already in 1551, the Englishman John Hart complained of English writing's 'vices' which caused it to be 'learned hard and evil to read'. Over the centuries, many alternative orthographies have been proposed.

The 1800s in particular saw three basic types of abrupt reform emerge: *standardizing*, calling for a more regular use of familiar letters; *supplementing*, adding new letters to the alphabet; and *supplanting*, creating all new letters.

From 1828, the American Noah Webster successfully began to reform US orthography with a standardization popularized by his own dictionary of American English; among other changes, he introduced such lasting innovations as *-our* (as in *honour*) becoming US *-or* (*honor*), and *-re* (*theatre*) becoming US *-er* (*theater*). In 1844, Isaac Pitman proposed a supplementing 'Phonotypy' in Britain. Americans founded the Spelling Reform Association in 1876; the Simplified Spelling Board was founded in 1906 and the Simplified Spelling Society in 1908 in Britain. This latter Society presented a standardized spelling reform as a bill to Parliament in 1949 that was defeated by 87 votes to 84. Four years later, a similar bill was actually passed – only to succumb to the Ministry of Education.

Current reform proposals include New Spelling, Simpler Spelling, Regularized English and World English Spelling, among others. George Bernard Shaw (1856–1950) left a sum in his will for the Public Trustee of Great Britain to hold a competition for the 'Proposed British Alphabet' of at least 40 new letters (this was to be a supplanting reform), thus enabling English to be written without groups of letters – or diacritical marks – for single sounds. The winning entry, by Kingsley Read, was ingenious ... and subsequently forgotten.

There are advantages to an English spelling reform, such as the reduction of learning time which may encourage the language's international diffusion. But there seem to be more disadvantages: the impracticability, loss of tradition, cost, the phonetic spellings creating too much ambiguity between dialects (recall Australian 'die') and loss of etymological markings (*sign/signature*), the lack of consensus as to what type of reform would be best and so on. Also, English is not as irregular as is often alleged. One study has shown that 84 per cent of English words were normally spelt according to a regulated usage, and only 3 per cent (around four hundred of the most frequently written words) so unpredictably that they had to be learned by rote.[13]

Written French maintains many historical spellings often held to be 'unnecessary'. For example, -*s* and -*t* at the ends of words are often not pronounced: *les garçons* ('the boys') and *petit garçon* ('small boy'). However, before vowels they are pronounced, as in *les élèves* ('the pupils') and *petit élève* ('small pupil'). In the first example, unpronounced -*s* and -*t* appear to serve no function; nonetheless, they are graphically marking lexemes – that is, they are providing visual cues to word recognition beyond phonetic reality. The 'unnecessary' letters of written French are almost always necessary, just for this reason.

The conflict of 'orthographic deficiency versus systemic regulation' is also waged in German, where a similar adequate resolution obtains. German spelling simply ignores the devoicing rule of word endings: *Hund* ('dog', pronounced HOONT) but plural *Hunde* ('dogs', HOONDEH). It also ignores the glottal stop in front of beginning vowels and between junctured vowels: *(ʔ)alles* ('all') and *The(ʔ)ater* ('theatre'). Germans simply 'fill these in' when reading aloud. The devoicing and glottal rules are system-wide, so there is no need to specially mark them in German writing. 'Phonetic fidelity' would be pointless here.

However, German spelling has other problems. For one, Austria's spelling conventions differ from Germany's, though not to the systemic extent that US spelling differs from Commonwealth spelling: German *Abnutzung*, Austrian *Abnützung* ('abrasion'); G. *karätig*, A. *karatig* ('[24]-carat'); G. *fauchen*, A. *pfauchen* ('hiss'); and so forth. Most differences are minor and only sporadic. And most have been addressed in the recent German spelling reform, the first in nearly a century.

On 1 July 1996, after years of careful planning, official delegates representing all of the German-speaking nations convened in Vienna to issue the Joint Declaration Towards a Reform of German Orthography. Their stated intent was to simplify, through a standardizing reform, the learning of written German and to alter the rules laid down by the Second Orthographic Conference in Berlin in 1901 to suit modern requirements. Directly affecting over a hundred million readers and writers in many countries – but principally in Germany, Austria and Switzerland – the reform had no intention of drastically changing the traditional German script derived, like

English, from the Latin alphabet. Instead, it concentrated on eliminating violations against German's principle of word-roots, seeking to maintain the same spelling of a root in all possible combinations of its written occurrence for easier visual identification (like the English example *sign/signature* above). Many other spelling changes and writing conventions were effected, too, such as *ss* for old *ß* in all instances, or the general separation of verbal compounds. In this way, old *Stengel* ('stalk') became new *Stängel* (from root *Stange* 'pole'), old *Kuß* ('kiss') became new *Kuss*, and old *kaltbleiben* ('to remain unperturbed') became new *kalt bleiben*.

Not everyone has been happy with the reform. Besides spelling chaos, it has caused, as critics pointed out almost immediately, the loss of important distinctions in the German language. For example, one is now to write *kalt bleiben* for what used to be either *kalt bleiben* ('to remain cold [weather]') or *kaltbleiben* ('to remain unperturbed'). Pre-reform German spelling used space/no space to mark semantic distinctions. By now using only space in verbal compounds, the new German spelling reform has increased ambiguity in this and in other cases. Humorists have pointed out that, if *Stengel* must be *Stängel*, then shouldn't Berlin become *Bärlin*? (*Bär* is 'bear' in German.) Within a year of the reform's introduction, major German-language publications were returning to the old system, claiming too much confusion and ambiguity had resulted.

'The "fundamental fallacy" of all spelling reformers', Sir Alan Herbert once affirmed in the British Parliament, 'is that the function of the printed or written word is to represent the spoken word. The true function of the printed or written word is to convey meaning, and to convey the same meaning to as many people as possible.'[14] Spelling reformers do indeed habitually champion spoken language without appreciating the special position, characteristics and benefits of written language, which are altogether different. Writing systems are usually one of two types: 'shallow phonographic' or 'deep phonographic'.[15] Because natural languages change over time while writing's inherent inertia causes increasing conservatism, 'shallow' automatically turns to 'deep'. When this happens, it is not really necessary to change the orthography, since the changes in spoken language already hold innate systemic markers permitting fluent reading and writing. Most generative phonologists – linguists who believe that languages are analyzed in terms of two levels of organization, known as *deep structure* and *surface structure* – are convinced that, in the process of reading and writing, the human mind applies particular rules to a mental lexicon in order to easily use otherwise 'incorrect' spellings. A major spelling reform might actually backfire: by introducing features incompatible with the internal patterns that have developed over time, it could create greater ambiguity. To those who wish to reform English spelling in order to 'improve' the language's accessibility, generative phonologists have countered that 'conventional [English] orthography is ... a near optimal system for the lexical representation of English words.'[16]

It is true that most alphabetic scripts display a deficit as regards the vowels of their respective language. This is because the vocalic phonemes in the language nearly always outnumber available letters of the alphabet, forcing 'doubling up' (as with English *a*, as we have seen). However, most alphabetic scripts manage to strike a successful compromise between spoken and written language, between 'accuracy to the mouth and intelligibility to the mind'.[17] Abrupt reforms are seldom needed with alphabetic scripts, because these, using a panoply of devices such as gradual adjustment and redundancy, are able to maintain comprehension and usefulness over many centuries.

One of the greatest, and least known, obstacles to a successful spelling reform is its failure to address the essential dichotomy between reading and writing, judging both to be one and the same process. In fact, reading and writing are separately processed cerebral activities. Writing is spelling, and many people who spell excellently read only poorly, while many who read excellently spell poorly. This is because these processes involve different learning strategies in the human brain. Writing is an active linguistic activity that demands both the visual and the phonetic component, appealing directly to phonological essentials. Reading is a passive visual activity, linking graphic art directly to meaning, most often bypassing speech altogether. No spelling reform could ever adequately reconcile two such disparate neural capacities.

Stenography or shorthand is a method of rapid writing using special symbols or abbreviations for common letters or words. It lies in a separate category of writing, because it is limited to special circumstances – the quick, short-term preservation of speech – and to special practitioners. It is an ancient practice. The Greek historian Xenophon (*c.* 430–354 BC) wrote the memoirs of Socrates in a form of shorthand. The Roman freeman Marcus Tullius Tiro devised a shorthand to record the speeches of Cicero in 63 BC; this Latin version was used for over a thousand years. Ignored during the High Middle Ages, shorthand was only revived in the 1500s. One century later, various systems were invented for use in school and church. The Industrial Revolution of the 1700s saw shorthand benefiting office work, and in the 1800s the principal systems were devised that still prevail. The two most popular in English are those of Isaac Pitman – Britain's main system – and John Robert Gregg – the US's main system, also used for several other languages.

Over four hundred shorthand systems have been devised just for English. Today, its most common use is in press reporting and clerical and secretarial work. Normally, about 65 letters are used: 25 single consonants, 24 double consonants and 16 vowels (though most vowels are omitted, as their presence is usually obvious). The stenotype machine, invented by the American court reporter W. S. Ireland in 1906, is principally used to record verbatim legal proceedings and legislative meetings. Very few people customarily command shorthand, whose use has diminished in recent years because of new technology.

Some scholars wonder whether alphabetic writing could become more efficient if more logograms were introduced to create a mixed system like Chinese morpheme-syllabic writing. The German philosopher and mathematician Gottfried Wilhelm Leibniz (1646–1716) believed that one could elaborate a universal script, apart from any of the world's natural languages; as with mathematics and music, it should also be generally implementable. This has long been a dream of those who do not understand writing systems' fundamental dependence on phonography. Writing has always been, and will always be, language-bound. Each language in history has elaborated, through borrowing, the script that 'best' reproduces its particular sounds. Even ancient Egyptian hieroglyphs contain a sizable phonetic component that is indispensable in order to avoid ambiguity.

With the beginning of mass international travel in the 1970s, all countries perceived a need to communicate essential facilities using symbols that are universally obvious – that is, pictograms rather than language-based characters or signs (letters). A major American study was effected at the time which found those symbols to be efficient which easily identified objects – bus, taxi, woman, man. Less efficient were symbols indicating an activity, such as ticket sales, custom control and passport control; these were too ambiguous. The general conclusion was that symbols were indeed helpful, but capable of communicating only a highly limited range of things. International symbolic writing was subsequently introduced throughout the world with these findings in mind. It was not an attempt to 'return to pictographic writing', but merely the helpful supplementation of normal writing in international venues – airports, ports, train stations and other places – using a very restricted 'lexicon' of easily identifiable objects or situations.

Some modern researchers are now seeking a way to expand this inchoate system into Leibniz's universal writing system, believing that it may be possible to construct a non-linguistic pictography to replace writing as we know it. These researchers contend that text and pictures have grown interdependent in our culture, in such a way that they might together be regarded as an autonomous language: a 'visual language'.[18] This would not be the symbol-writing of airports and train stations, they are careful to point out, but the marriage of visuality and writing, a separate hybrid phenomenon. The process of visual textual presentation may be a more efficient means of conveying complex ideas than our current practice, as it will allow us to cope better with the inundation of written data to which each person must respond daily. Visual language could achieve this by greatly reducing the period of digestion of complex material, they believe.

Regarding information overload not as a problem of volume

but of perceptual management, these researchers wish to convey complex ideas simply. This can be achieved, they insist, through more than a mere combining of words and pictures, charts and timelines. Holding visual language to be an actual language – that is, possessing formal rules of syntax and semantics – they claim that it commands a freedom in the expression of these rules that natural languages do not display, bestowing on visual language its unique strength. The most significant conclusion of the proponents of visual language is that images and their standardized placement in text do indeed help to convey complex ideas more simply than conventional writing. This is attributable, some claim, to the fact that the human brain uses different pathways to process verbal and non-verbal information – a reader using both channels at once will understand better and more quickly and be able to recall more.

Visual language is, in fact, now present everywhere. Most of us take it for granted, aware neither of its existence nor of its increasing infiltration throughout modern society. Merely sitting in our cars, we are besieged by visual language: speedometer, odometer, fuel gauge, battery indicator, seatbelt sign, radio programme, temperature and so on. Much of this comes with text (letters, numbers) 'read' as visual language, not as spoken text. In this way, an enormous amount of data can be processed almost at a glance. The shortcomings of visual language are that it is weak in detail and precision. It certainly cannot convey the full range of human thought. However, mainly because of new technology, visual language has shown itself to be an essential supplement to complete writing. With it, the world's writing systems have acquired a new dimension.

THE FUTURE OF WRITING

Efficiency and simplicity do not determine a script's future – the prestige and power of those using it do. Languages evolve naturally; writing systems and scripts do not. These are purposefully borrowed, changed and abandoned primarily for social and psychological reasons that have little to do with speech or orthography. In this way, the descendants of the writers of ancient hieroglyphs and cuneiforms now use the Arabic consonantal alphabet. And the people who carved and painted the logosyllabic glyphs of Mesoamerica now write in an alphabetic script the ancient Romans once used. Neither of these instances represents the triumph of a 'superior' writing system.

Politics have played a massive role in writing's history. In the early 1800s, for example, Russia acquired Azerbaijan, whose people wrote using the Arabic consonantal alphabet. Around 1929, Joseph Stalin, suspecting the Azerbaijanis' loyalty, actively sought to have them abandon Arabic for the Latin alphabet. But in the 1930s, Stalin became convinced that the Azerbaijanis were linking up with the Turks, who had just adopted the Latin alphabet themselves, and so he ordered the Azerbaijanis to adopt Russia's Cyrillic alphabet instead. Today's citizens of Azerbaijan, independent since 1991, write their national tongue using two scripts: all street signs and commodity labels are in the Latin alphabet while all newspapers are in the Cyrillic alphabet (Arabic has disappeared). Azerbaijan's current regime is planning to encourage the wider use of the Latin alphabet in order to reflect the country's professed non-sectarian openness.

Other forms of writing have survived for mercenary reasons. Most countries have a law insisting that a production date be displayed in public broadcasting. In Western countries, at least, Roman numerals still announce the production dates of TV and film programmes simply because few people can read them, thus preventing viewers from realizing just how old a re-sold programme truly is – as one British producer recently confessed.[19]

Despite the general unpredictability of such things, certain broad trends are recognizable in writing's future. Though many writing directions and orientations have obtained in the past – right-to-left linear, top-to-bottom vertical, spirals, boustrophedon and many more – increasingly the writing systems of the world (including Chinese, Korean and Japanese) are being written in imitation of the Latin arrangement, horizontally, from left to right, in uni-directional lines proceeding from the top of a page to the bottom. This will evidently be Earth's only writing arrangement within a few centuries, though some scripts (like

Arabic and Hebrew) might preserve traditional right-to-left writing for as long as they are written.

Of greater significance to the future of writing is the Latin alphabet's advance, which began with the conquests of the Roman Empire over two thousand years ago and is now accelerating as never before. This has little to do with the Latin alphabetization of hitherto scriptless languages, preserving them as one preserves species from an endangered rain-forest, a peripheral activity. The main metropolitan languages of the planet – Chinese, English, Spanish and Portuguese, those spoken by most of humankind and thus likely to survive the next four hundred years – will determine writing's future, one that appears, at least at the onset of the computer age, to be boldly Latin-alphabetic.

This has several explanations. First of all, three of the above languages already use the Latin alphabet, and China is actively encouraging the use of Pinyin (Chinese written in the Latin alphabet; see Chapter 5). Further, a single world language, International Standard English, is emerging that is written in the Latin alphabet. And the computer, developed by a culture using the Latin alphabet, is redefining our modern world in this script; anyone who wishes to share the tool must command its keyboard.

Computers and on-line networking operate best in the Latin alphabet principally because their invention and diffusion, as writing-based procedures, occurred in it. Other alphabets, and even entire writing systems, can of course be programmed. However, these will remain peripheral as they are generally foreign to the system and incompatible with mainline computing and networking – that is, with the Latin alphabet that most of the world is currently using for this activity. If the future lies with computer-based societies and economies, then non-Latin alphabetic systems will have to adapt or suffer the economic and social consequences. Computers are now 'forcing' the world itself to romanize, in other words.

The Latin alphabet is certainly not writing's pinnacle, but it is clearly writing's crest. It alone is now meeting the unprecedented requirements of our modern world, leaving all other writing systems and scripts behind – those who choose to use it and join the new technology will be those who profit. It is an uncontested election at this point in history, indeed, some would say, an ultimatum, understandably rousing among many peoples sentiments akin to those of losing one's native tongue. However, as seen with Chinese Pinyin, romanization is not tantamount to adopting a global language, with loss of one's tongue and ethnic 'identity'. On the contrary, both a culture and its language are preserved by romanization, through the enabled or continued reading and writing of the respective language, which otherwise might fall to a metropolitan aggressor. In this case, a supplanting reform becomes an essential social mechanism for the preservation of a culture ... the reality that the Chinese are currently confronting.

It is possible, however, that the trend towards one writing system and script for the world will become in the end merely a handmaiden of English-language 'imperialism'. Around four thousand languages are spoken at present; in a hundred years, perhaps only a thousand of these will be left.[20] All metropolitan languages are encroaching rapidly on all non-metropolitan tongues, English apparently more aggressively than others, for a variety of reasons. Romanization could ultimately participate in this historical process. Though the Chinese actively support romanization and the Japanese use *rōmaji* with increasing frequency, Arabic and Hebrew speakers appear unlikely ever to romanize, chiefly for religious but also for practical reasons: without vowels, the Arabic script, for one, can transmit a far greater number of dialects than the Latin script, a complete alphabet. Many cultures might be bi-scriptural in future, using traditional writing for local needs and the Latin alphabet for everything else. Within two or three centuries, only a small number of minority writing systems and scripts will survive, however, whereas the Latin alphabet will dominate the planet. It will be the World Script.

A book published in 2301 will probably be almost identical in appearance to this one, in whatever 'hard' or 'soft' format it may appear: the same alphabetic system with the same letters in the same direction and orientation, even in Roman type. Only the language will seem 'odd', with many unknown words. Indeed, the Latin alphabet's increased international, and in time interplanetary, use will mean accelerated fossilization. In time, like the Egyptian hieroglyphs, the World Script will become a written monolith.

Writing's use in society, however, will change dramatically. As a result of the personal computer, one can witness this transformation even now. An ever-increasing number of people are spending more hours per day using written – that is, keyboard – language rather than spoken language.[21] This is especially true of students, office workers, journalists, editors, writers, researchers, computer programmers, pensioners and many others. (In the Middle Ages, only scribes, who comprised a very small percentage of the population, were to be found in the scriptoria.) Within a few years, computers will be enriching nearly every household of the developed world. Human life in these countries is centring on, and contracting to, electronic texts and international networking, and moving away from speech. Soon, written language might be more prominent worldwide than spoken language. A different sort of language is emerging from this artificial interfacing: an 'oral written language' occupying a special position between spoken and written language.[22] Computers now regularly communicate with one another, too, through writing – that is, through written programming languages – without human mediation. Writing has, in this way, transcended humanity itself. We have redefined the very meaning of 'writing'.

At the beginning of the 2000s, as the number of writing systems and scripts is diminishing, the amount of writing is soaring and that of writing materials and techniques abounds. Laser lettering now types our correspondence. Mid-air holographic writing emblazons open-air concerts. 'E-ink', electronic ink that fills a sheet composed of microscopic spheres – one hemisphere with a positive charge, the other negative – changing colour when subjected to an electron pulse, can now instantaneously transform the Bible, for example, into the *Bhagavad Gita* with one mouse click. Until fairly recently, our society and its fundamental economic processes depended largely on the multiplication of *physical* things, such as the printed word. This no longer obtains, and what is replacing it is unknown territory. We are not only redefining writing but re-inventing its place in society.

SIGN   **SOUND**

reading   *(word in language)*

174 Writing's future: Will only reading be left? (Compare illus. 14, 16.)

Some believe that there may be no place for writing in future. At the same time as electronic texting supersedes physical printing, writing itself is challenged: computer voice-recognition systems could eventually replace writing altogether, leaving only the one arrow – reading (illus. 174). But even reading might vanish, once computer voice-response systems are perfected. Then one need never again write one's name ... or read a poem.

However, the benefits and joys of reading and writing will probably still outweigh those of computer voice-recognition systems for many centuries, because writing is innate in most literate cultures. Modern societies everywhere are dependent on the written word for nearly every aspect of human interaction. A starship commander of the 2400s may depend on voice commands and response with her vessel's main computer, granted; but one would expect her, in the privacy of her quarters, to open for pleasure a volume of Whitman, Bashō or Cervantes indistinguishable from one we might read today.

That starship commander might well be the same one who will retrieve humankind's first attempt to communicate with aliens through writing. The Pioneer 10 spacecraft, launched in 1972, bore on its antenna a 15-by-23-cm gold-anodized aluminium plate (illus. 175) designed by the American astronomer Carl Sagan and 'written in the only language we share with the recipients: Science'. Now beyond our Solar System, the plate's 'text' pinpoints the craft's exact origin, its date in relation to the Milky Way galaxy (in 1970) and its makers (both genders). The plate's inscription is not complete writing as we know it but, through pictograms and pulse signals, conveys what should be, at least according to human scientists, a 'universally understandable message'. Ironically, noted Sagan, 'the human beings are the most mysterious part of the message.'

It is possible that by the time Pioneer 10's plate is discovered or retrieved, little will have radically altered humankind's most

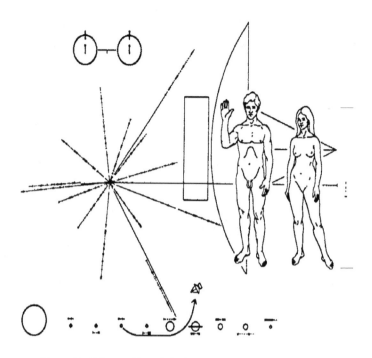

175 Humankind's interstellar epistle: the Pioneer 10 inscription launched in 1972.

fundamental relationship with writing. Those with intelligence and understanding will always appreciate that, as linguist Florian Coulmas has written, 'The skills of reading and writing provide access to knowledge, and knowledge is power.'[23]

So writing is much more than the 'painting of the voice'. At Pelkor Chode monastery in Gyangze, Tibet, pilgrims still crawl underneath stacks of holy texts as they have done for centuries in a gesture believed to absorb the wisdom of Buddhist scriptures. The very act of writing about one's feelings, recent studies have revealed, can rid one of depression, boost the immune system and lower blood pressure – recalling Aristotle's belief that writing could express 'affections of the soul'. And spacecraft beyond the Solar System now respond to written commands received from Earth's computers. However imperfect,

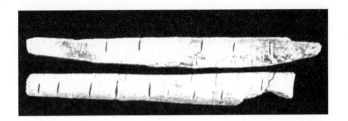

176 'Leaving a mark on creation that imparts a form of thought': bird-bone tubes incised at regular intervals by Neandertals around 30,000 years ago.

writing has become an indispensable expression of our social species as we begin to venture beyond all known limits. Yet to leave a mark on creation that imparts a form of thought itself – this impulse characterizes not only us but also our immediate antecedants of tens of thousands of years ago (illus. 176). As writing continues to serve and advance humankind with multiform wonder, it is defining and creating a new humanity.

Whatever form writing may take in future, it will remain central to the human experience, empowering and memorializing. As an Egyptian scribe brushed in ink some four thousand years ago: 'A man has perished and his body has become earth. All his relatives have crumbled to dust. It is writing that makes him remembered.'

References

ONE · FROM NOTCHES TO TABLETS

1 Henri-Jean Martin, *The History and Power of Writing*, trans. Lydia G. Cochrane (Chicago and London, 1994).
2 John DeFrancis, *Visible Speech: The Diverse Oneness of Writing Systems* (Honolulu, 1989).
3 David Diringer, *Writing* (London, 1962).
4 Adapted from Florian Coulmas, *The Writing Systems of the World* (Oxford and New York, 1989), who presents these as 'formal characteristics', not criteria.
5 Steven Roger Fischer, *A History of Language* (London, 1999).
6 Marcel Cohen, *La Grande Invention de l'écriture et son évolution*, 2 vols (Paris, 1958).
7 Leonhard Bloomfield, *Language* (New York, 1933).
8 Ignace J. Gelb, *A Study of Writing* [1952], rev. edn (Chicago and London, 1963).
9 Kaj Birket-Smith, 'The Circumpacific Distribution of Knot Records', *Folk*, VIII (1966), pp. 15–24.
10 Hans Prem and Berthold Riese, 'Authochthonous American Writing Systems: The Aztec and Maya Examples', in F. Coulmas and K. Ehlich, eds, *Writing in Focus* (Berlin, Amsterdam and New York, 1983), pp. 167–86.
11 Paul Bahn and Jean Vertut, *Images of the Ice Age* (London, 1988).
12 Robert Claiborne, *The Birth of Writing* (New York, 1974).
13 M. D. McLeod, *The Asante* (London, 1981), cited in Albertine Gaur, *A History of Writing*, rev. edn (London, 1992).
14 Carl Meinhof, 'Zur Entstehung der Schrift', *Zeitschrift für ägyptische Sprache*, XLIX (1911), pp. 1–14; Johannes Friedrich, *Geschichte der Schrift* (Heidelberg, 1966).
15 A. J. Abraham, *String Figures* (Algonac, MI, 1988).
16 Claiborne, *The Birth of Writing*.
17 J. D. Bernal, *Science in History*, 4 vols (London, 1954).
18 Martin, *The History and Power of Writing*.
19 Shan M. M. Winn, *Pre-Writing in Southeast Europe: The Sign System of the Vinča Culture, ca. 4000 B.C.* (Calgary, 1981).
20 M. S. F. Hood, 'The Tartaria Tablets', *Antiquity*, XLI (1967), pp. 99–113.
21 Janos Makkay, 'The Late Neolithic Tordos Group of Signs', *Alba Regia*, X (1969), pp. 9–50.

22 Emilia Masson, "L' Ecriture" dans les civilisations danubiennes
   néolithiques', *Kadmos*, XXIII (1984), pp. 89–123.
23 Gelb, *A Study of Writing*.
24 Julius Jordan, 'Uruk, vorläufige Berichte', *Abhandlungen der Preußischen
   Akademie der Wissenschaften, philosophisch-historische Klasse* (Berlin, 1932).
25 A. Leo Oppenheim, 'On an Operational Device in Mesopotamian
   Bureaucracy', *Journal of Near Eastern Studies*, XVIII (1959), pp. 121–8, first
   recognized the system. Pierre Amiet, 'Il y a 5000 ans les Elamites inven-
   taient l'écriture', *Archeologia*, XII (1966), pp. 20–22, described the oldest
   bullæ and suggested that their outside markings resembled their contents. Denise Schmandt-Besserat has been the leading proponent of the
   theory; among her many publications, of particular interest are 'The
   Earliest Precursors of Writing', *Scientific American*, CCXXXVIII (1978),
   pp. 50–59; and *Before Writing*, 2 vols (Austin, 1992).
26 Roy Harris, *The Origin of Writing* (London, 1986); Piotr Michalowski,
   'Early Mesopotamian Communicative Systems: Art, Literature, and
   Writing', in Ann C. Gunther, ed., *Investigating Artistic Environments in
   the Ancient Near East* (Washington, DC, 1990), pp. 53–69; Piotr
   Michalowski, 'Tokenism', *American Anthropologist*, XLV (1993),
   pp. 996–9; Paul Zimansky, 'Review of *Before Writing* by Denise
   Schmandt-Besserat', *Journal of Field Archæology*, XX (1993), pp. 513–17.
27 Zimansky, 'Review of *Before Writing*'.
28 Coulmas, *The Writing Systems of the World*.
29 Gelb, *A Study of Writing*; Friedrich, *Geschichte der Schrift*; Hans Jensen,
   Sign, Symbol and Script (New York, 1969); Geoffrey Sampson, *Writing
   Systems* (London, 1985); Coulmas, *The Writing Systems of the World*.
30 Jensen, *Sign, Symbol and Script*.
31 Andrew Robinson, *The Story of Writing* (London, 1995). For the relation
   of units of speech to units of writing – that is, how language-specific seg-
   ments are resolved through graphic representation – see the excellent
   description by Coulmas, *The Writing Systems of the World*, pp. 37–54.

TWO · TALKING ART

 1 Andrew Robinson, *The Story of Writing* (London, 1995). Robinson maintains that the introduction of phonography 'turned proto-writing into
   full writing'.
 2 Peter T. Daniels, 'The First Civilizations', in Peter T. Daniels and
   William Bright, eds, *The World's Writing Systems* (New York, 1996),
   pp. 21–32.
 3 Robert Claiborne, *The Birth of Writing* (New York, 1974).
 4 W. V. Davies, *Egyptian Hieroglyphs*, Reading the Past (London, 1987).
 5 Steven Roger Fischer, *A History of Language* (London, 1999).
 6 John D. Ray, 'The Emergence of Writing in Egypt', *World Archaeology*,
   XVII/3 (1986), pp. 307–16.
 7 Robert K. Ritner, 'Egyptian Writing', in Daniels and Bright, eds, *The
   World's Writing Systems*, pp. 73–84.
 8 Among the many useful publications describing Egyptian hieroglyphs

are E. A. Wallis Budge, *An Egyptian Hieroglyphic Dictionary*, 2 vols
(Mineola, NY, 1978); Davies, *Egyptian Hieroglyphs*; David P. Silverman,
Language and Writing in Ancient Egypt, Carnegie Series on Egypt
(Oakland, CA, 1990); Jaromir Malek, *The ABC of Hieroglyphs: Ancient
Egyptian Writing* (Gilsum, NH, 1995); Hilary Wilson, *Understanding
Hieroglyphs: A Complete Introductory Guide* (Lincolnwood, IL, 1995).

9 Davies, *Egyptian Hieroglyphs*.
10 Ritner, 'Egyptian Writing'.
11 Davies, *Egyptian Hieroglyphs*.
12 Robinson, *The Story of Writing*.
13 Maurice W. M. Pope, 'The Origin of Near Eastern Writing', *Antiquity*,
XL (1965), pp. 17–23; Thorkild Jacobson, *Toward the Image of Tammuz
and Other Essays on Mesopotamian History and Culture* (Oslo, 1970); Piotr
Michalowski, 'Mesopotamian Cuneiform', in Daniels and Bright, eds,
The World's Writing Systems, pp. 33–6.
14 Henri-Jean Martin, *The History and Power of Writing*, trans. Lydia G.
Cochrane (Chicago and London, 1994).
15 Marvin A. Powell, 'Three Problems in the History of Cuneiform
Writing: Origins, Direction of Script, Literacy', *Visible Language*, XV/4
(1981), pp. 419–40.
16 C. B. F. Walker, *Cuneiform*, Reading the Past, vol. III (Berkeley and Los
Angeles, 1989).
17 M. W. Green, 'The Construction and Implementation of the Cuneiform
Writing System', *Visible Language*, XV/4 (1981), pp. 345–72.
18 Florian Coulmas, *The Writing Systems of the World* (Oxford and New
York, 1989).
19 Ignace J. Gelb, *A Study of Writing* [1952], rev. edn (Chicago and London,
1963).
20 Jerrold S. Cooper, 'Sumerian and Akkadian', in Daniels and Bright, eds,
The World's Writing Systems, pp. 37–57; M. Civil and R. Biggs, 'Notes sur
des textes sumériens archaïques', *Revue d'Assyriologie*, LX (1966).
21 David Diringer, *The Alphabet: A Key to the History of Mankind*, third edn
(London, 1968).
22 Gene B. Gragg, 'Other Languages', in Daniels and Bright, eds, *The
World's Writing Systems*, pp. 58–72.
23 Christel Rüster, *Hethitische Keilschrift-Paläographie* (Wiesbaden, 1972).
24 Stanislav Segert, *A Basic Grammar of the Ugaritic Language* (Berkeley,
1984).
25 Coulmas, *The Writing Systems of the World*.
26 Friedrich Wilhelm König, *Die elamischen Königsinschriften* (Graz, 1965).
27 Johannes Friedrich, *Geschichte der Schrift* (Heidelberg, 1966).
28 Maurice Pope, *The Story of Decipherment: From Egyptian Hieroglyphic to
Linear B* (London, 1975).
29 Hans Jensen, *Sign, Symbol and Script* (New York, 1969).
30 Coulmas, *The Writing Systems of the World*.
31 Carl C. Lamberg-Karlovsky, 'The Proto-Elamites on the Iranian
Plateau', *Antiquity*, LII (1978), pp. 114–20.

32 Robert K. Englund, 'The Proto-Elamite Script', in Daniels and Bright, eds, *The World's Writing Systems*, pp. 160–64.

33 F. Vallat, 'Les Documents épigraphiques de l'acropole (1969-1971)', *Cahiers de la délégation archéologique française en Iran*, I (1971), pp. 235–45; 'Les Tablettes proto-elamites de l'acropole (campagne 1972)', *Cahiers de la délégation archéologique française en Iran*, III (1973), pp. 93–105; Piero Meriggi, *La scrittura proto-elamica*, 3 vols (Rome, 1971–4).

34 Lamberg-Karlovsky, 'The Proto-Elamites on the Iranian Plateau'.

35 Asko Parpola, *Deciphering the Indus Script* (Cambridge, 1994).

36 Asko Parpola, 'The Indus Script', in Daniels and Bright, eds, *The World's Writing Systems*, pp. 165–71.

37 Parpola, *Deciphering the Indus Script*. See also Gregory L. Possehl, *The Indus Age: The Writing System* (Philadelphia, 1996).

38 Walter A. Fairservis, Jr, 'The Script of the Indus Valley Civilization', *Scientific American* (March 1983), pp. 41–9.

39 Asko Parpola, 'The Indus Script: A Challenging Puzzle', *World Archaeology*, XVII/3 (1986), pp. 399–419.

40 Parpola, *Deciphering the Indus Script*.

41 Albertine Gaur, *A History of Writing*, rev. edn (London, 1992).

42 Archibald A. Hill, 'The Typology of Writing Systems', in W. M. Austin, ed., *Papers in Linguistics in Honor of Léon Dostert* (The Hague, 1967), pp. 92–9.

THREE · SPEAKING SYSTEMS

1 Henri-Jean Martin, *The History and Power of Writing*, trans. Lydia G. Cochrane (Chicago and London, 1994).

2 Florian Coulmas, *The Writing Systems of the World* (Oxford and New York, 1989).

3 Gordon Childe, *What Happened in History* [1942] (Harmondsworth, 1982).

4 George E. Mendenhall, *The Syllabic Inscriptions from Byblos* (Beirut, 1985).

5 Brian E. Colless, 'The Proto-Alphabetic Inscriptions of Canaan', *Abr-Nahrain*, XXIX (1991), pp. 18–66; 'The Byblos Syllabary and the Proto-Alphabet', *Abr-Nahrain*, XXX (1992), pp. 55–102.

6 Mendenhall, *The Syllabic Inscriptions from Byblos*.

7 See the discussion in Colless, 'The Byblos Syllabary and the Proto-Alphabet'.

8 *Ibid.*

9 Ignace J. Gelb, *Hittite Hieroglyphs* (London, 1931); *A Study of Writing* [1952] (Chicago and London, 1963).

10 H. Craig Melchert, 'Anatolian Hieroglyphs', in Peter T. Daniels and William Bright, eds, *The World's Writing Systems* (New York, 1996), pp. 120–24.

11 *Ibid.*

12 Albertine Gaur, *A History of Writing*, rev. edn (London, 1992).

13 Martin, *The History and Power of Writing*.

14 This section follows the recent theory that Minoan Greeks elaborated Crete's hieroglyphic and Linear A scripts, as detailed in Steven Roger Fischer, *Evidence for Hellenic Dialect in the Phaistos Disk* (Berne *et al.*, 1988); a popular version of this is Steven Roger Fischer, *Glyphbreaker* (New York, 1997). Readers are also encouraged to read the traditional and standard theories, which hold that Greeks borrowed syllabic writing from pre-Greek Minoans, outlined in Emmett L. Bennett, Jr, 'Aegean Scripts', in Daniels and Bright, eds, *The World's Writing Systems*, pp. 125–33; John Chadwick, *Linear B and Related Scripts*, second edn (London, 1989).

15 For a full description of the Phaistos Disk, see Yves Duhoux, *Le Disque de Phaestos* (Louvain, 1977). For its decipherment and content, see Fischer, *Evidence for Hellenic Dialect in the Phaistos Disk*.

16 Fischer, *Evidence for Hellenic Dialect in the Phaistos Disk*.

17 Louis Godart and Jean-Pierre Olivier, *Recueil des inscriptions en linéaire A*, Etudes crétoises 21/1–5 (Athens, 1976–85).

18 Michael Ventris and John Chadwick, *Documents in Mycenæan Greek*, second edn (Cambridge, 1973).

19 Thomas G. Palaima, 'Cypro-Minoan Scripts: Problems of Historical Context', in Yves Duhoux, Thomas G. Palaima and John Bennet, eds, *Problems in Decipherment*, Bibliothèque des cahiers de l'Institut de Linguistique de Louvain 49 (Louvain, 1989), pp. 121–87.

20 Hans Jensen, *Sign, Symbol and Script* (New York, 1969).

21 G. R. Driver, *Semitic Writing: From Pictograph to Alphabet* [1948] (London, 1976).

22 W. V. Davies, *Egyptian Hieroglyphs*, Reading the Past (London, 1987).

23 David Diringer, *The Alphabet: A Key to the History of Mankind*, third edn (London, 1968).

24 M. O'Connor, 'Epigraphic Semitic Scripts', in Daniels and Bright, eds, *The World's Writing Systems*, pp. 88–107.

25 Colless, 'The Proto-Alphabetic Inscriptions of Canaan'.

26 Coulmas, *The Writing Systems of the World*.

27 Johannes Friedrich, *Geschichte der Schrift* (Heidelberg, 1966); Diringer, *The Alphabet*.

28 O'Connor, 'Epigraphic Semitic Scripts'.

29 Coulmas, *The Writing Systems of the World*.

30 M. O'Connor, 'The Berber Scripts', in Daniels and Bright, eds, *The World's Writing Systems*, pp. 112–16.

31 O'Connor, 'Epigraphic Semitic Scripts'.

32 S. A. Birnbaum, *The Hebrew Script* (Edinburgh, 1971).

33 Jensen, *Sign, Symbol and Script*.

34 Coulmas, *The Writing Systems of the World*.

35 D. Navon and J. Shimron, 'Reading Hebrew: How Necessary is the Graphemic Representation of Vowels?', in L. Henderson, ed., *Orthographies and Reading* (London, 1984), pp. 91–102.

36 Diringer, *The Alphabet*.

37 Coulmas, *The Writing Systems of the World*.

38 F. E. Sommer, *The Arabic Writing in Five Lessons, with Practical Exercises and Key* (New York, 1942).

39 *Ibid.*; Farhat J. Ziadeh and R. Bayly Winder, *An Introduction to Modern Arabic* (Princeton, 1957); David Cowan, *An Introduction to Modern Literary Arabic* (Cambridge, 1964); J. R. Smart, *Arabic: A Complete Course for Beginners* (London, 1986).

40 Youssef Mahmoud, 'The Arabic Writing System and the Sociolinguistics of Orthography Reform', PhD diss., Georgetown University, Washington, DC, 1979.

41 Friedrich, *Geschichte der Schrift*.

42 Coulmas, *The Writing Systems of the World*.

43 D. P. Pattanayak, 'The Problem and Planning of Scripts', in G. Sambasiva Rao, ed., *Literacy Methodology* (Manasagangotri, Mysore, 1979), pp. 43–59.

44 V. Kannaiyan, *Scripts in and around India* (Madras, 1960).

45 *Ibid.*

46 Steven Roger Fischer, *A History of Language* (London, 1999).

47 Coulmas, *The Writing Systems of the World*.

48 Lachman M. Khubchandani, *Plural Languages, Plural Cultures* (Honolulu, 1983).

49 William Bright, 'The Devanagari Script', in Daniels and Bright, eds, *The World's Writing Systems*, pp. 384–90.

50 Mary Haas, *The Thai System of Writing* (Washington, DC, 1956).

51 J. G. de Casparis, *Indonesian Palæography* (Leiden, 1975).

52 Wolfgang-Ekkehard Scharlipp, *Einführung in die tibetische Schrift* (Hamburg, 1984).

53 Francis Britto, *Diglossia: A Study of the Theory with Application to Tamil* (Washington, DC, 1986).

54 Fischer, *A History of Language*.

FOUR · FROM ALPHA TO OMEGA

1 Pierre Swiggers, 'Transmission of the Phoenician Script to the West', in Peter T. Daniels and William Bright, eds, *The World's Writing Systems* (New York, 1996), pp. 261–70.

2 Geoffrey Sampson, *Writing Systems* (London, 1985).

3 Roger D. Woodard, *Greek Writing from Knossos to Homer: A Linguistic Interpretation of the Origin of the Greek Alphabet and the Continuity of Ancient Greek Literacy* (Oxford, 1997). David Diringer, *The Alphabet: A Key to the History of Mankind*, third edn (London, 1968), believes that the Greeks borrowed the Phoenician alphabet around 1000 BC. Florian Coulmas, *The Writing Systems of the World* (Oxford and New York, 1989), endorses the tenth century, 'at the latest'. Already in 1907, W. Larfeld, *Handbuch der griechischen Epigraphik* (Leipzig, 1907), estimated the date as the eleventh century BC. More conservative classicists, such as Swiggers, 'Transmission of the Phoenician Script to the West', believe that the borrowing occurred in Greece between 800 and 775 BC. Semitists generally assume a much earlier date, from 1750 to 1100 BC;

the leading proponent of early borrowing (albeit at a conservative 1100 BC) is Joseph Naveh, *Early History of the Alphabet*, second edn (Leiden, 1987).

4 Edward Maunde Thompson, *Handbook of Greek and Latin Palæography* (London, 1906).

5 Lilian Hamilton Jeffery, *The Local Scripts of Archaic Greece: A Study of the Origin of the Greek Alphabet and Its Development from the Eighth to the Fifth Centuries B.C.*, second edn rev. A. W. Johnston (Oxford, 1990).

6 Michael S. Macrakis, ed., *Greek Letters from Tablets to Pixels* (New Castle, DE, 1996).

7 P. Kyle McCarter, Jr, *The Antiquity of the Greek Alphabet and the Early Phoenician Scripts* (Missoula, MT, 1975).

8 Coulmas, *The Writing Systems of the World*.

9 Leslie Threatte, 'The Greek Alphabet', in Daniels and Bright, eds, *The World's Writing Systems*, pp. 271–80.

10 Sampson, *Writing Systems*.

11 See Hans Jensen, *Sign, Symbol and Script* (New York, 1969), for the extensive literature on the origin of Greek's supplementary letters. There are two main hypotheses: that these represent the differentiation of existing Greek letters, or that they are borrowings from non-Greek sources.

12 Pierre Swiggers and Wolfgang Jenniges, 'The Anatolian Alphabets', in Daniels and Bright, eds, *The World's Writing Systems*, pp. 281–7.

13 W. V. Davies, *Egyptian Hieroglyphs*, Reading the Past (London, 1987).

14 Karl-Heinz Priese, 'Zur Entstehung der meroitischen Schrift', in Fritz Hintze, ed., *Sudan im Altertum*, Meroitica I (Berlin, 1973), pp. 273–306.

15 N. B. Millet, 'The Meroitic Script', in Daniels and Bright, eds, *The World's Writing Systems*, pp. 84–6.

16 Robert K. Ritner, 'The Coptic Alphabet', in Daniels and Bright, eds, *The World's Writing Systems*, pp. 287–90.

17 Walter C. Till, *Koptische Grammatik* (Leipzig, 1955).

18 Walter E. Crum, *A Coptic Dictionary* (Oxford, 1939).

19 Albertine Gaur, *A History of Writing*, vol. 2, rev. edn (London, 1992).

20 'Etruscan Text Find', in *Archaeology*, LII/5 (1999), p. 16.

21 Larissa Bonfante, 'The Scripts of Italy', in Daniels and Bright, eds, *The World's Writing Systems*, pp. 297–311.

22 Ambros Pfiffig, *Die etruskische Sprache: Versuch einer Gesamtdarstellung* (Graz, 1969).

23 Giuliano Bonfante and Larissa Bonfante, *The Etruscan Language: An Introduction* (Manchester, 1983).

24 Sampson, *Writing Systems*.

25 John F. Healey, *The Early Alphabet*, Reading the Past (London, 1990).

26 Sampson, *Writing Systems*.

27 W. S. Allen, *Vox Latina* (Cambridge, 1965).

28 Coulmas, *The Writing Systems of the World*.

29 Pierre Swiggers, 'The Iberian Scripts', in Daniels and Bright, eds, *The World's Writing Systems*, pp. 108–12.

30 Jürgen Untermann, *Monumenta Linguarum Hispanisarum* (Wiesbaden, 1975–90).

31 Ernst Ebbinghaus, 'The Gothic Alphabet', in Daniels and Bright, eds, *The World's Writing Systems*, pp. 290–93.

32 Ernst Ebbinghaus, 'The Origin of Wulfila's Alphabet', *General Linguistics*, XIX (1979), pp. 15–29.

33 Erdmute Schultze, 'Die Runen', in Bruno Krüger, ed., *Die Germanen*, vol. 2 (Berlin, 1986), pp. 315–26.

34 Gaur, *A History of Writing*.

35 Ralph W. V. Elliott, 'The Runic Script', in Daniels and Bright, eds, *The World's Writing Systems*, pp. 333–9.

36 Raymond I. Page, *Runes*, Reading the Past (London, 1987).

37 Raymond I. Page, *An Introduction to English Runes* (London, 1973).

38 Klaus Düwel, *Runenkunde*, second edn (Stuttgart, 1983).

39 Damian McManus, 'Ogham', in Daniels and Bright, eds, *The World's Writing Systems*, pp. 340–45.

40 James Carney, 'The Invention of the Ogom Cipher', *Ériu (Journal of the Royal Irish Academy)*, XXVI (1975), pp. 53–65.

41 Damian McManus, *A Guide to Ogam*, Maynooth Monographs 4 (Maynooth, 1991).

42 Paul Cubberley, 'The Slavic Alphabets', in Daniels and Bright, eds, *The World's Writing Systems*, pp. 346–55.

43 Leon Stilman, *Russian Alphabet and Phonetics*, twelfth edn (New York, 1960).

44 Paul Cubberley, 'Alphabets and Transliteration', in Bernard Comrie and Greville G. Corbett, eds, *The Slavonic Languages* (London, 1993), pp. 20–59.

FIVE · THE EAST ASIAN 'REGENESIS'

1 William G. Boltz, 'East Asian Writing Systems', in Peter T. Daniels and William Bright, eds, *The World's Writing Systems* (New York, 1996), pp. 189–90.

2 Herrlee G. Creel, *Chinese Writing* (Washington, DC, 1943).

3 Cheung Kwong-yue, 'Recent Archaeological Evidence Relating to the Origin of Chinese Characters', in David N. Keightley, ed., *The Origins of Chinese Civilization* (Berkeley and Los Angeles, 1983), pp. 323–91.

4 C. J. Ball, *Chinese and Sumerian* (London, 1913); A. Ungnad, 'Sumerische und chinesische Schrift', *Wiener Zeitschrift für die Kunde des Morgenlandes*, XXXIV (1927).

5 William G. Boltz, *The Origin and Early Development of the Chinese Writing System*, American Oriental Series 78 (New Haven, 1994).

6 Suzanne Wen-Pu Yao, *Ostasiatische Schriftkunst* (Berlin, 1981).

7 Bertrand Russell, *The Problem of China* (London, 1922).

8 Yuen Ren Chao, *Language and Symbolic Systems* (Cambridge, 1968).

9 Florian Coulmas, *The Writing Systems of the World* (Oxford and New York, 1989).

10 John DeFrancis, *The Chinese Language: Fact and Fantasy* (Honolulu, 1984).
11 Boltz, *The Origin and Early Development of the Chinese Writing System*.
12 Viviane Alleton, *L'Ecriture chinoise* (Paris, 1970).
13 Victor H. Mair, 'Modern Chinese Writing', in Daniels and Bright, *The World's Writing Systems*, pp. 200–208.
14 Albertine Gaur, *A History of Writing*, rev. edn (London, 1992).
15 Mair, 'Modern Chinese Writing'.
16 *Ibid.*
17 Victor H. Mair, 'Cheng Ch'iao's Understanding of Sanskrit: The Concept of Spelling in China', in *A Festschrift in Honour of Professor Jao Tsung-i on the Occasion of His Seventy-fifth Anniversary* (Hong Kong, 1993), pp. 331–41.
18 DeFrancis, *The Chinese Language*.
19 Nguyen Dinh-Hoa, 'Vietnamese', in Daniels and Bright, eds, *The World's Writing Systems*, pp. 691–5.
20 Gaur, *A History of Writing*.
21 Lee Sangbaek, *A History of Korean Alphabet and Movable Types* (Seoul, 1970).
22 Ross King, 'Korean Writing', in Daniels and Bright, eds, *The World's Writing Systems*, pp. 218–27.
23 Geoffrey Sampson, *Writing Systems* (London, 1985).
24 King, 'Korean Writing'.
25 Gari Keith Ledyard, 'The Korean Language Reform of 1446: The Origin, Background and Early History of the Korean Alphabet', PhD diss., University of California at Berkeley, 1966.
26 Ross King, 'The Korean Elements in the Manchu Script Reform of 1632', *Central Asiatic Journal*, XXXI (1987), pp. 197–217.
27 Coulmas, *The Writing Systems of the World*.
28 Insup Taylor, 'The Korean Writing System: An Alphabet?', in Paul A. Kolers, Merald E. Wrolstad and Herman Bouma, eds, *Processing of Visible Language*, vol. 2 (New York, 1980), pp. 67–82.
29 Lee Sangbaek, *A History of Korean Alphabet and Movable Types*.
30 Sampson, *Writing Systems*.
31 King, 'Korean Writing'.
32 Sampson, *Writing Systems*.
33 Janet S. Smith, 'Japanese Writing', in Daniels and Bright, eds, *The World's Writing Systems*, pp. 209–17.
34 Hans Jensen, *Sign, Symbol and Script* (New York, 1969).
35 G. B. Sansom, *Japan: A Short Cultural History* (New York, 1962).
36 Smith, 'Japanese Writing'.
37 Sampson, *Writing Systems*.
38 See particularly Coulmas, *The Writing Systems of the World*, in this regard.
39 Smith, 'Japanese Writing'.
40 Sampson, *Writing Systems*.
41 Coulmas, *The Writing Systems of the World*.

42 *Ibid.*

SIX · THE AMERICAS

1 John S. Justeson and Terrence Kaufman, 'A Decipherment of Epi-
Olmec Hieroglyphic Writing', *Science*, CCLIX (1993), pp. 1703–11.
2 Virginia Morell, 'New Light on Writing in the Americas', *Science*, CCLI
(1991), pp. 268–70.
3 Florian Coulmas, *The Writing Systems of the World* (Oxford and New
York, 1989).
4 Steven Roger Fischer, *A History of Language* (London, 1999).
5 Joyce Marcus, *Mesoamerican Writing Systems: Propaganda, Myth, and
History in Four Ancient Civilizations* (Princeton, 1992).
6 As, for example, Peter T. Daniels, 'The Invention of Writing', in Peter
T. Daniels and William Bright, eds, *The World's Writing Systems* (New
York, 1996), pp. 579–86.
7 Michael D. Coe, cited in Morell, 'New Light on Writing in the
Americas'.
8 Michael D. Coe, *Breaking the Maya Code* (London, 1992).
9 *Ibid.*
10 Joyce Marcus, 'The First Appearance of Zapotec Writing and
Calendrics', in Kent V. Flannery and Joyce Marcus, eds, *The Cloud
People: Divergent Evolution of the Zapotec and Mixtec Civilizations* (New
York, 1983), pp. 91–6.
11 Morell, 'New Light on Writing in the Americas'.
12 Janet Catherine Berlo, 'Early Writing in Central Mexico: *In Tlilli, In
Tlapalli* before A.D. 1000', in Richard A. Diehl and Janet Catherine
Berlo, *Mesoamerica after the Decline of Teotihuacan A.D. 700-900*
(Washington, DC, 1989), pp. 19–47.
13 Marcus, *Mesoamerican Writing Systems*.
14 Justeson, cited in Morell, 'New Light on Writing in the Americas'.
15 Marcus, cited in Martha J. Macri, 'Maya and Other Mesoamerican
Scripts', in Daniels and Bright, *The World's Writing Systems*, pp. 172–82.
16 Justeson and Kaufman, 'A Decipherment of Epi-Olmec Hieroglyphic
Writing'.
17 *Ibid.*
18 Coe, *Breaking the Maya Code*.
19 Linda Schele and Nikolai Grube, *Notebook for the XIXth Maya
Hieroglyphic Workshop at Texas, March 9–18, 1995* (Austin, TX, 1995).
20 John S. Justeson *et al.*, *The Foreign Impact on Lowland Mayan Language
and Script*, Middle American Research Institute, Publication 53 (New
Orleans, 1985).
21 Marcus, *Mesoamerican Writing Systems*.
22 Schele and Grube, *Notebook*.
23 Macri, 'Maya and Other Mesoamerican Scripts'.
24 Coe, *Breaking the Maya Code*.
25 Schele and Grube, *Notebook*.
26 Coe, *Breaking the Maya Code*.

27 Michael D. Coe, *The Maya Scribe and His World* (New York, 1973).
28 Michael D. Coe and Justin Kerr, *The Art of the Maya Scribe* (London, 1998).
29 Cecil H. Brown, 'Hieroglyphic Literacy in Ancient Mayaland: Inferences from Linguistic Data', *Current Anthropology*, XXXII (1991), pp. 489–96.
30 Coe, *Breaking the Maya Code*.
31 Marcus, *Mesoamerican Writing Systems*.
32 Coe, *Breaking the Maya Code*.
33 Christopher L. Moser, *Ñuiñe Writing and Iconography of the Mixteca Baja*, Vanderbilt University Publications in Anthropology 19 (Nashville, 1977).
34 James C. Langley, 'The Forms and Usage of Notation at Teotihuacan', *Ancient Mesoamerica*, II (1991), pp. 285–98.
35 Berlo, 'Early Writing in Central Mexico'.
36 Macri, 'Maya and Other Mesoamerican Scripts'.
37 A full documentation of these fascinating pictorial manuscripts is available in John B. Glass, 'A Survey of Native Middle American Pictorial Manuscripts', in Howard F. Cline, ed., *Guide to Ethnohistorical Sources*, pt 3, Handbook of Middle American Indians 14 (Austin, 1975), pp. 3–80; 'A Census of Native Middle American Pictorial Manuscripts', in Cline, ed., *Guide to Ethnohistorical Sources*, pp. 81–252.
38 Morell, 'New Light on Writing in the Americas'.
39 Mary Elizabeth Smith, 'The Mixtec Writing System', in Kent V. Flannery and Joyce Marcus, eds, *The Cloud People: Divergent Evolution of the Zapotec and Mixtec Civilizations* (New York, 1983), pp. 238–45.
40 Marcus, *Mesoamerican Writing Systems*.
41 Coulmas, *The Writing Systems of the World*.
42 Marcus, *Mesoamerican Writing Systems*.
43 Victoria de la Jara, 'Vers le déchiffrement des écritures anciennes du Pérou', *Science progrès – La Nature*, XCV (1967), pp. 241–7.
44 Albertine Gaur, *A History of Writing*, rev. edn (London, 1992).
45 Marcel Cohen, cited in de la Jara, 'Vers le déchiffrement des écritures'.
46 Marcus, *Mesoamerican Writing Systems*.

SEVEN · THE PARCHMENT KEYBOARD

1 *St. Augustine's Confessions, with an English Translation by William Watts, 1631* (Cambridge, MA, and London, 1989).
2 Joseph Balogh, 'Voces paginarum', *Philologus*, LXXXII (1926–7), pp. 84–100; Bernard M. Knox, 'Silent Reading in Antiquity', *Greek, Roman and Byzantine Studies*, IX/4 (1968), pp. 421–35.
3 R. Reed, *Ancient Skins, Parchments and Leather* (London, 1972).
4 Arthur S. Osley, ed., *Calligraphy and Palæography* (London, 1965).
5 Michelle P. Brown, *A Guide to Western Historical Scripts from Antiquity to 1600* (London, 1990).
6 John Woodcock and Stan Knight, *A Book of Formal Scripts* (London, 1992).

7 Henri-Jean Martin, *The History and Power of Writing*, trans. Lydia G. Cochrane (Chicago and London, 1994).

8 Stan Knight, *Historical Scripts* (London, 1984).

9 Geoffrey Sampson, *Writing Systems* (London, 1985).

10 *Ibid.*

11 Stan Knight, 'The Roman Alphabet', in Peter T. Daniels and William Bright, eds, *The World's Writing Systems* (New York, 1996), pp. 312–32.

12 Martin, *The History and Power of Writing*.

13 S. Harrison Thomson, *Latin Bookhands of the Later Middle Ages* (Cambridge, 1969).

14 Albinia C. de la Mare, *The Handwriting of the Italian Humanists* (London, 1973).

15 James Wardrop, *The Script of Humanism* (Oxford, 1963).

16 Berthold L. Ullman, *The Origin and Development of Humanistic Script*, second edn (Rome, 1974).

17 Knight, *Historical Scripts*.

18 Martin, *The History and Power of Writing*.

19 Knight, *Historical Scripts*.

20 T. A. M. Bishop, *English Caroline Minuscule* (Oxford, 1971).

21 Alfred J. Fairbank, *A Handwriting Manual* (Leicester, 1932); Joyce Irene Whalley, *English Handwriting, 1540–1853* (London, 1969).

22 Florian Coulmas, *The Writing Systems of the World* (Oxford and New York, 1989).

23 *New Scientist* (15 July 2000).

24 R. H. Clapperton, *Paper: An Historical Account* (Oxford, 1934).

25 Albertine Gaur, *A History of Writing*, rev. edn (London, 1992).

26 *Ibid.*

27 Beatrice Warde, 'Foreword', in S. H. Steinberg, *Five Hundred Years of Printing*, second edn (London, 1961).

28 Steven Roger Fischer, *Glyphbreaker* (New York, 1997).

29 Thomas Francis Carter, *The Invention of Printing in China and Its Spread Westwards* (New York, 1925).

30 David Chibbett, *The History of Japanese Printing and Book Illustration* (Tokyo, 1977).

31 Gaur, *A History of Writing*.

32 *Ibid.*

33 Knight, *Historical Scripts*.

34 Steinberg, *Five Hundred Years of Printing*.

35 *Ibid.*

36 Gaur, *A History of Writing*.

37 Knight, *Historical Scripts*.

38 Steinberg, *Five Hundred Years of Printing*.

39 W. L. Heilbronner, *Printing and the Book in 15th-Century England* (Charlottesville, 1967).

40 Steinberg, *Five Hundred Years of Printing*.

41 Arthur S. Osley, ed., *Calligraphy and Palæography* (London, 1965).

42 Stanley Morison, *A Tally of Types* (Cambridge, 1973).

43 Joseph Blumenthal, *Art of the Printed Book, 1455–1955* (New York and Boston, 1973).
44 Daniel Berkeley Updike, *Printing Types: Their History, Forms, and Use*, second edn (Cambridge, 1937).
45 Warren Chappell, *A Short History of the Printed Word* (New York, 1970).
46 *Ibid.*
47 A. F. Johnson, *Type Designs*, third edn (London, 1966).
48 Updike, *Printing Types*.
49 Sebastian Carter, *Twentieth Century Type Designers* (New York, 1987).
50 *Ibid.*
51 Steinberg, *Five Hundred Years of Printing*.
52 Wilfred A. Beeching, *Century of the Typewriter* (New York, 1974).
53 Peter T. Daniels, 'Analog and Digital Writing', in Daniels and Bright, eds, *The World's Writing Systems*, pp. 883–92.
54 Elizabeth L. Eisenstein, *The Printing Press as an Agent of Change: Communications and Cultural Transformations in Early-Modern Europe* (Cambridge, 1979).
55 Steinberg, *Five Hundred Years of Printing*.
56 *Ibid.*
57 Alfred Schmitt, 'Die Bamum-Schrift', *Studium Generale*, XX (1967), pp. 594–604.
58 David Dalby, 'Further Indigenous Scripts of West Africa: Manding, Wolof and Fula Alphabets and Yoruba "Holy" Writing', *African Language Studies*, X (1969), pp. 161–81.
59 Saul H. Riesenberg and Shigeru Kaneshiro, *A Caroline Islands Script*, Smithsonian Institution Bureau of American Ethnology *Bulletin* 173; Anthropological Papers 60 (Washington, DC, 1960), pp. 273–333.
60 J. Park Harrison, 'Note on Five Hieroglyphic Tablets from Easter Island', *Journal of the Royal Anthropological Institute of Great Britain and Ireland*, V (1876), pp. 248–50.
61 Steven Roger Fischer, *Rongorongo: The Easter Island Script: History, Traditions, Texts*, Oxford Studies in Anthropological Linguistics 14 (Oxford, 1997); *idem*, *Glyphbreaker*.
62 Steven Roger Fischer, *A History of Language* (London, 1999).
63 Knight, *Historical Scripts*.
64 John Man, *Alpha Beta: How Our Alphabet Changed the Western World* (London, 2000).

EIGHT · SCRIPTING THE FUTURE

1 Edward S. Tylor, *Anthropology* (New York, 1881).
2 David Diringer, *The Alphabet: A Key to the History of Mankind*, third edn (London, 1968).
3 Henri-Jean Martin, *The History and Power of Writing*, trans. Lydia G. Cochrane (Chicago and London, 1994).
4 Geoffrey Sampson, *Writing Systems* (London, 1985).
5 Steven Roger Fischer, *A History of Language* (London, 1999).
6 M. W. Sugathapala De Silva, *Diglossia and Literacy* (Manasagangotri,

Mysore, 1976).

7 Karl Krumbacher, *Das Problem der neugriechischen Schriftsprache* (Munich, 1902).

8 One of the best general treatments of diglossia is Francis Britto, *Diglossia: A Study of the Theory with Application to Tamil* (Washington, DC, 1986).

9 Florian Coulmas, *The Writing Systems of the World* (Oxford and New York, 1989).

10 Madhav M. Deshpande, *Critical Studies in Indian Grammarians*, Michigan Series in South and Southeast Asian Languages and Linguistics, No. 2 (Ann Arbor, 1979).

11 Florian Coulmas, 'What Writing Can Do to Language', in S. Battestini, ed., *Georgetown University Roundtable on Languages and Linguistics 1986* (Washington, DC, 1987), pp. 107–29.

12 Fischer, *A History of Language*.

13 P. R. Hanna, R. E. Hodges and J. S. Hanna, *Spelling: Structure and Strategies* (Boston, 1971).

14 S. H. Steinberg, *Five Hundred Years of Printing*, second edn (London, 1961).

15 Sampson, *Writing Systems*.

16 Noam Chomsky and Morris Halle, *The Sound Pattern of English* (New York, 1968).

17 Andrew Robinson, *The Story of Writing* (London, 1995).

18 Robert Horn, *Visual Language* (Bainbridge Island, WA, 1998).

19 *New Scientist* (12 February 2000).

20 Fischer, *A History of Language*.

21 *Ibid.*

22 Seppo Tella, *Talking Shop Via E-Mail: A Thematic and Linguistic Analysis of Electronic Mail Communication* (Helsinki, 1992).

23 Coulmas, *The Writing Systems of the World*.

Select Bibliography

Albright, W. F., *The Proto-Sinaitic Inscriptions and Their Decipherment* (Cambridge, MA, 1966)

Albrow, K. H., *The English Writing System: Notes towards a Description* (London, 1972)

Allen, W. S., *Vox Latina* (Cambridge, 1965)

Alleton, Viviane, *L'Ecriture chinoise* (Paris, 1970)

André, Béatrice, *L'Invention de l'écriture* (Paris, 1988)

Arntz, H. *Die Runenschrift* (Halle, 1938)

Augst, Gerhard, ed., *New Trends in Graphemics and Orthography* (Berlin and New York, 1986)

Bahn, Paul, and Jean Vertut, *Images of the Ice Age* (London, 1988)

—, *Journey through the Ice Age* (London, 1997)

Ball, C. J., *Chinese and Sumerian* (London, 1913)

Bankes, George, *Moche Pottery from Peru* (London, 1980)

Barthel, Gustav, *Konnte Adam Schreiben: Weltgeschichte der Schrift* (Köln, 1972)

Beeching, Wilfred A., *Century of the Typewriter* (New York, 1974)

Benson, Elizabeth P., and Gillett G. Griffin, eds, *Maya Iconography* (Princeton, 1988)

Birnbaum, S. A., *The Hebrew Script* (Edinburgh, 1971)

Bishop, T. A. M., *English Caroline Minuscule* (Oxford, 1971)

Bloomfield, Leonhard, *Language* (New York, 1933)

Blumenthal, Joseph, *Art of the Printed Book, 1455–1955* (New York and Boston, 1973)

Boltz, William G., *The Origin and Early Development of the Chinese Writing System*, American Oriental Series 78 (New Haven, 1994)

Bonfante, Giuliano, and Larissa Bonfante, *The Etruscan Language: An Introduction* (Manchester, 1983)

Bonfante, Larissa, *Etruscan* (London, 1990)

Britto, Francis, *Diglossia: A Study of the Theory with Application to Tamil* (Washington, DC, 1986)

Brown, Michelle P., *A Guide to Western Historical Scripts from Antiquity to 1600* (London, 1990)

Budge, E. A. Wallis, *An Egyptian Hieroglyphic Dictionary*, 2 vols (Mineola, NY, 1978)

Campbell, George L., *Handbook of Scripts and Alphabets* (London, 1997)

Carter, Sebastian, *Twentieth Century Type Designers* (New York, 1987)

Carter, Thomas Francis, *The Invention of Printing in China and Its Spread Westwards* (New York, 1925)

Casparis, J. G. de, *Indonesian Palæography* (Leiden, 1975)

Chadwick, John, *Linear B and Related Scripts*, 2nd edn (London, 1989)

Chappell, Warren, *A Short History of the Printed Word* (New York, 1970)

Chibbett, David, *The History of Japanese Printing and Book Illustration* (Tokyo, 1977)

Chiera, Edward, *They Wrote on Clay* (Chicago and London, 1938)

Chomsky, Noam, and Morris Halle, *The Sound Pattern of English* (New York, 1968)

Claiborne, Robert, *The Birth of Writing* (New York, 1974)

Clapperton, R. H., *Paper: An Historical Account* (Oxford, 1934)

Coe, Michael D., *The Maya Scribe and His World* (New York, 1973)

—, *Breaking the Maya Code* (London, 1992)

—, and Justin Kerr, *The Art of the Maya Scribe* (London, 1998)

Cohen, Marcel, *La Grande Invention de l'écriture et son évolution*, 2 vols (Paris, 1958)

Coulmas, Florian, *The Writing Systems of the World* (Oxford and New York, 1989)

—, *The Blackwell Encyclopædia of Writing Systems* (Oxford, 1996)

—, and K. Ehlich, eds, *Writing in Focus* (Berlin, Amsterdam and New York, 1983)

Cowan, David, *An Introduction to Modern Literary Arabic* (Cambridge, 1964)

Coyaud, Maurice, *L'Ambiguité en japonais écrit* (Paris, 1985)

Creel, Herrlee G., *Chinese Writing* (Washington, DC, 1943)

Crum, Walter E., *A Coptic Dictionary* (Oxford, 1939)

Daniels, Peter T., and William Bright, eds, *The World's Writing Systems* (New York, 1996)

Davies, W. V., *Egyptian Hieroglyphs*, Reading the Past (London, 1987)

DeFrancis, John, *The Chinese Language: Fact and Fantasy* (Honolulu, 1984)

—, *Visible Speech: The Diverse Oneness of Writing Systems* (Honolulu, 1989)

Desbordes, Françoise, *Idées romaines sur l'écriture* (Lille, 1990)

Deshpande, Madhav M., *Critical Studies in Indian Grammarians*, Michigan Series in South and Southeast Asian Languages and Linguistics, No. 2 (Ann Arbor, 1979)

De Silva, M. W. Sugathapala, *Diglossia and Literacy* (Manasagangotri, Mysore, 1976)

Dietrich, M., and O. Lorentz, *Die Keilalphabete: Die phoenizisch-kanaanäischen und altarabischen Alphabete in Ugarit* (Münster, 1988)

Diringer, David, *Writing* (London, 1962)

—, *The Alphabet: A Key to the History of Mankind*, 3rd edn (London, 1968)

—, *A History of the Alphabet*, 2nd edn (London, 1977)

Dreyfuss, Henry, *Signs, Images, Symbols* (New York, 1966)

Driver, G. R., *Semitic Writing: From Pictograph to Alphabet*, rev. edn (London, 1976)

Duhoux, Yves, *Le Disque de Phaestos* (Louvain, 1977)

Düwel, Klaus, *Runenkunde*, 2nd edn (Stuttgart, 1983)

Eisenstein, Elizabeth L., *The Printing Press as an Agent of Change: Communications and Cultural Transformations in Early-Modern Europe*

(Cambridge, 1979)

Evans, Arthur, *Scripta Minoa I* (Oxford, 1909)

—, *Scripta Minoa II* (Oxford, 1952)

Fairbank, Alfred J., *A Handwriting Manual* (Leicester, 1932)

Falkenstein, A., *Das Sumerische* (Leiden, 1964)

Feldbusch, Elisabeth, *Geschriebene Sprache: Untersuchungen zu ihrer Herausbildung und Grundlegung ihrer Theorie* (Berlin and New York, 1985)

Février, J.-G., *Histoire de l'écriture* (Paris, 1959)

Fischer, Steven Roger, *Evidence for Hellenic Dialect in the Phaistos Disk* (Berne et al., 1988)

—, *Glyphbreaker* (New York, 1997)

—, *Rongorongo: The Easter Island Script: History, Traditions, Texts*, Oxford Studies in Anthropological Linguistics 14 (Oxford, 1997)

—, *A History of Language* (London, 1999)

Fishman, Joshua A., ed., *Advances in the Creation and Revision of Writing Systems* (The Hague, 1977)

Földes-Papp, K., *Vom Felsbild zum Alphabet* (Stuttgart, 1966)

Follick, M., *The Case for Spelling Reform* (London, 1965)

Friedrich, Johannes, *Geschichte der Schrift unter besonderer Berücksichtigung ihrer geistigen Entwicklung* (Heidelberg, 1966)

Frith, Uta, ed., *Cognitive Processes in Spelling* (London, 1980)

Gardiner, A. H., and T. A. Peet, *The Inscriptions of Sinai* (London, 1955)

Gaur, Albertine, *A History of Writing*, rev. edn (London, 1992)

Gelb, Ignace J., *Hittite Hieroglyphs* (London, 1931)

—, *A Study of Writing: The Foundations of Grammatology*, rev. edn (Chicago and London, 1963)

Gibson, E. J., and A. Levin, *The Psychology of Reading* (Cambridge, MA, 1975)

Green, Margaret W., and Hans J. Nissen, *Zeichenliste der archaischen Texte aus Uruk*, Ausgrabungen der Deutschen Forschungsgemeinschaft in Uruk-Warka 11 (Berlin, 1987)

Günther, K. B., and H. Günther, eds, *Schrift, Schreiben, Schriftlichkeit* (Tübingen, 1983)

Haas, Mary, *The Thai System of Writing* (Washington, DC, 1956)

Haas, W., ed., *Alphabets for English* (Manchester, 1969)

—, ed., *Standard Languages, Spoken and Written* (Manchester, 1982)

Hanna, P. R., R. E. Hodges and J. S. Hanna, *Spelling: Structure and Strategies* (Boston, 1971)

Harris, Roy, *The Language Makers* (Ithaca, NY, 1980)

—, *The Origin of Writing* (London, 1986)

—, *Signs of Writing* (London, 1995)

Healey, John F., *Early Alphabet*, Reading the Past (London, 1990)

Heilbronner, W. L., *Printing and the Book in 15th-Century England* (Charlottesville, 1967)

Henderson, L., *Orthography and Word Recognition in Reading* (London and New York, 1982)

—, ed., *Orthographies and Reading* (London, 1984)

Horn, Robert, *Visual Language* (Bainbridge Island, WA, 1998)

Hosking, R. F., and G. M. Meredith-Owens, eds, *A Handbook of Asian Scripts*

(London, 1966)

Houston, S. D., *Maya Glyphs* (London, 1989)

Irwin, C., *The Romance of Writing* (New York, 1956)

Isaac, Peter C., *Development of Written Language and Early Writing Materials* (Newcastle upon Tyne, 1989)

Jackson, Donald, *The Story of Writing* (New York, 1981)

Jean, Georges, *L'Ecriture: Mémoire des hommes* (Paris, 1987)

Jeffery, Lilian Hamilton, *The Local Scripts of Archaic Greece: A Study of the Origin of the Greek Alphabet and Its Development from the Eighth to the Fifth Centuries B.C.*, 2nd edn rev. A. W. Johnston (Oxford, 1990)

Jensen, Hans, *Geschichte der Schrift* (Hannover, 1925)

—, *Sign, Symbol and Script* (New York, 1969)

Johnson, A. F., *Type Designs*, 3rd edn (London, 1966)

Justeson, John S., *et al.*, *The Foreign Impact on Lowland Mayan Language and Script*, Middle American Research Institute, Publication 53 (New Orleans, 1985)

Kannaiyan, V., *Scripts in and around India* (Madras, 1960)

Kéki, Bela, *5000 Jahre Schrift* (Leipzig, 1976)

Khubchandani, Lachman M., *Plural Languages, Plural Cultures* (Honolulu, 1983)

Kindaichi, Haruhiko, *Nihongo [Japanese]* (Tokyo, 1957)

Knight, Stan, *Historical Scripts* (London, 1984)

Koenig, Viviane, and Claire Laporte, *Vers 3000 av. J.-C.: La Naissance de l'écriture* (Paris, 1990)

Kohrt, M., *Theoretische Aspekte der deutschen Orthographie* (Tübingen, 1987)

König, Friedrich Wilhelm, *Die elamischen Königsinschriften* (Graz, 1965)

Krumbacher, Karl, *Das Problem der neugriechischen Schriftsprache* (Munich, 1902)

Labat, R., and F. Malbran-Labat, *Manuel d'épigraphie akkadienne*, 6th edn (Paris, 1988)

Larfeld, W., *Handbuch der griechischen Epigraphik* (Leipzig, 1907)

Ledyard, Gari Keith, 'The Korean Language Reform of 1446: The Origin, Background and Early History of the Korean Alphabet', PhD diss., University of California at Berkeley, 1966

Lee Sangbaek, *A History of Korean Alphabet and Movable Types* (Seoul, 1970)

Lülfing, Hans, *An der Wiege des Alphabets* (Leipzig, 1977)

McCarter, P. Kyle, Jr, *The Antiquity of the Greek Alphabet and the Early Phoenician Scripts* (Missoula, MT, 1975)

McManus, Damian, *A Guide to Ogam*, Maynooth Monographs 4 (Maynooth, 1991)

Macrakis, Michael S., ed., *Greek Letters from Tablets to Pixels* (New Castle, DE, 1996)

Mahmoud, Youssef, 'The Arabic Writing System and the Sociolinguistics of Orthography Reform', PhD diss., Georgetown University, Washington, DC, 1979

Malek, Jaromir, *The ABC of Hieroglyphs: Ancient Egyptian Writing* (Gilsum, NH, 1995)

Mallery, Garrick, *Picture-Writing of the American Indians* (Washington, DC, 1893)

Man, John, *Alpha Beta: How Our Alphabet Changed the Western World* (London, 2000)

Marcus, Joyce, *Mesoamerican Writing Systems: Propaganda, Myth, and History in Four Ancient Civilizations* (Princeton, 1992)

Mare, Albinia C. de la, *The Handwriting of the Italian Humanists* (London, 1973)

Martin, Henri-Jean, *The History and Power of Writing*, trans. Lydia G. Cochrane (Chicago and London, 1994)

Massey, W., *The Origin and Progress of Letters* (London, 1963)

Masson, O., *Les Inscriptions chypriotes syllabiques* (Paris, 1961)

Mendenhall, George E., *The Syllabic Inscriptions from Byblos* (Beirut, 1985)

Mercer, S. A. B., *The Origin of Writing and the Alphabet* (London, 1959)

Miller, D. Gary, *Ancient Scripts and Phonological Knowledge*, Amsterdam Studies in the Theory and History of Linguistic Science (Amsterdam, 1994)

Miller, Roy Andrew, *The Japanese Language* (Chicago and London, 1967)

Moltke, E., *Runes and Their Origin* (Copenhagen, 1985)

Moorhouse, A. C., *The Triumph of the Alphabet* (New York, 1953)

Morison, Stanley, *A Tally of Types* (Cambridge, 1973)

Moser, Christopher L., *Ñuiñe Writing and Iconography of the Mixteca Baja*, Vanderbilt University Publications in Anthropology 19 (Nashville, 1977)

Naveh, Joseph, *Early History of the Alphabet*, 2nd edn (Leiden, 1987)

Ogg, O., *The 26 Letters*, 2nd edn (London, 1961)

Okii, Hayashi, ed., *Zusetsu nihongo [Graphic Japanese]* (Tokyo, 1982)

Osley, Arthur S., ed., *Calligraphy and Palæography* (London, 1965)

Page, Raymond I., *An Introduction to English Runes* (London, 1973)

—, *Runes*, Reading the Past (London, 1987)

Parpola, Asko, *Deciphering the Indus Script* (Cambridge, 1994)

Petrucci, A., *Breve storia della scrittura latina* (Rome, 1989)

Pettersson, John Sören, *Critique of Evolutionary Accounts of Writing* (Uppsala, 1991)

Pfiffig, Ambros, *Die etruskische Sprache: Versuch einer Gesamtdarstellung* (Graz, 1969)

Pope, Maurice, *Aegean Writing and Linear A* (Lund, 1964)

—, *The Story of Decipherment: From Egyptian Hieroglyphic to Linear B* (London, 1975)

Possehl, Gregory L., *The Indus Age: The Writing System* (Philadelphia, 1996)

Ramsey, S. Robert, *The Languages of China* (Princeton, NJ, 1990)

Reed, R., *Ancient Skins, Parchments and Leather* (London, 1972)

Reynolds, Joyce, *Latin Inscriptions* (London, 1991)

Riesenberg, Saul H., and Shigeru Kaneshiro, *A Caroline Islands Script*, Smithsonian Institution Bureau of American Ethnology *Bulletin* 173 (Washington, DC, 1960)

Robinson, Andrew, *The Story of Writing* (London, 1995)

Rüster, Christel, *Hethitische Keilschrift-Paläographie* (Wiesbaden, 1972)

Saas, B., *The Genesis of the Alphabet and Its Development in the Second Millennium BC* (Wiesbaden, 1988)

Sampson, Geoffrey, *Writing Systems: A Linguistic Introduction* (London,

1985)

Sansom, G. B., *Japan: A Short Cultural History* (New York, 1962)

Sato Habein, Yaeko, *The History of the Japanese Written Language* (Tokyo, 1984)

Scharlipp, Wolfgang-Ekkehard, *Einführung in die tibetische Schrift* (Hamburg, 1984)

Schele, Linda, and Nikolai Grube, *Notebook for the XIXth Maya Hieroglyphic Workshop at Texas, March 9–18, 1995* (Austin, TX, 1995)

Schmandt-Besserat, Denise, *Before Writing: From Counting to Cuneiform* (Austin, TX, 1992)

—, *How Writing Came About* (Austin, TX, 1997)

Schmitt, Alfred, *Untersuchungen zur Geschichte der Schrift* (Leipzig, 1940)

—, *Entstehung und Entwicklung der Schriften*, ed. Claus Haebler (Cologne, 1980)

Schneider, Stuart, and George Fischler, *The Illustrated Guide to Antique Writing Instruments* (New York, 1997)

Scholderer, Victor, *Johann Gutenberg, the Inventor of Printing*, 2nd edn (London, 1970)

Scragg, D. G., *A History of English Spelling* (Manchester, 1974)

Senner, Wayne M., ed., *The Origins of Writing* (Lincoln, NB, 1991)

Sethe, Kurt, *Vom Bild zum Buchstaben: Die Entstehungsgeschichte der Schrift*, Untersuchungen zur Geschichte und Altertumskunde Ägyptens 12 (Leipzig, 1939)

Seyboldt, Peter, and Gregory K. Chiang, *Language Reform in China: Documents and Documentary* (White Plains, NY, 1979)

Silverman, David P., *Language and Writing in Ancient Egypt*, Carnegie Series on Egypt (Oakland, CA, 1990)

Smart, J. R., *Arabic: A Complete Course for Beginners* (London, 1986)

Sommer, F. E., *The Arabic Writing in Five Lessons, with Practical Exercises and Key* (New York, 1942)

Söden, W. von, *Das akkadische Syllabar* (Rome, 1967)

Steinberg, S. H., *Five Hundred Years of Printing*, 2nd edn (London, 1961)

Steindorff, G., *Lehrbuch der koptischen Grammatik* (Chicago, 1951)

Stilman, Leon, *Russian Alphabet and Phonetics*, 12th edn (New York, 1960)

Stubbs, Michael, *Language and Literacy* (London, 1980)

Taylor, Isaac, *The History of the Alphabet: An Account of the Origin and Development of Letters*, 2 vols (London, 1899)

Tella, Seppo, *Talking Shop Via E-Mail: A Thematic and Linguistic Analysis of Electronic Mail Communication* (Helsinki, 1992)

Thompson, Edward Maunde, *Handbook of Greek and Latin Palæography* (London, 1906)

Thomson, S. Harrison, *Latin Bookhands of the Later Middle Ages* (Cambridge, 1969)

Till, Walter C., *Koptische Grammatik* (Leipzig, 1955)

Tsien, Tsuen-hsuin, *Written on Bamboo and Silk* (Chicago, 1962)

Tylor, Edward S., *Anthropology* (New York, 1881)

Ullman, Berthold L., *The Origin and Development of Humanistic Script*, 2nd edn (Rome, 1974)

Untermann, Jürgen, *Monumenta Linguarum Hispanisarum* (Wiesbaden,

1975–90)

Updike, Daniel Berkeley, *Printing Types: Their History, Forms, and Use*, 2nd
    edn (Cambridge, 1937)

Vachek, J., *Written Language: General Problems and Problems of English* (The
    Hague, 1973)

Venezky, R. L., *The Structure of English Orthography* (The Hague, 1972)

Ventris, Michael, and John Chadwick, *Documents in Mycenæan Greek*, 2nd
    edn (Cambridge, 1973)

Vervliet, Hendrik, ed., *The Book Through Five Thousand Years* (London, 1972)

Walker, C. B. F., *Cuneiform*, Reading the Past, III (Berkeley and Los Angeles,
    1989)

Wardrop, James, *The Script of Humanism* (Oxford, 1963)

Wellisch, Hans H., *The Conversion of Script: Its Nature, History and Utilization*
    (College Park, MD, 1978)

Wen-Pu Yao, Suzanne, *Ostasiatische Schriftkunst* (Berlin, 1981)

Whalley, Joyce Irene, *English Handwriting, 1540–1853* (London, 1969)

White, John L., ed., *Studies in Ancient Letter Writing* (Atlanta, GA, 1983)

Widmann, H., ed., *Der gegenwärtige Stand der Gutenberg-Forschung*
    (Stuttgart, 1977)

Wilson, Hilary, *Understanding Hieroglyphs: A Complete Introductory Guide*
    (Lincolnwood, IL, 1995)

Winn, Shan M. M., *Pre-Writing in Southeast Europe: The Sign System of the
    Vinča Culture, ca. 4000 B.C.* (Calgary, 1981)

Woodard, Roger D., *Greek Writing from Knossos to Homer: A Linguistic
    Interpretation of the Origin of the Greek Alphabet and the Continuity of
    Ancient Greek Literacy* (Oxford, 1997)

Woodcock, John, and Stan Knight, *A Book of Formal Scripts* (London, 1992)

Yuen Ren Chao, *Language and Symbolic Systems* (Cambridge, 1968)

Ziadeh, Farhat J., and R. Bayly Winder, *An Introduction to Modern Arabic*
    (Princeton, 1957)

Illustration Acknowledgements

The author and publisher wish to express their thanks to the following sources of illustrative material and/or permission to reproduce it. (Where illustrations have been drawn from previously published material, full citations are provided in the Select Bibliography.)

Institut Royale des Sciences Naturelles de Belgique, Brussels: 2; drawing after an original by the Abbé Henri Breuil in *Four Hundred Centuries of Cave Art* (1952): 3; from Garrick Mallery, *Picture-Writing of the American Indians* (1893): 4; adapted from Georg Möller, *Hieratische Paläographie* (1936): 24; from *Description de l'Égypte ou Recueil des Observations et des Recherches qui ont été faites en Égypte pendant l'expédition de Vivant Denon* (1809–30): 25; British Museum, London: 27, 31, 40 129; adapted from Green and Nissen (1987): 29; from M. Civil and R. D. Biggs, *Revue d'assyriologie*, LX (1966): 33; Iraklion Archaeological Museum, Crete: 47; reproduction by H. Duc de Luynes from *Numismatique et inscriptions chypriotes* (1852): 51; adapted from Diringer (1968): 68; adapted from Jensen (1969): 74, 125; adapted from Jensen (1925): 75; Deutsches Archäologisches Institut, Athens: 95; from Bonfante and Bonfante (1983): 105; Museo de Antropología, Xalapa, Veracruz, Mexico: 140; after Stephen D. Houston, *Maya Glyphs* (1989): 143; from Fischer (1999): 172.

Index